Business Plans
FOR
DUMMIES®

by Paul Tiffany and Steven D. Peterson

Adapted for the UK by Colin Barrow

JOHN WILEY & SONS, LTD

Business Plans For Dummies®

Published by
John Wiley & Sons, Ltd
The Atrium
Southern Gate
Chichester
West Sussex
PO19 8SQ
England
E-mail (for orders and customer service enquires): cs-books@wiley.co.uk

Visit our Home Page on www.wileyeurope.com

Wiley also publishes its books in a variety of electronic formats. Some content that appears in print may not be available in electronic books.

British Library Cataloguing in Publication Data: A catalogue record for this book is available from the British Library

ISBN-10: 0-7645-7026-9 (pbk.)
ISBN-13: 978-0-7645-7026-1 (pbk.)

Printed and bound in Great Britain by TJ International, Padstow, Cornwall

10 9 8 7 6 5

WILEY

About the Authors

Paul Tiffany is the managing director of Paul Tiffany & Associates, a Santa Rosa, California-based firm that has offered management training and consulting services to organizations throughout the world for the past fifteen years. In addition, he has taught business planning courses at some of the top business schools in the country, including Stanford, Wharton, and The Haas School of Business at the University of California, Berkeley, where he currently serves as adjunct professor. He holds an MBA from Harvard University and a PhD from Berkeley.

Steven Peterson is a senior partner and founder of Home Planet Technologies, a management training company specializing in hands-on software tools designed to enhance business strategy, business planning, and general management skills. He is the creator and designer of The Protean Strategist, a state-of-the-art computer-based business simulation. The simulation creates a dynamic business environment where participants run companies and compete against each other in a fast-changing marketplace. Each management team in the simulation is responsible for developing its own strategy, business plan, and program to make the plan work.

Steven has used The Protean Strategist to add excitement, hands-on experience, teamwork, and a competitive challenge to corporate training programs around the world. He has worked with both large and small companies on products and services in industries ranging from telecommunications to financial services and from high technology to consumer goods and industrial equipment.

When he's not planning his own business, Steven is planning to remodel his 80-year old house or to redesign the garden. And he confesses that of the three, the garden proves to be the most difficult. Steven holds advanced degrees in mathematics and physics, receiving his doctorate from Cornell University. He teaches part-time at the Haas School of Business, University of California at Berkeley, and lives in the Bay Area with his long-time companion, Peter, and their long-lived canine, Jake.

Colin Barrow is Head of the Enterprise Group at Cranfield School of Management, where he teaches entrepreneurship on the MBA and other programmes. He is also a visiting professor at business schools in the US, Asia, France and Austria. His books on entrepreneurship and small business have been translated into fifteen languages including Russian and Chinese. He worked with Microsoft to incorporate the business planning model used in his teaching programmes into the software program, Microsoft Business Planner, now bundled with Office. He is a regular contributor to newspapers, periodicals, and academic journals such as *The Financial Times*, *The Guardian*, *Management Today* and the *International Small Business Journal*.

Thousands of students have passed through Colin's start-up and business growth programmes, raising millions in new capital and going on to run successful and thriving enterprises. He is a non-executive director of two venture capital funds, on the board of several small businesses and serves on a number of Government Task Forces.

Dedication

Paul Tiffany:

For the thousands of students and executives whom I have taught in the past, and who have provided me with constant inspiration and insight about the challenges facing management in the modern world.

Steven Peterson:

To my parents, Mary and Pete, for always being there to encourage and support me in whatever path I chose to pursue. Your love and devotion to each other and our family are beyond measure. And to my sister, Susie, for her deep and constant friendship, and for giving me the chance to be a big brother and an uncle.

Authors' Acknowledgements

First we would like to express our gratitude to Peter Jaret for the many hours he spent reading, editing, asking questions, and making suggestions. His insights were always on the mark, and the book reflects his own immense talents as a writer. We would also like to thank Rick Oliver for his care in reviewing the book, and for all his astute comments and advice. His continued enthusiasm for the book is gratifying and greatly appreciated.

Special thanks go out to three of our editors. To Barb Terry for starting us out on the right track. And to Tere Drenth and Colleen Rainsberger for keeping us on course and on schedule. While we didn't always show it at the time, we really appreciate all their energy and hard work.

We are grateful to John Kilcullen and Kathy Welton, our publishers, for giving us the chance to write the book in the first place, and for allowing us the extra time to make it as good as it is.

We would also like to thank the talented staff at our publisher for taking care of all the important details. To Kathy Simpson for copy editing and Donna Love for assisting with several chapters. To Joyce Pepple and Heather Dismore for dealing with all the permissions. And to Ann Miller for seeing that the bills got paid.

Paul would also like to thank his family for their support during this project – for Janet, and for his children, Ann, Rafael, Roland, Brandon, and Mariah.

— Paul and Steven

I would like to thank everyone at Wiley Publishing, especially Jason Dunne, Daniel Mersey, and Samantha Clapp, for the opportunity to write this book – as well as their help, encouragement, feedback, and tireless work to make this all happen.

— Colin

Publisher's Acknowledgements

We're proud of this book; please send us your comments through our Dummies online registration form located at www.dummies.com/register/.

Some of the people who helped bring this book to market include the following:

Acquisitions, Editorial, and Media Development

Executive Editor: Jason Dunne

Executive Project Editor: Caroline Walmsley

Project Editors: Daniel Mersey, Amie Tibble

Content Editor: Rachael Chilvers

Editorial Assistant: Samantha Clapp

Technical Reviewer: Laurence Thomas

Cover Photos: © Peter Scholey/Getty Images

Cartoons: Ed McLachlan

Production

Project Coordinator: Erin Smith

Layout and Graphics: Jonelle Burns, Denny Hager, Joyce Haughey, Michael Kruzil, Jacque Schneider

Proofreaders: Laura Albert, Andy Hollandbeck, Carl William Pierce, Brian H. Walls

Indexer: TECHBOOKS Production Services

Publishing and Editorial for Consumer Dummies

> **Diane Graves Steele,** Vice President and Publisher, Consumer Dummies

> **Joyce Pepple,** Acquisitions Director, Consumer Dummies

> **Kristin A Cocks,** Product Development Director, Consumer Dummies

> **Michael Spring,** Vice President and Publisher, Travel

> **Brice Gosnell,** Associate Publisher, Travel

> **Kelly Regan,** Editorial Director, Travel

Publishing for Technology Dummies

> **Andy Cummings,** Vice President and Publisher, Dummies Technology/General User

Composition Services

> **Gerry Fahey,** Vice President of Production Services

> **Debbie Stailey,** Director of Composition Services

Contents at a Glance

Table of Contents

Introduction

· ·

So you pulled this book off the shelf and decided to give us a try. Good move. You've come to the right place. Believe it or not, we don't need to read tea leaves to know a bit about your background. In fact, we'd go so far as to suggest that you probably find yourself in one of the following situations:

- ✔ You have a great idea for a brand-new gadget and can't wait to get your own company up and running.
- ✔ Your boss just turned over a new leaf and wants a business plan from you in three weeks.
- ✔ You've always run the business without a business plan, and you're the one who turned over the new leaf.
- ✔ You thought you had a business plan for the company, but it doesn't seem to be doing the job that it should.

Are we close? Whatever your situation, you're not going to need those tea leaves to make a business plan, just read this book instead. We can't tell you the future of your business. But the business plan that we help you put together prepares you for the future. And we'll be with you every step of the way.

Why You Need This Book

You may not know how to make a business plan just yet, but you're smart enough to know that a plan is important. We know, from years of working with companies large and small, that a business plan is crucial – it's the only way that you can get where you want to go.

This book helps you create your business plan step by step. Along the way, you may discover things about your business that you never realised – things that just may help you beat the competition. We even throw in a few laughs as well.

Sure, for some of you, a business plan is something that you're required to put together to raise money for a startup company. At best, it's a formality; at worst, it's a real pain in the neck. But a business plan isn't just there to raise money; it's also a powerful tool – one that's bound to make your company a better place to work and your business a more successful operation.

Is a business plan magic? No – no sorcery here. A business plan works because it forces you to stop and think about what you're doing. It prompts you to figure out what you want your company to be in the future and how you intend to make the future happen. Then your plan acts as a template, guiding you through the steps required to meet your goals. For example:

- A business plan requires you to look carefully at your industry, your customers, and the competition to determine what your real opportunities are and what threats you face.

- A business plan takes a good hard look at your company as well, so that you can honestly and objectively recognise its capabilities and resources, its strengths and weaknesses, and its true advantages.

- A business plan coaxes a financial report, a forecast, and a budget out of you, so that you know where you stand today and what the future holds.

- A business plan prepares you for an uncertain future by encouraging you to come up with business strategies and alternatives to increase your chances of success down the road.

How to Use This Book

a fist have to time and Leern about the water befor a Lern how to make a bota

Business Plans For Dummies will help your business succeed no matter who you are or what your job description is, whether you're part of a large corporation or a one-person show. Depending on your situation, you may find yourself dipping into and out of the book in different ways:

- If business plans are new to you, you may want to start at the beginning and let us be your guides. We take you from your company mission all the way through to making your business plan work, and we keep your head above water the whole way.

- If you're a little more experienced, you may want to head straight for one of the more interesting watering holes: how to recognise the critical success factors in your business, for example, or where to look for your company's strengths and weaknesses. After dipping in anywhere along the way, you'll most likely discover yet another section where you want to spend some time.

Just remember – no matter where you find yourself, it's never too late to start a business plan, and it's never too late to make the one that you have even better. In each case, you can find what you're looking for between these bright-yellow covers.

How This Book Is Organised

Business Plans For Dummies is divided into six parts, based on the major elements of your business plan. You don't have to read all the parts, however, and you certainly don't have to read them in order. Each chapter is devoted to a particular business-planning topic, and you may need some chapters more than you do others. Feel free to skip around; pick and choose what you're really interested in.

Part 1: Determining Where You Want to Go

Before you can put together a business plan, you have to decide where you want to end up in the future. This part helps you get on track right away by establishing a mission for your company, along with business goals and objectives. Then we help you examine your company's values and your vision for the future.

Part II: Sizing Up Your Marketplace

To make a useful plan for your business, you have to know something about the market you're going after. In this part, we help you examine your industry and figure out what it takes to be successful by identifying where your opportunities and threats come from. We also help you analyse your customers, so that you can understand who they are, what they need, and how you can group them to better serve them. Finally, we help you scope out your competition, trying to determine exactly what you need to win.

Part III: Weighing Your Company's Prospects

In this part we turn our full attention to your company. We help you look as objectively as you can at your capabilities and resources, identifying the strengths that you can count on and the weaknesses that you need to deal with. We also help you zero in on what you do best, enabling you to figure out the real value that you provide for your customers and the true advantage that you have over your competitors. Finally, we guide you through your finances and help you put together a financial forecast and a budget.

Part IV: Looking to the Future

The main reason why you make a business plan in the first place is to get ready for what lies ahead for your business. Part IV helps you look into your future and prepares you for change. We introduce several standard alternatives and show you how you can use them to come up with strategies of your own. And we consider the different directions that you can take as your company grows bigger.

Part V: A Planner's Toolkit

Your business plan is no good if you can't put it to work. In this part, we help you shape your company to be as efficient and effective as it can be. We also help you prepare the people in your company so that they have the skills they need to accomplish the goals set out in your plan. Finally, we show you a sample of a real business plan, so that you know – start to finish – what you're aiming for.

Part VI: The Part of Tens

The Part of Tens is a collection of reminders, hints, observations, and warnings about what to do – and not to do – as you work through your business plan. These chapters focus on the big picture, so look at them whenever you need a little perspective on where you stand and where you're headed.

Icons Used in This Book

To guide you through your business plan preparation, we include icons in the left margins of the book. Here's what they mean:

This icon indicates tips to put you way ahead of the competition.

Wherever you see this icon, you find definitions of business-guru terms.

This icon calls your attention to illuminating examples from the business world.

 This icon flags situations that apply mostly to large companies, but that may help small companies as well.

 Ouch! You may get burned unless you heed these warnings.

 This icon serves as a friendly reminder that the topic at hand is important enough for you to note down for the future.

Where to Go from Here

Take a minute to thumb through this book and get comfortable with what's inside. Then pick out one or two chapters that tickle your fancy. Better yet, turn to a chapter that you already know something about. Or, if you're really daring, turn the page and start at the beginning.

Don't forget to use the table of contents for a chapter-by-chapter breakdown. The index is also an excellent place to turn to find a specific topic right away.

Part I
Determining Where You Want to Go

"In a previous life, before I became a lemming,
I was a small company without a business plan"

In this part . . .

No matter what you'd like to finish, from wallpapering the bedroom to hooking up the DVD, it's awfully easy to pass over all the preliminary stuff and jump right into the thick of the project. Let's face it, the preliminaries are a bit boring. But for the really important things in life – and in business – preparation is everything. So *preparing* to do your business plan ranks right up there in importance with each of the other major steps as you create a plan.

In this part, we help you prepare to plan by looking at what a business plan is all about. First, we look at how to establish a mission for your company and develop business goals and objectives. We also point out why values are so important to your company, and show you how you can use your company's values. Finally, we look at how a vision for your company gives you something to aim for and a direction to take.

Chapter 1

Starting Your Business Plan

* *

In This Chapter

▶ Getting the most out of your plan

▶ Using your plan as a record of the past and a guide to the future

▶ Making your plan function as your company description

▶ Figuring out who makes the plan

▶ Checking out what the written plan looks like

* *

Most of us go through life thinking ahead. We plan to paint the house, plan to go back to university, plan to take a holiday, and plan for retirement – we always have a plan or two in the works. Why do we plan so much? We certainly can't predict what's going to happen, so why bother? Certainly, none of us knows the future. But each of us knows that tomorrow will be different from today, and today isn't the same as yesterday. Planning for those differences is one way to move forward and face things that are unfamiliar and uncertain. Planning is a strategy for survival.

Companies make business plans for many of the same reasons. Planning is a strategy to improve the odds of success in a business world that's constantly changing. Business plans are not a guarantee of success, of course. Business planning isn't a science that offers you right and wrong answers about the future. But business planning is a process that gets you ready for what's to come. And making a plan increases the likelihood that down the road, your company will be in the right place at the right time.

In this chapter, we explore what planning is all about, how you can use your business plan, and why having a plan is so important. We talk about your business plan as a guide to your company's future, as well as a record of where you've been and how you've done. Because your plan is a ready-made description of your company, we also talk about the kinds of people who may be interested in seeing your business plan. Then we help you get a handle on who should be involved in putting your plan together, depending on how big your company is. Finally, we show you what your business plan should look like on paper.

Getting the Most Out of Your Plan

A *plan* originally meant only one thing: a flat view of a building, viewed from above. If you've ever had a house built or remodelled, you know that this kind of plan is still around (and still expensive). Over the centuries, however, the meaning of the word *plan* has expanded to include time as well as space. A *plan* in the modern sense also refers to a view of the future, seen from the present. You make plans for a birthday party next week or a business trip next month.

A *business plan* is a particular view of your company's future, describing the following things:

- ✔ What your industry will look like
- ✔ What markets you'll compete in
- ✔ What competition you'll be up against
- ✔ What products and services you'll offer
- ✔ What value you'll provide customers
- ✔ What long-term advantages you'll have
- ✔ How big and profitable your company will become

To create a detailed view of the future, you have to make a lot of predictions about what's going to happen down the road. If your company manufactures crystal balls, of course, you're in luck. If not, you have to find other ways to make some basic business assumptions about the future, which we share with you throughout this book.

In the end, your business plan is only as good as all the assumptions you put into it. To make sure that your assumptions make sense, much of your planning should involve trying to understand your surroundings today – what's going on right now in your own industry and marketplace. By making these assumptions, you can better predict your business and its future. Will your predictions actually come true? Only time will tell. Fortunately, the planning process makes you better prepared for whatever lies ahead.

Looking forward

A business plan provides a view of the future. Whether your company is large or small, whether you're just starting a business or are part of a seasoned company, you still need some sort of planning process to point you in the right direction and guide you along the way.

✔ A brand-new company makes a business plan to get its bearings and often uses the plan to get funding.

✔ An up-and-running company uses a plan to be better prepared.

✔ A large company needs a plan so that everybody sees the same view ahead.

✔ A small company makes a plan if it wants to make sure that it survives those crucial first two years.

In fact, a small company needs a business plan most of all. If you own or manage a small business, you already know that you're the jack-or-jill-of-all-trades. You hardly have enough time to get your daily business tasks done, much less plan for next week, next month, or next year. But because you run a small business, you simply can't afford *not* to plan.

When a giant company stumbles, it usually has the financial reserves to break the fall and get back on its feet. If your resources are limited, however, a single mistake – such as exaggerating the demand for your products or underestimating how long you have to wait to get paid – can spell the end of everything you've invested in and worked so hard to achieve. A business plan points out many dangers, alerting you to the hazards and obstacles that lie ahead, so that you can avoid such pitfalls. Remember: two-thirds of all new businesses cease trading within their first two or three years.

Looking back

A business plan paints a picture of where your company has been and how it has changed over the years. By reviewing past performance, you can use your plan to figure out what worked and what didn't. In effect, your business plan offers you an opportunity to keep score, allowing you to set goals for your company and then keep track of your achievements. For example

✔ Your plan creates a view of the future. In years to come, you can use old copies of your plan to look back and determine just how good you are at seeing what lies ahead.

✔ Your plan maps out a direction to go in and the route to take. You can use it to gauge how skilful you are at accomplishing what you set out to do.

✔ Your plan forecasts where you want to be. You can use it to check out how close you have come to your targets for the industry, your market, and your finances.

Your history, as described in your business plan, teaches you important lessons about the business you're in – so you aren't doomed to make the same mistakes over and over. If you can't remember exactly where your company has been, you probably won't see where it's headed.

Looking around

You can use your business plan to tell the world (or at least anyone out there who's interested) all about your company. No matter who you're dealing with or why, your plan has a ready-made description to back up the claims you make. Your plan comes in handy when you're dealing with the following people:

✔ Suppliers you are asking to extend you credit and offer you terms

✔ Distributors that want to add your product or service to their line-ups

✔ Big customers that hope to establish long-term business relationships with you

✔ The board of directors or other advisers who want to offer support

✔ Outside consultants you bring in to help out with specific issues

✔ Bankers who decide on whether or not to lend you money

✔ Investors who are interested in taking a stake in your company

All these people have their own special reasons for wanting more information about you, and each probably is interested in a different part of your plan. A well-written business plan satisfies all these groups and makes your company stronger in the process.

✔ A business plan improves your company's chances of success.

✔ A business plan shows you where your company has been and how it has changed.

✔ A business plan provides a blueprint for the future.

✔ Business planning is an ongoing process.

Naming Your Planners

Okay, a business plan is essential. Who's supposed to put the wretched thing together? In some sense, the answer depends on how big your company is.

✔ **Small businesses:** If your business is really just you – or maybe you and a couple of other people – you already know exactly who's responsible for making a plan for the company. That's not such a bad thing, when you think about it. Who better to create a view of the future and set business goals and objectives than the people who are also responsible for reaching the goals and making the future happen?

✔ **Medium-sized companies:** If your company is a bit bigger, you probably don't want to go it alone when it comes to putting together your business plan. First of all, putting together a plan is a big job. But more than that, involving all the key people in the planning process has a certain advantage: everyone involved in the plan has a stake in making sure that your company succeeds.

✔ **Large companies:** If you're part of a big company, you may need serious help to make a business plan that's complete and always up-to-date. To get all the work done, you may have to hire people who have nothing to do but tend to your company's business plan full time. Unfortunately, creating a planning staff involves a real danger: Your plan can take on a life of its own and get completely divorced from what's really happening with your business. Remember: You have to make sure that your planners don't create plans all by themselves. To be of any use in the long run, the planning staff must support the managers who actually have to carry out the business plan.

Putting Your Plan on Paper

When you put together a business plan, your efforts take you in many directions. You face all sorts of issues related to the business that you're in. Right off the bat, for example, you need to answer basic questions about your company and what you want it to be in the future. Then you have to decide what targets to aim for as you look ahead and set business goals and objectives.

A large part of creating a business plan requires only a dose of good common sense on your part. But if you want to make sure that your business plan succeeds, you also have to take the time to do the following:

✔ Look closely at your industry

✔ Get to know your customers

✔ Check out your competitors

✔ List all your company's resources

✔ Note what makes your company unique

✔ List your company's advantages

✔ Figure out your basic financial condition

✔ Put together a financial forecast and a budget

In addition, you have to be prepared for everything to change down the road. So you also need to think about other options and alternatives and be on the lookout for new ways to make your company prosper.

You don't want to scare people – yourself included – with a written plan that's too long. The longer your plan is, in fact, the less likely people are to read it. Ideally, for a small or medium-sized company, your written plan should be 15 or 20 pages maximum. Remember that you can always support the main text with all the exhibits, appendixes, and references that you think it needs. If you want to glance at a sample business plan, jump to Chapter 16.

To remind yourself (and other people) that your written plan is forever a work in progress, we suggest that you keep it in a three-ring binder, or its electronic equivalent. That way, you can add or delete pages, and swap entire sections in or out, as your business plan changes – and we're certain that it *will* change. Fortunately, however, the format you use – all the major sections of a business plan – will stay the same.

Before you get your business plan under way, take a moment to review the following sections.

Executive summary

Your executive summary touches on everything that's important in your business plan. It's more than just a simple introduction; it's the whole plan, only shorter. In many cases, the people who read your plan won't need to go any further than the executive summary; if they do, the summary points them to the right place.

The executive summary isn't much longer than a page or two, and you should wait until the rest of the business plan is complete before you write it. That way, all you have to do is review the plan to identify the key ideas you want to convey.

If you want to make sure that people remember what you tell them, you have to say what you're going to say, say it, and then say what you've said. The executive summary is where you say what you're going to say.

Company overview

The company overview provides a place to make important observations about the nature of your business. In the overview, you discuss your industry, your customers, and the products and services you offer or plan to develop. Although you should try to touch on your company's business history and major activities in the overview, you can leave many of the details for the later sections.

To put together this kind of general company overview, you should draw on several key planning documents, including the following:

- **Mission statement:** A statement of your company's purpose, establishing what it is and what it does.
- **Goals and objectives:** A list of all the major goals that you set for your company, along with the objectives that you have to meet to achieve those goals.
- **Values statement:** The set of beliefs and principles that guide your company's actions and activities.
- **Vision statement:** A phrase or two that announces where your company wants to go or paints a broad picture of what you want your company to become.

To begin constructing these statements, turn to Chapters 2 and 3.

Business environment

The section of your business plan that deals with your business environment should cover all the major aspects of your company's situation that are beyond your immediate control, including the nature of your industry, the direction of the marketplace, and the intensity of your competition. You should look at each of these areas in detail to come up with lists of both the opportunities that your business environment offers and the threats that your company faces. Based on your observations, you can then describe what it takes to be a successful company.

Pay special attention to how your industry operates. You should describe the primary business forces that you see out there, as well as the key industry relationships that really determine how business gets done. Next, you should talk about your marketplace and your customers in more detail, perhaps even dividing the market into segments that represent the kinds of customers you serve. Finally, spend some time on the competition, describing what those companies are, what they're like, how they work, and what they're likely to be up to in the future.

For more information on how to explore your business circumstances and the overall environment that your company competes in, check out Chapters 4, 5, 6, and 7.

Company description

In the company description, you go into much more detail about what your company has to offer. The description should include some information about your management, the organisation, new technology, your products and services, company operations, your marketing potential – in short, anything special that you bring to your industry.

In particular, you should look carefully and objectively at the long list of your company's capabilities and resources. Sort out the capabilities that represent strengths from those that are weaknesses. In the process, try to point out where you have real advantages over your competitors.

Examining your company through your customers' eyes helps. With this viewpoint, you sometimes can discover customer value that you didn't know you were providing, and as a result, you can come up with additional long-term ways to compete in the market.

To start to put together all the things that your company brings to the table, flip to Chapters 8 and 9.

Company strategy

The section on company strategy brings together everything that you know about your business environment and your own company to come up with your projections of the future.

You want to take time in this section to map out your basic strategies for dealing with the major parts of your business, including the industry, your markets, and the competition. Talk about why the strategy is the right one, given your business situation. Describe how the strategy will play out in the future. Finally, point out specifically what your company needs to do to ensure that the strategy succeeds.

Everybody knows that the future is uncertain, so you should also talk about ways in which your business world may be different in the future than it is today. List alternative possibilities, and in each case, describe what your company is doing to anticipate the changes and take advantage of new opportunities.

To begin to prepare for change in your business world and get some help on how to think more strategically about your company's future, skip to Chapters 12, 13, and 14.

Financial review

Your financial review covers both where you stand today and where you expect to be in the future.

You should describe your current financial situation by using several standard financial statements. True, these statements don't make for the liveliest reading, but the people who are interested in this part of your business plan expect to see them. The basic financial statements include:

- ✓ **Profit and loss account:** A list of numbers that adds up all the revenue that your company brings in over a month, a quarter, or a year and then subtracts the total costs involved in running your business. What's left is your *bottom line* – the profit that you make during the period.

- ✓ **Balance sheet:** A snapshot of your financial condition at a particular moment, showing exactly what things your company owns, what money it owes, and what your company is really worth

- ✓ **Cash-flow statement:** A record that traces the flow of cash in and out of your company over a given period, tracking where the money comes from and where it ends up. The cash-flow statement only tracks money when you actually receive it or spend it.

Your projections about your future financial situation use exactly the same kind of financial statements. But for projections, you estimate all the numbers in the statements, based on your understanding of what's going to happen. Because nothing is certain, make sure to include all the assumptions you made to come up with your estimates in the first place.

To get a jump start on your company's financial planning, turn to Chapters 10 and 11.

Action plan

Your action plan lays out how you intend to carry out your business plan. This section should point out proposed changes in management or the organisation itself, for example, as well as new policies or procedures that you expect to put in place. You should also include any additional skills that you, your managers, and your employees may need to make the plan work. Finally, you want to talk a bit about how you're going to generate excitement for your business plan inside your company, so as to create a culture that supports what you're trying to accomplish. Only then can you have real confidence that your business plan is going to succeed.

For more background on how to make your business plan work after you put it all together, go straight to Chapter 15.

- ✔ The executive summary touches on all the important parts of your plan.

- ✔ The company overview describes the nature of your business, using your mission, values, and vision statements.

- ✔ Your business plan should analyse your business environment.

- ✔ The company description identifies your company's specific capabilities and resources.

- ✔ The plan should discuss your current business strategy.

- ✔ A financial review includes a profit and loss account, balance sheet, and cash-flow statement.

Chapter 2

Charting the Proper Course

*Y*ou probably have a pretty good idea of what you want to do with your business. But how do you make your idea a reality? You start by defining the business activities that your company plans to engage in, the goals that you expect to meet, and the ways in which you are going to measure success.

In this chapter, we help you create a basic overview of your company and its activities, shaping the description into your company's mission statement. We introduce goals and objectives, and show you how to use them to measure the results that you expect to achieve. We also examine business efficiency versus effectiveness, as well as management by objectives, and we help you prepare to set your own company's goals and objectives.

Creating Your Company's Mission Statement

True, no one jumps up and down with excitement at the idea of a mission statement. Too many of us have seen mission statements turning yellow on the cafeteria notice-board, completely ignored by everyone but the people who wrote them. But it doesn't have to be that way.

Your company's *mission statement* is meant to communicate the purpose of your business to people both inside and outside the organisation. It establishes who you are and what you do. To be effective, your mission statement must do the following things:

- Highlight your company's business activities, including the markets that it serves, the geographic areas that it covers, and the products and services that it offers.

- Emphasise the things your company does that set it apart from every other business out there.

- Include the major accomplishments that you anticipate you will achieve over the next few years.

- Convey what you have to say in a clear, concise, informative, and interesting manner. (A little inspiration doesn't hurt, either.)

Getting started

We know that creating a mission statement for your company can sound like an impossible task – the Mount Everest of business-planning chores. Some preparation up front, however, can make the process a little easier. Ask yourself the following background questions as you get ready to work on your company's mission statement. It's okay if the answers are fairly general at this point, because you're only interested in the basics right now. (If you feel that you need some help getting started, take a closer look at your customers in Chapters 5 and 6.)

- Which customers or groups of customers does your company plan to serve?

- What products or services does your company plan to provide?

- What needs do you satisfy?

- How do your company's products differ from the competition's?

- What extra value or benefits do customers receive when they choose your company over the competition?

- How fast are these answers changing?

In other words, a well-crafted mission statement answers a basic question:

> *What is your business?*

Need more help? That's not at all surprising. To create a mission statement that's worth anything requires the involvement of managers who are familiar with all aspects of your business. Follow these steps to begin the process:

1. **Get together a small group of people whose responsibilities cover all major functions and activities that the company is involved in.**

2. **Ask the group members to prepare for this assignment by coming up with their own answers to the background questions listed earlier in this section.**

3. **Review the reasons for having a company mission in the first place, and go over what the mission statement should include.**

4. **Schedule several informal meetings in which group members can present their own perspectives, brainstorm a bit, and begin to form a consensus.**

5. **Create, revise, and review the company's mission in as many formal meetings as it takes for everyone to be satisfied with the final mission statement.**

Capturing your business (in 50 words or less)

Your company's mission statement has to draw a compelling picture of what your business is all about. We often refer to this picture as creating a *tangible image* of the company. We'll begin with a first stab at a mission statement:

> *Our gizmos bring unique value to people, wherever they may be.*

Now, this statement is not a bad start; it says a little something about geography and a bit about being different. But it's far from complete. To work toward communicating the company's activities, accomplishments, and capabilities with more clarity and punch, we suggest expanding the statement as follows:

> *We provide the highest-quality gizmos, with unmatched value, to the global widget industry, allowing our customers to be leaders in their own fields.*

This statement tells you what the company does (provide highest-quality gizmos), who it serves (global widget industry), and what sets it apart from its competitors (unmatched value, which allows customers to lead their own fields). Its energy makes it a far more compelling mission statement than the earlier version.

How do real companies go about capturing their purpose clearly and concisely, in 50 words or less? The following examples provide useful insights:

Tesco (leading food retailer): We go the extra mile for customers, making shopping better, simpler, cheaper in every store, in every country in which we operate. Every little helps.

Otis Elevator (a leading manufacturer of lifts): Our mission is to provide any customer a means of moving people and things up, down, and sideways over short distances with higher reliability than any similar enterprise in the world.

Blooming Marvellous (fashionable clothes for mothers-to-be, by mail order and via the Internet): We aim to provide a wide choice of stylish, practical and good value maternity wear and children's wear, and the best in safe, innovative and stimulating nursery goods.

IBM: At IBM we strive to lead the world in the creation, development and manufacture of the industry's most advanced information technologies, including computer systems, software, networking systems, storage devices and microelectronics. We translate these advanced technologies into value for our customers through our professional solutions and services business worldwide.

International Red Cross (an international humanitarian organisation): The mission of the Red Cross is to improve the quality of human life; to enhance self-reliance and concern for others; and to help people avoid, prepare for, and cope with emergencies.

(Source: Company annual reports)

✔ A mission statement establishes what your company is and what it does.

✔ When you create your mission statement, involve people who represent all aspects of your business.

✔ Make your mission statement clear, concise, informative, and interesting.

Introducing Goals and Objectives

Your mission statement is a giant step forward; in it, you articulate the purpose of your company by defining the business that you're in. But that's just the first step. Have you ever planned a holiday trip by car? Choosing the destination is essential (and often painful, especially if the children want to go mad at Alton Towers and you want to relax into the gentle pace of life at Walton-on-the-Naze). The real effort starts, however, when you begin to work out an itinerary, carefully setting up mileage goals and sightseeing objectives so that you won't see your three-week getaway turn into a *Carry On* plot. Goals and objectives are just as important to successful business planning.

We bet that you're eager to jump right in here and get on with your business plan. We'd like to take a few moments up front, however, to introduce some important ideas that you can take advantage of when you begin setting your own goals and objectives.

Why bother?

Who needs goals, anyway? You may be the type who plans a trip by filling the camper van with petrol, stopping at the cash machine en route, and flipping a coin as you head out of town. Why waste time trying to decipher a map when you're just out for the ride? Maybe your approach is fine for a quick getaway adventure, but for a company, failing to set business goals can lead to rather more serious consequences.

If your company doesn't have goals to work toward, all directions are equal, every effort is useful, and any activity represents progress.

If your business opportunities are so obvious and so overwhelming that you don't need to define a particular course of action to reach your ultimate destination, you've won the business planner's lottery. It's far more likely, however, that you're going to run into one hazardous crossroad after another, and a lack of careful planning can be dangerous indeed.

- ✔ The Lloyd's of London debacle, which cost most of its 32,000 names (as those providing capital to the insurance market are known) almost their entire personal wealth, resulted from a failure to create prudent financial goals and objectives across an entire industry.

- ✔ Monumental planning blunders have been partly blamed for the collapse of the previously world-class UK motorcycle industry. The failure to anticipate and react to the Japanese market entry and superior product quality was a by-product of an industry that lacked a culture of planning.

Setting business goals and objectives provides an important insurance policy for your business: the opportunity to plan a successful course of action and then keep track of progress.

Goals versus objectives

After you complete a mission statement, your business goals lay out a basic itinerary for getting there. As a result, you often state those goals in terms of general business intentions. You may define your company's goals by using phrases such as 'becoming the market leader' or 'being the low-cost provider of choice'. These aims are clear enough to focus the company's activities without being so narrowly defined that they stifle creativity or limit flexibility.

Goals are broad business results that your company is absolutely committed to achieving. In working toward its goals, your company must be willing to come up with the resources – the money and the people – required to attain the intended results. The goals that you set for your company should ultimately dictate your business choices, driving decision making throughout your organisation. Goals should forge an unbreakable link between your company's actions and its mission.

Simply setting a general goal for your company isn't the end of the story. If that goal is to be reached, your company must also provide some guidance on how to get there. So your company must follow up its goal with a series of objectives: operational statements that specify exactly what must be done to reach the goal.

Objectives are specific statements that relate directly to a particular goal; they supply the details of what must be done and when. Objectives often have numbers and dates attached to them. In every case, it should be easy to verify that you've reached a given objective. Objectives never stand alone. Outside the context of their larger goals, they have little meaning. In fact, they can be downright confusing.

The goal 'Improve employee morale', for example, is much too general without specific objectives to back it up. Yet 'Reduce employee grievances by 35 per cent over the coming year' can be misinterpreted, if it's stated by itself. (One way to achieve this single objective is to terminate some employees and terrorise the rest of the workforce.) When the goal and objective are taken together, however, their meaning becomes clear.

Whirlpool Corporation and its Asian goal

Whirlpool Corporation is a leading manufacturer and marketer of home appliances. In a recent annual report, the company stated several business goals, including eventual market leadership in Asia. Japanese firms operating in the region have enjoyed that position for many years.

Whirlpool is organised into four regional units around the globe: North America, Europe, Latin America, and Asia. All regions but Asia recently posted higher earnings. Yet rather than pursue ways to cut costs and bring its Asia earnings up, the company invested in that region, positioning itself for the future. The goal of market leadership has clearly shaped Whirlpool's behaviour as it commits resources to the area.

The company supports its Asian goal with five key objectives:

- Partnering with solid local companies
- Positioning its brands in the region
- Transferring best practices into the region
- Leveraging its global scale of operations
- Developing human resources in the region

Whirlpool believes that it can achieve eventual market leadership in Asia by aggressively pursuing these five key objectives as a way to clarify its intentions and measure progress.

Want an easy way to keep the difference between goals and objectives straight? Remember the acronym *GOWN:* G for goals, O for objectives, W for words, and N for numbers. For goals, we use *words* – sketching in the broad picture. For objectives, we use *numbers* – filling in the specific details.

If you use different definitions for goals and objectives, don't worry, you're not going crazy. What's crazy is the lack of any standard definition of terms when it comes to business planning. The important thing is to settle on the definitions that you want to use and stick with them in a consistent manner. That way, you prevent any unnecessary confusion within your company.

Efficiency versus effectiveness

All this talk about goals and objectives provides us with the perfect opportunity to bring up another pair of business terms that have been bandied back and forth for years: *efficiency* and *effectiveness*. The terms were first thrown together in an absolutely captivating business classic, *Functions of the Executive,* written by Chester Barnard back in 1939. Old Chester was president of the New York Telephone Company, and we're afraid that he had a bit too much time on his hands. But he did come up with one notion that's still useful for working with your company's goals and objectives: efficiency versus effectiveness.

We all strive to be both efficient and effective in our individual work, of course. *Effectiveness* is often described as 'doing the right thing', whereas *efficiency* can be described as 'doing things right'. Chester came up with the idea that these concepts can also be applied to a company and its activities.

In this context, effectiveness – doing the right thing – has a great deal to do with choosing the right goals to pursue. For example, Global Gizmos Company's mission statement may emphasise becoming customer-focused and market-driven in all product areas. If Global Gizmos is to be effective, management must set goals that encourage product designers and engineers to be in touch with their customers *first* and to be aware of market demands *before* they start designing and creating new products.

Efficiency – doing things right – is concerned more with how well the company is applying resources in pursuit of its goals. To be efficient, Global Gizmos' employees must have objectives that ensure that the company can achieve its goals of becoming customer-focused and market-driven. Among other things, these objectives should lead to a proper allocation of the research budget among design, product development, and market testing. Resources are always scarce, and Global Gizmos Company can't afford to squander them.

Successful organisations are not just one or the other – either effective or effi-cient. The best companies are *both* efficient and effective on a consistent basis. These companies get that way by taking goal-setting and the development of clear, measurable objectives seriously in the relentless pursuit of the com-pany's mission.

Management by objectives

When you think about it, all the heroic efforts that you put into defining your company's mission and then setting goals and objectives are really aimed at improving the overall efficiency and effectiveness of your organisation. To a large extent, that also means getting the people in your company to march to the beat of the same drummer – ideally, one who's in step with your mission, goals, and objectives.

In 1954, another management guru, Peter Drucker, came up with a novel way to generate and communicate a company's intentions – its mission, goals, and objectives – simply by involving all the employees who have to actually carry them out. Not surprisingly, he also coined a term for his method, calling it *management by objectives* (or MBO).

In his hefty work, *The Practice of Management*, Drucker observed that a com-pany's goals and objectives are too often set in place at the highest levels of an organisation and eventually trickle down to middle managers, supervisors, and everybody else. Senior management assumes that its pearls of business wisdom are gratefully received with a cheerful 'Heigh-ho, heigh-ho, it's off to work we go' attitude.

MBO at Cyprus Semiconductor

Cyprus Semiconductor is a high-tech company that's been a consistent performer, in part because the company has embraced a com-puterised form of management by objectives called Turbo MBO. How does it work? Every week, the computer system tracks thousands of objectives for the company's several hundred employees. Each Monday, workgroups review the accomplishments of the preceding week, enter their results into the system, and get back to work. On Tuesday, managers look over the results and adjust their employees' objectives. On Wednesday, senior managers assess the general status of all goals, investigate problems, and come up with appropriate solutions.

Although Turbo MBO is carried out weekly, the process actually involves only a few hours of each manager's time. The company estimates that Turbo MBO has cut product development and delivery time in half, substantially increas-ing revenue and profits.

But, of course, not all the loyal subjects who are expected to carry out these lofty goals necessarily agree with them. Often, these same employees are closer to the issues and have a better perspective on what really has to be done than company leaders do. Accordingly, Drucker suggested MBO, a collaborative process in which all levels of the organisation are involved in setting the company's goals and objectives.

Management by objectives turned out to be a wildly successful idea when it was introduced. By the mid-1970s, more than half of the US Fortune 500 companies were using the technique. Granted, not everybody was happy with the process. Some companies baulked at the time and effort that it took to set MBO goals and related objectives. Other companies failed to carry out the paperwork that the system requires. Still other companies found the entire concept of shared decision making to be just plain weird and the new culture to be too alien.

For companies that are committed to using it correctly, MBO has proved to be a valuable management tool – a process capable of generating new ideas, communicating business intentions, and focusing the company's energy on an agreed-upon set of goals and objectives. Management by objectives works because it involves people in fashioning their own future. Employees are more committed to that future, because they have a greater stake in the process that's going to get them there. As you begin to work on your own company's goals and objectives, invest some well-spent hours in figuring out ways to bring the spirit of MBO into your collaborative process.

- ✔ *Goals* are the broad results that your company is committed to achieving.

- ✔ *Objectives* are the steps that you need to take to reach your goals.

- ✔ The right goals make your company more effective. The right objectives make your company more efficient.

- ✔ By giving everybody in your company a role in setting objectives, you stand a better chance of success.

Setting Your Own Goals and Objectives

Your company's goals and objectives reflect your primary business intentions, and they determine both the itinerary and timetable for getting you there. In other words, your goals and objectives focus the company on the important work at hand and provide a mechanism for measuring your progress.

Goals and objectives are ultimately meant to make your company more efficient and effective. But how can you see to it that setting them is also as efficient and effective as it can be? Like so much of business planning, this process involves a large dose of common sense.

Guidelines for setting goals

Goals are the broad business results that your company is committed to achieving. To jump start the process of setting your company's goals, here's a useful set of guidelines:

- ✔ Determine who will be involved in setting your company's goals. Because goals are the core of your company's business, the group members should include the people who are responsible for all your major business activities. If you're going it alone in business, try to develop a core group of advisers who can meet with you periodically to set goals.

- ✔ Develop a procedure for monitoring your company's goals on a routine basis, revising or reworking them as business circumstances change.

- ✔ Create individual goals that clarify your company's business activities without limiting flexibility and creativity.

- ✔ Confirm that your company's goals, taken together, provide an effective blueprint for achieving your broad business intentions.

- ✔ Make sure that your company's stated goals are closely tied to your company's mission statement.

- ✔ Use the goals to communicate your business intentions to people both inside and outside your company.

Guidelines for setting objectives

This set of guidelines provides a useful template when your company starts to develop business objectives. Remember – objectives are the statements that fill in the details, specifying exactly how you're going to reach each of your company's goals. As much as possible, your objectives should be tied to cold, hard numbers: the number of new customers you want, for example, or products sold, or money earned:

- ✔ Determine who will set business objectives in your company. Objectives determine what must be done and when, and should involve every employee.

- ✔ Develop a system for setting, reviewing, and managing business objectives throughout your company.

- ✔ Make sure that objectives are achievable and verifiable by including numbers and dates where appropriate.

- ✔ Create business objectives that are clearly linked to, and that advance, larger company goals.

✔ Confirm that your company's objectives, taken together, result in an efficient use of resources – money and people – in pursuit of broader business intentions.

✔ Consider using a formal method, such as management by objectives (MBO) or Investors In People (IIP) to involve everyone in your company in the continuous process of setting, reviewing, and meeting business objectives. Check out the sidebar 'Investing in Your Staff' for a little more information on IIP.

Getting it right

We've said it over and over, but it's so important that it deserves repeating one more time: Your company's goals and objectives must be closely tied to your mission.

Too many companies become near-sighted and simply forget their broad business intentions when they go about the nitty-gritty work of setting goals and tying them to measurable objectives. Managers start with whatever's close at hand. They look at employee activities and behaviour, and come up with incentives and rewards that seem to do the right thing at the moment, motivating workers toward specific (and maybe even laudable) objectives. But these types of goals and objectives tend to be near-sighted, and may be totally out of kilter with the larger aims of the company.

Investing in Your Staff

Investors in People sets standards of good practice for preparing and developing your employees to meet your business objectives. The development goes far beyond simple training activities. There are four main principles.

1. Commitment: An Investor in People is fully committed to developing its people in order to achieve its aims and objectives.

2. Planning: An Investor in People is clear about its aims and objectives and what its people need to do to achieve them.

3. Action: An Investor in People develops its people effectively in order to improve its performance.

4. Evaluation: An Investor in People understands the impact of its investment in people on its performance.

A series of 'indicators' are used by an external body to assess whether your company meets the IIP standards. A copy of the IIP Standard, the indicators, and related publications are available from the Investors in People UK order line on 01268 888238 (fax: 01268 417163). For more information on IIP call 0207 4671946. You can also visit their Web site at www.iipuk.co.uk.

Suppose that a PC mail-order business finds that its margins are squeezed. As a result, the company sets objectives and offers incentive bonuses to managers who can reduce expenses by 15 per cent during the next six-month reporting period. The manager in charge of customer service, being a rational team player, mandates an immediate reduction in the average time that service reps can spend on the phone with customer inquiries. He delivers this mandate even though the company has built its reputation on helping customers with confusing software purchases, and even though the company mission states 'The organisation is committed to offering the best customer service in the industry.'

Hurried conversations inevitably lead to disgruntled customers. Even worse, these objectives send a clear signal to employees that efficiency and cost-cutting efforts are what really count – not customer satisfaction. If goals and objectives had taken the company's mission into account, perhaps the customer service manager would have come up with a more innovative solution – introducing an automated fax-back system, for example. By allowing customers the option of receiving faxes that answer the most common software questions, the system could have reduced calls to the service reps and enhanced service at the same time.

Goals with a mission

Innovex, a £50 million sales recruitment and management business operating in the health care market before its sale to Quintiles, operated throughout the UK and provided a flexible menu of sales and marketing services ranging from a long-term strategic partnership to a temporary increase in sales force headcount to hundreds of clients.

Innovex: Our Mission

Innovex's Mission is to be the preferred provider for health sales support services in the communities we serve. Our customers will choose us because we provide high-quality, cost-effective, customer-responsive care and services.

Innovex: Long-range Strategic Goals

✔ Become a £250 million diversified health care company within five years

✔ Develop a market-driven organisation

✔ Create a quality-centred culture

✔ Build value in our company by investing in our people

✔ Create exceptional value for our shareholders

(Source: Company Business Plan)

Given the company's mission, Innovex's goals make perfect sense. By pursuing the goals of becoming market-driven and quality-centred, for example, the company understands that it will better serve customers and thus achieve part of its mission: becoming customers' preferred provider.

Avoiding the pitfalls

Setting your company's goals and objectives is really about influencing human behaviour. Goals and objectives are meant to motivate everyone in your organisation. They also see to it that everyone's activities are channelled in the same direction, with the same results in mind. Whenever human nature is involved, nothing is certain. But you can improve the odds that your actions will have the expected results by avoiding several common pitfalls as your company works on its business goals and objectives.

Don't set pie-in-the-sky goals for yourself. If you don't have a prayer of achieving a goal, you may as well not bother setting it. Goals are meant to motivate; impossible goals tend to discourage. You don't want to mess up a knockout business opportunity just because you need a little more time, resources, and energy.

Don't sell your organisation short. Although trying to reach too far with your goals can be dangerous, you don't want to wimp out, either. Goals often become self-fulfilling prophecies. Companies set them, attain them, and then relax – coasting along on automatic pilot – until they get around to setting new goals. If anything, try to err a bit on the high side, creating goals that will expand your organisation's capabilities. You may be surprised by the skills and expertise that you discover in your own company.

Be careful what you aim for. It's awfully important that your goals clearly state what you want to see happen. If your goals are unclear or off the mark, you and your employees may actually end up pursuing misguided aims in a determined manner. Goals that are out of sync with a company's larger mission may lead to behaviour that makes little sense from the broader perspective and purpose of the company.

Beware of too many words or too many numbers. Remember – a goal is a broad statement of a business intention that flows directly from your company's mission. Objectives are more narrowly defined and are always tied to a specific goal; they fill in the details, specify time frames, and include ways of verifying success. As we've said, goals tend to be defined in words; objectives, in numbers. But no rule is hard and fast. In reality, well-designed goals and objectives often mix words and numbers. Words alone are sometimes too vague to carry any real meaning, and not all hoped-for outcomes can be reduced to pure numbers.

Don't keep your goals and objectives a secret. If goals and objectives are meant to focus and direct your organisation's behaviour, everyone has to know about them. We know, we know – this statement seems to be so obvious that it sounds downright silly. But you'd be amazed at the number of managers and owners who carefully set goals and objectives and then go to great lengths to hide them from everyone else. They protect the goals as though they were corporate jewels. But these jewels have no value unless they are communicated to and embraced by everybody in the company.

Timing is everything

What's the proper timeframe for your goals and objectives? How far out should your planning horizon be – one year, three years, maybe five? (Until the fall of communism, five-year plans were all the rage.) The answer is . . . it depends.

Certain industries remain almost tortoise-like in their pace. Many furniture companies in the UK, for example, operate today much as they did 50 years ago. Consumer tastes have changed only slowly, and the types of materials used and levels of craftsmanship required have stayed pretty much the same. Change may be on the horizon, however, with producers overseas matching style, materials, and quality at significantly lower costs.

Change is perhaps the only constant for other industries. Take health care, for example. The world of doctors and hospitals was once a predictable universe in which business goals and objectives could be developed years in advance. Now the industry is going through a sea of change. Predicting where the rough waters are going to be is often an exercise in frustration. If you're in hospital management today, you're not worried about five-year horizons; your planning cycles and reviews are now more likely to be measured in months.

What change means for business planners is that you don't want to go too far out on a limb when trying to predict the future. You really have no choice but to set business goals and follow them up with verifiable objectives, but don't get into a position where you construct rigid guidelines over impossibly long time frames. Build in flexibility so that you have the opportunity to revisit your goals and objectives, trimming and tacking to avoid being capsized by all the uncertainty.

Identify the forces of change in your own industry. What are they? How fast are they moving? Chapter 4 points out how to look for opportunities and threats out there. Look at Chapter 12 for more guidance in preparing for change.

  ✔ Make sure that your company's goals are closely tied to its mission statement.

  ✔ Ambitious goals motivate; impossible goals only discourage.

  ✔ Settle on objectives that are both achievable and measurable.

  ✔ Communicate your goals and objectives to everybody in your company.

Chapter 3

Setting Off in the Right Direction

● ●

In This Chapter

▶ Understanding why a set of values is so important

▶ Figuring out who your stakeholders are

▶ Identifying your company's current beliefs and principles

▶ Putting together your company values statement

▶ Creating a vision statement for your company

● ●

*Y*ou may ask yourself why on earth you're reading a chapter on values and vision in a book on business planning. We can hear what you're thinking: Hey, it's the twenty-first century. Today's business ethics revolve around survival in the marketplace: Cater to your customers, beat the competition (hey, demolish them!), make 'loadsamoney', and run.

Yet even in a business world dominated by market economies, global competition, and the laws of the jungle, values still matter. In fact, we're convinced that successful business plans must start with a statement of company values.

Now, don't get us wrong here – we have no quarrel with profits. We absolutely love them, and we expect to earn lots for ourselves over time. But short-term profits don't go far over the long haul. Values and a vision keep everybody in your company – even if there are only two of you – on course and heading in the same direction. What if you're a company of one? Taking time to establish your values and vision will still keep you on track as your business grows.

In this chapter, we point out why values are so important in the first place. We help you identify your company's values by noting who has a stake in your business and discovering the beliefs and business principles that you already hold. Then we show you how to put together a values statement and create a vision statement for your company.

Why Values Matter

Your company faces all sorts of options, alternatives, and decisions every day that you're in business. If you take the time to define your company's values, these principles and beliefs can guide your managers, employees, or just you (if you're in business for yourself) as you face complicated issues that don't have easy answers. When the unexpected happens, you'll be able to react quickly and decisively, based on a clear sense of what's important.

Tough choices

Consider a scenario. Frank Little is an independent consultant working for a large UK-based petrochemical firm that we'll call Bigg Oil. He's conducting market analysis for one of the company's largest divisions and is involved in an important project concerning the development of new overseas business.

Frank's good at what he does, and he sketches out several options for the production, distribution, and pricing of petrochemicals in three countries. In one of his most promising scenarios, the numbers for a country that we'll call Friedonia yield substantially higher short-term profits than the other two – primarily because that nation doesn't yet have expensive pollution-control procedures in place. The other two nations have environmental laws similar to those in the UK.

Here's Frank's dilemma: By introducing its product line into Friedonia, Frank's client can make huge profits. Sure, the resulting pollution may cause ecological damage that could possibly be traced back to Bigg Oil. But there is nothing illegal in the company's activities, according to Friedonia's current laws, and Frank stands to get a lot more business from Bigg Oil if the project goes ahead.

He agonises over the situation and his report. What should Frank recommend to senior management?

- ✔ Go for the short-term bucks.
- ✔ Voluntarily enact procedures to control pollution, even though the company is not legally required to do so.
- ✔ Forget Friedonia until the country has stronger environmental laws.

Maybe you can relate to our friend Frank's quandary, having faced similar kinds of ethical questions and trade-offs in your own business.

If Frank had a set of values written down, those values could help him out of his quandary. Values provide a framework to guide people who are confronted with difficult choices.

Having no fundamental guidelines to follow – or, worse yet, being told to play it safe or 'don't rock the boat' – businesspeople in Frank's position are forced to choose the safest path, and that path is often determined by profits alone. But the easiest path is not always the best.

Lost and unprepared

What happens when disaster strikes? We all remember headline-grabbing stories in which unexpected troubles tarnished the images of all sorts of companies, such as the following:

- ✔ **Exxon (oil manufacturer and exporter):** The infamous oil tanker *Valdez* spilled millions of gallons of crude oil into a pristine Alaskan bay, causing incalculable environmental damage.

- ✔ **Perrier (natural carbonated water bottler):** In 1989, French-based Perrier was the market leader in bottled mineral water, its name synonymous with purity and quality. Perrier water was on the tables of virtually every high-class restaurant around the world. Sales peaked at 1.2 billion bottles a year. The plant at Vergèze, near Nimes, was tooled up for 1.5 billion, with capital investment and personnel to match. The Perrier water benzene contamination incident in 1990 wiped out a lifetime investment in promoting the images of purity and quality.

- ✔ **Intel (computer chip manufacturer):** A flaw in its Pentium chip (which was or wasn't really significant, depending on who you talked to) led to corporate apologies and product replacement.

These companies all stumbled over so-called externalities (to use economics doublespeak). *Externalities* refer to those circumstances that extend beyond a firm's immediate control to issues that are deeper than simply making a mint. Over time, the failure to see the power of these outside forces – and to account for social and ethical values when you make decisions – can result in serious or even disastrous consequences for your company. As the examples illustrate, we're not talking about one unhappy customer, folks; we're talking about big-time trouble.

Our list of examples could include episodes involving companies of every size in all industries. Faced with unexpected events, unprepared companies often react as though they are in total disarray. When a company lacks a set of stated values that everybody subscribes to, the interpretation of important issues is left up to anyone and everyone in the company. Then the company is likely to find itself speaking with many voices and going in several directions, resulting in confused employees, unhappy customers, an angry public, and maybe, disappointed investors.

The value of having values

A *values statement* is a set of beliefs and principles that guides the activities and operations of a company, no matter what its size. The people at the top of your company must exemplify your stated values, and your company's incentive and reward systems should lead all employees to act in ways that support your company's values.

Here's an example of just how important a values statement can be. In the summer of 1985, the United States experienced what was described by many people as a terrorist attack. Someone in the Chicago area tampered with bottles of Tylenol, the best-selling pain reliever from McNeil Laboratories, a subsidiary of the health care giant Johnson & Johnson. An unknown number of Tylenol capsules were laced with cyanide, and eight people died. The tragedy created a business crisis for Johnson & Johnson.

Johnson & Johnson reacted quickly and decisively to the threat against its customers. The company pulled every bottle of Tylenol from retail shelves throughout America – a massive undertaking that ultimately cost the company more than $100 million – and it did so immediately upon learning of the problem.

When the crisis was finally over, Johnson & Johnson became a corporate role model. The company's lightning-fast response to the Tylenol incident earned it a reputation as one of the most responsible companies in the world, one that takes its civic duties seriously and is willing to put the public good ahead of its own profits. Johnson & Johnson's many businesses benefited accordingly.

Why did Johnson & Johnson behave so well when so many other companies find themselves paralysed in similar situations? The reasons are summed up in the company's statement of values, an extraordinary document called the Johnson & Johnson Credo (see the 'The Johnson & Johnson Credo' sidebar).

For more than half a century, the credo has successfully guided behaviour and actions across the sprawling Johnson & Johnson empire, currently a £17 billion worldwide corporation employing more than 109,500 people.

The Johnson & Johnson Credo

'We believe our first responsibility is to the doctors, nurses, and patients, to mothers and all others who use our products and services. In meeting their needs, everything we do must be of high quality. We must constantly strive to reduce our costs in order to maintain reasonable prices. Customers' orders must be serviced promptly and accurately. Our suppliers and distributors must have an opportunity to make a fair profit.

We are responsible to our employees, the men and women who work with us throughout the world. Everyone must be considered as an individual. We must respect their dignity and recognize their merit. They must have a sense of security in their jobs. Compensation must be fair and adequate, and working conditions clean, orderly, and safe. Employees must feel free to make suggestions and complaints. There must be equal opportunity for employment, development, and advancement for those qualified. We

must provide competent management, and their actions must be just and ethical.

We are responsible to the communities in which we live and work and to the world community as well. We must be good citizens – support good works and charities and bear our fair share of taxes. We must encourage civic improvements and better health and education. We must maintain in good order the property we are privileged to use, protecting the environment and natural resources.

Our final responsibility is to our stockholders. Business must make a sound profit. We must experiment with new ideas. Research must be carried on, innovative programs developed and mistakes paid for. New equipment must be purchased, new facilities provided and new products launched. Reserves must be created to provide for adverse times. When we operate according to these principles, the stockholders should realize a fair return.'

The Johnson & Johnson Credo works so well because each employee takes it seriously. With the active encouragement and involvement of top management, from the chairperson on down, the credo is invoked, praised, and communicated throughout the company. Old-timers and new employees alike are continually reminded of the importance of the message. Promotions depend, in part, on how well managers live up to and disseminate the values of the credo within their areas of responsibility. The credo is a significant factor in Johnson & Johnson's continued performance near the top of its industry – and an indication of why the company is so well regarded by so many people.

    ✔ A values statement is a set of beliefs and principles to guide your company's activities.

    ✔ Clearly stated values can help your company react quickly and decisively when the unexpected strikes.

    ✔ Everybody in your company must embrace the company's values.

Identifying Your Company's Values

Values statements often address several audiences. The Johnson & Johnson Credo (refer to the preceding section), for example, speaks to doctors, patients, customers, suppliers, distributors, employees, stockholders, and the community at large. As you begin to work on your own company's values, you should think about different groups, each of which has some relationship with your company.

Stakeholders are groups of people who have some claim or interest in how you operate your business. The stakes involved can be tangible and legally binding, or they may be informal arrangements or expectations that have developed over time. Although all of these interested parties have a stake in what you do, stakeholders may have different ideas and rather strong feelings about what values your company should embrace.

You're going to put together a values statement primarily for the benefit of employees, of course (or just for yourself, if you operate a business alone). But your company's values are going to have an obvious impact on all your stakeholders, including owners, shareholders, customers, suppliers, regulators – and even your mother, if she loaned you £10,000 to start your business. As you start to identify the values that are most important to your company, you're going to have to consider different viewpoints, including the following:

✔ The demands of your shareholders (if you have any)

✔ The interests and expectations of all your stakeholders

✔ The beliefs and principles that you and your company already hold

In the following sections, we take a closer look at each of these factors. When you come up with a preliminary list of company values that you feel are most important, you'll be in a good position to go on and create a values statement.

Investors

Economists argue that when it comes to company values, you really have to worry about only one significant group: the shareholders. On paper, at least, the shareholders are the true owners of the firm, and they deserve your undivided attention. In this view of the world, managers are simply paid agents of those who own the company, no matter how far removed those owners may be, and you don't need to know much more about values except to carry out your shareholders' wishes.

A short values statement that works

McKinsey provide a marvellous example of a set of values which have been strongly and clearly articulated for over 60 years in such a way that any member of the professional staff who is or ever has been employed with McKinsey, anywhere in the world, can instantly, seriously, and passionately tell you what the company stands for. This is done through a set of 'guiding principles':

Serving clients

✔ Adhere to professional standards

✔ Follow the top management approach

✔ Assist the client in implementation and capability building

✔ Perform consulting in cost-effective manner

Building the firm

✔ Operate as one firm

✔ Maintain a meritocracy

✔ Show a genuine concern for our people

✔ Foster an open and non-hierarchical working atmosphere

✔ Manage the firm's resources responsibly

Being a member of the professional staff

✔ Demonstrate commitment to client service

✔ Strive continuously for superior quality

✔ Advance the state of the art of management

✔ Contribute to a spirit of partnership through teamwork and collaboration

✔ Profit from the freedom and assume the responsibility associated with self-governance

✔ Uphold the obligation to dissent

Now, we can't really argue with this picture, as far as it goes, but it doesn't square with the intentions of many shareholders out there today. For starters, your company may not have any investors, unless you count yourself and the bank account that you wiped out to start your company. In addition, pension funds and unit trusts now control the majority of publicly-held shares, and the investors who buy these funds are mainly interested in making their own personal nest eggs grow. These shareholders are absentee owners. They seldom demand a serious say in management decision making. When something goes wrong with the company or with their fund, they simply sell the shares and get on with their next investment.

So what's our point? Although shareholders obviously are an important bunch, deserving the attention of companies that have shareholders, their demands shouldn't necessarily crowd out all other voices. Remember – your shareholders have the luxury of selling off shares and moving on to other choices when things go wrong. As a manager or owner, you don't have that option.

Your company will be much better off in the long run if you take a broader view, acknowledging not just the shareholders, but also all the stakeholders, giving each group the attention that it deserves.

The rest of the crew

If you think about it, you may be surprised at how many types of people are involved in what your company does – everyone from suppliers to distributors and from bankers to customers. Each group has its own set of interests and looks to your company to fulfil a series of promises. The explicit promises that you make may take the form of legal agreements, licences, freelance agreements, or purchase orders. Your implicit promises represent the unwritten expectations of the various groups that have dealings with your company.

For each group of stakeholders that you identify, you should ask two basic questions:

✔ What are these people most interested in?

✔ What do these people expect from my company?

In other words, what is their stake in the activities and behaviour of your company? At first glance, it may seem that your interests conflict with your stakeholders' interests. *You* may want to maximise profits over time as one of your company's key values, for example. You may decide that serving customers is important as well. But what do your *customers* want? They certainly have a stake in your business, and it's probably safe to say that they are looking for quality products and services at reasonable prices.

Do these two values conflict with each other? Not necessarily. Wouldn't most customers rather buy from companies that they trust, companies that they feel comfortable with, companies that have served them well in the past? In addition, customers don't really like the uncertainty and time wasted in trying new products or services, and they won't make a change unless they're really pushed to do so. In other words, most of your customers don't want to deny you profits, because they realise that your business – and their favourite goods and services – won't be around for long if you can't make any money. (For the lowdown on figuring out your customers, check out Chapters 5 and 6.)

At the same time, customers aren't stupid and certainly don't want to be taken advantage of. We've all heard stories about food and hardware shops that try to make a quick buck after floods, hurricanes, or earthquakes. Although competition usually keeps prices in check, scarcity creates opportunity and the temptation to overcharge customers. But again, customers are stakeholders in the business, with interests and expectations. After a disaster is over and the clean-up is behind them, those same customers often take their cash elsewhere, rewarding stores that may have behaved more responsibly in the crisis.

It's time to bring together all your information on the people who have a stake in your company and to create a stakeholder profile. Follow these steps:

1. **List all interest groups that have a relationship with your company.**

   Don't forget to include the less-obvious candidates. Your list may include customers, owners, shareholders, banks, creditors, suppliers, distributors, business partners, industry associates, regulatory agencies, advocacy groups, and so on.

2. **Rank the stakeholders by importance to the business.**

   How does each group affect your business goals?

3. **Record what you think are the interests of each group.**

4. **Record what you think are the expectations of each group.**

Do your company's actions fit with what you have identified as being your key stakeholders' expectations? You should always be aware of how your business decisions are perceived by the general public. How do those decisions look from the other side? Do you see satisfied customers, contented employees, helpful creditors, responsive suppliers, and eager distributors? If not, how is your company going to respond to those stakeholders who feel that you are letting them down?

Ideally, of course, you want to plan ahead when it comes to your dealings with all stakeholders. The secret to responding before molehills become mountains lies in having a clear understanding of each group's expectations and a set of values that acknowledges each group's interests.

Existing beliefs and principles

Drawing up a list of abstract beliefs and principles is one thing, putting those beliefs to the test is another. Tough choices come along, forcing you to examine your beliefs closely. If you run a one-person company, you already know something about what you stand for. If you're part of a bigger company, chances are that certain beliefs and values are inherent in the way in which your company does business. The best way to get to the heart of those beliefs and principles is to imagine how youd respond to tough dilemmas.

Think about the situations described in the Beliefs and Principles Questionnaire (see Figure 3-1). Ask other people in your company, or trusted colleagues from outside your business, how they'd react to these situations. Chances are you'll wish that the questionnaire included a box marked *Other* or *Don't know*. But the whole point of situations that put your values to the test is that they're not always easy.

Keep in mind that there are no right or wrong answers; no one's going to send a note home or give anyone a bad mark. You're simply trying to identify the basic values that your company already feels comfortable with. Completed questionnaires give insights into the general beliefs and principles that your company considers to be important.

- Many people, ranging from employees to customers, have a stake in what your company does.

- Different stakeholders may have different viewpoints when it comes to your company's values.

- It's important for your company to acknowledge as many stakeholder perspectives as possible.

- Company values should be tied to the beliefs and principles that you already hold.

Beliefs and Principles Questionnaire

Situation	Possible response
A disgruntled customer demands a full sales refund on a product. The product isn't defective but can't be resold. The customer insists that it just doesn't work correctly. Would you be more inclined to:	❏ Send the customer away, keeping the sale on the books ❏ Refund the customer's money, absorbing the loss but betting on repeat business and loyal customers
You are faced with filling a key position in your company. Would you be more inclined to:	❏ Recruit a person from the outside who has the necessary job skills but little experience in your industry ❏ Promote an experienced and loyal employee, providing job-skills training
You are forced to let one of your employees go. Would you tend to dismiss:	❏ The young, recently hired university graduate, inexperienced but energetic ❏ The 55-year-old manager with 20 years at the company, solid and hard-working but somewhat set in his or her ways
You find out that a long-term supplier has been routinely undercharging you for services, increasing your own profit margins. Would you be inclined to:	❏ Let the matter pass, assuming that it's ultimately the supplier's mistake and responsibility ❏ Take the initiative to correct the invoice error in the future ❏ Offer to not only correct the mistake, but also pay back the accumulated difference

(continued)

Beliefs and Principles Questionnaire *Continued*

Situation	Possible response
You have a brilliant and creative employee. Unfortunately, this employee continually flouts the rules and disrupts the entire company. Would you tend to:	❑ Tolerate the behaviour ❑ Work on ways to correct the situation ❑ Sack the employee
An employee is faced with a personal dilemma. To meet a deadline on an important project, the employee must work overtime and miss a child's birthday celebration. Which do you tend to think of as the "better" employee:	❑ The one who willingly agrees to work overtime ❑ The one who declines to come in and instead attends the birthday party
To meet your profit target for the coming quarter, you are faced with reducing costs. Would you lean toward:	❑ Cutting back on customer-service expenses ❑ Reducing current investment in new product development ❑ Missing the quarterly target, concluding that the long-term investments are both necessary and justified
When developing the compensation packages for managers in your company, would you support:	❑ Incentives based primarily on rewarding individual effort ❑ Compensation systems that promote attainment of group or team-based goals
You discover that one of your products doesn't quite meet its published specifications. Would your likely response be to:	❑ Immediately alert your customers to the discrepancy ❑ Invest some time and effort in understanding the problem before informing customers ❑ Quietly correct the error, assuming that if customers were having problems, they would have already come to you
Rank the following in terms of their importance to you in your business:	❑ Maximize profits ❑ Satisfy customers ❑ Create jobs ❑ Promote new technologies ❑ Win product-quality awards ❑ Beat the competition ❑ Maintain long-term growth ❑ Dominate markets

Figure 3-1:
Beliefs and
Principles
Question-
naire.

Answers to the questionnaire point to the beliefs and principles that your company's managers and employees already hold.

Putting Together the Values Statement

When you have a good idea of just who your company's stakeholders are, and when you have got to grips with the general beliefs and principles that your company already holds, you have to bring these two worlds together. But how do you create a written statement of values based on those general beliefs and principles that will also guide your company toward doing the right thing in the eyes of all your stakeholders?

First, keep in mind that your company's values statement represents more than a quick to-do list. Your values reach beyond quarterly goals or even yearly targets. They're meant to guide you through those tough decisions as you build a sustainable business that will last and grow over years and decades.

Maybe your company already has some sort of values credo in place. If so, you're a step ahead of the game. (You lose points, however, if you have to glance at the dusty plaque on the office wall to read it.) If you can't dig up a ready-made values statement to start with, begin putting together your own. You have two options.

The quick way to develop a values statement

You may not have the luxury of spending weeks or months to develop a values statement, so we'll show you a quick way to create one that will set your company on the right track. If your company is small, you can follow the steps yourself or with one or two of your colleagues – no need for long meetings and careful review. If you're part of a larger company, however, you're going to have to go through a bit more rigmarole to get a consensus. Sorry.

1. **Meet with your company's chief decision-makers to talk about the general company values that should guide employee behaviour.**

2. **Prepare a first-draft list of all the values discussed in the meeting and circulate copies for review.**

3. **Schedule one or two follow-up meetings with senior managers to clarify and confirm a final set of values.**

4. **Create a values statement that captures the agreed-upon values clearly and concisely, and get it approved.**

5. **Meet with managers at all levels to make sure that they understand the importance of, and reasoning behind, the company values statement.**

6. **See that every employee gets a copy of the statement.**

The values statement that you come up with here may serve you well for a long time. At the very least, it should meet your needs while you work on a more complete and permanent version.

Make sure that every employee receives a copy of your company's values statement, along with an explanation of its purpose. If you're in business for yourself, place a framed copy of the values statement near your desk or (if you work from home) stick it on the fridge. Don't let it gather dust. For a bigger company, print the values statement on wallet-sized cards, and don't forget to include it in the annual report. It's important that your company's values are referred to, relied on, and understood to be a guiding force in the actions and activities of every person who represents your company.

The long way to develop a values statement

Why is the quick way to create a values statement not always good enough? If you're part of a large firm, the quick way relies heavily on the ideas and suggestions of people at the top of the organisation. Yet the best insights on company values often come from employees themselves – people from different backgrounds and various levels in the company who can draw on a range of business experiences.

The long way to create a values statement takes a little more effort, but getting these employees involved usually is worth it. Follow these steps:

1. **Select three or four representative groups of employees, including a mix of people from all levels and functions in your company.**

2. **Have the groups meet on a rather formal basis over a two- to three-month period to come up with values that should guide the behaviour of every employee in the firm.**

   You have to point the groups in the right direction at the beginning. Start by asking everyone to fill out the questionnaire shown in Figure 3-1 earlier in this chapter.

3. **Ask group members to create a short list of the values that they think are most important.**

   Encourage them to back up this list with their reasons, reminding them that values are often the tiebreakers when it comes to tough management decisions and difficult choices.

4. **Bring the lists together and create a priority ranking of all the values suggested.**

5. **Compose a statement, motto, or credo that includes the most significant and widely held values, along with compelling reasons for those values.**

6. **Have the groups review and ratify your values statement.**

When it's time to conduct those annual employee performance reviews (you know, the ones that everyone loves to hate), use them as an opportunity to promote your company's values. Bring out a copy of the values statement and ask each employee how well his or her individual activities reflect the company's values. At the same time, ask yourself whether the incentive and reward systems in your company work toward supporting those values.

- ✔ Even though you think that you know your values, getting them down on paper is worth the effort.
- ✔ The best insights on company values come from employees themselves.
- ✔ Make the values statement available to everybody in your company.

Creating Your Company's Vision Statement

After you identify the stakeholders in your company and create your company's values statement, it's time to come up with a *vision statement* – a precise, well-crafted set of words announcing where your company wants to go or painting a picture of what your company wants to become. To people inside and outside your company, your vision statement is your compass, showing the whole world the direction in which your company is headed.

A vision statement not only points the way to the future, but also makes you want to get up and go there. It represents your company's best hopes and brightest dreams. Now, we know that Karl Marx and his crew seldom come up in conversation at cocktail parties any longer, even in Moscow. But when you hear his message

> *Workers of the world, unite! You have nothing to lose but your chains!*

it's hard not to be roused, even today. Effective vision statements are, in part, inspirational calls to action. What if Marx had come up with something like this:

> *Hey, guys, let's all get together over here! Maybe we can figure out how to make you more dosh!*

Karl who? Forget that place in history.

Don't panic if you don't have the makings of a dynamic, charismatic leader in your back pocket. An insightful corporate vision is much more likely to develop out of a diverse team of hard-working folks than to spring mysteriously from an inspired moment in the life of a leader. And if you wait around for the person at the top to produce something, you may never see a vision statement. Tackle the task on your own, before it's requested from above, and you just may jump-start a process that's long overdue.

It shouldn't surprise you to learn that the best way to create a meaningful vision statement looks a lot like the best way to create a values statement. Just follow these steps:

1. **Select a small group of dedicated employees from various levels across your company.**

   If your company is small, get the whole gang together. If you're the chief cook and bottle washer all in one, you can represent yourself. Remember – the more people you involve, the broader the perspective and the better the chance you'll get a vision statement that truly reflects your company's future.

2. **Have the group reread your company's values statement and review the list of stakeholders who have an interest in your company.**

3. **Begin a verbal free-for-all.**

   Allow everybody to add his or her own two pennies' worth and to volunteer personal opinions and ideas about the company's future form and direction.

4. **After the vision team feels comfortable with its work, add the finishing touches and send the draft upstairs.**

   If it's to take on its rightful role, a vision statement must be embraced and promoted by managers at the top.

Keep these tips in mind when you create your vision statement:

✔ Make sure that no one dominates the discussion as the team begins to toss around ideas and the phrases that will form your company's vision. There's no faster way to kill off creativity than having every idea come from one person.

✔ Allow sufficient time for the words to grow on the group, permitting the deeper meanings to sink in. You can't accomplish the vision statement process in one quick take. Good vision statements have a tendency to evolve over time – and several meetings.

✔ Make sure that your company's vision statement is tied to your company's reality. Nothing is worse than creating a vision that has more to do with fantasy than with the future. Fantasy visions generate nothing but a sense of confusion and alienation among everyone involved.

Although your vision statement may be only a couple of sentences or even just a phrase, the vision statement is the compass that provides your company's direction into the future. Spend enough time with your statement to make sure that the north on your compass truly is north – that it does indeed point in the direction in which you want to go.

As a rule of thumb, you should assume that your vision statement will serve the company for the next decade. Does this mean that you can never change the statement? No – but you should change a vision statement only if business conditions truly warrant a new course of action. Keep in mind that the ideas you captured in your company's vision statement aren't meant to be crossed out or rewritten on a whim; they represent the lasting themes that guide your company at any time and under any circumstance.

But only diamonds are forever. If a changing environment throws you an unexpected curve, by all means alter your vision to reflect the new reality. If the words on paper no longer have meaning for your company, they are wasted on everyone. Again, the company's vision statement is useful only to the extent that it has the power to move your people forward into the future.

- ✔ A vision statement describes where your company intends to go and what it wants to become.

- ✔ The more people you involve in creating your company's vision statement, the broader its scope.

- ✔ Make sure that your company's vision is grounded in reality.

Part II
Sizing Up Your Marketplace

In this part . . .

The best way to succeed at anything is to figure out what you're getting into before you even start – especially the things that you can't control. Think about your garden, for example. If you plan to make that patch of dirt into a neighbourhood showcase, you have to do your gardening homework. You have to know something about the soil conditions and your climate. Is it shady or sunny? How cold does it get at night? What type of plants thrive? What combinations work well together? Which weeds do you have to watch out for? And what pests are you up against? And who said gardening was going to be easy anyway?

A business plan isn't much different. In this part we help you look out the window to see what your company's up against in its own backyard. First, we take a hard look at your industry to see what it really takes for you to be successful. And we get you prepared for business opportunities and threats that are bound to come your way. We spend a lot of time talking about your customers – what they need, what they want, and what makes them happy. We look at how you can divide your customers into groups with similar needs and wants, so that you can serve them even better. Finally, we talk about your competitors – who they are, what they're up to, and how you can plan to compete against them and win.

Chapter 4

Checking Out the Business Environment

*O*ne of the most important questions you can ask yourself as you prepare to create a business plan is 'What business am I really in?' The question may sound simple – even trivial. Maybe that's why it's too often ignored. But if you can answer this basic question correctly, you take the first giant step toward creating an effective business plan.

Remember when trains with elegant dining cars graced our railway lines? Probably not. But you can still catch an old film and become a bit nostalgic for a long-lost era. Railway companies in the 1930s, 1940s, and 1950s thought that they knew exactly what business they were in: the railway business. The question was a no-brainer. As it turns out, however, passengers were looking for something a little more general: basic transportation. Railways soon found that they had to compete with motorways, Morris Motors and Ford, British Airways, and international airports, finally joining forces with the likes of Virgin to run a mixture of rail and air services. The forces and players in the railway business extended well beyond ties and rails. The railways didn't see the big picture and never regained their former glory.

In this chapter, we help you capture your big picture by defining the business that you're really in. We analyse your industry, search for critical success factors, and then give you some pointers on preparing for the opportunities and threats that may appear on your horizon.

Defining the Business That You're In

Okay, so what business are you *really* in? Don't say that you're in the 'widget business', if widgets are what you produce; you have to go beyond the easy answer based simply on what you do or what you make. You have to dig a bit deeper and ask yourself what makes your industry tick:

- What basic needs do you fulfil?
- What underlying forces are at work?
- What role does your company play?

You can make sure that your company isn't like the railways by understanding the underlying forces that shape your own business environment. Start by analysing the industry that you're in. For a closer look at your customers, check out Chapters 5 and 6. The competition gets a once-over in Chapter 7. And we take a closer look at your own company in Chapters 8 and 9.

Eastman Kodak – no longer picture-perfect

Founded way back in 1880 by the entrepreneur George Eastman, Eastman Kodak quickly established itself as the leader in amateur still photography, selling cameras and film, and developing the prints that we've long since stuffed into albums, drawers, boxes, and entire cupboards. Where did the company make its money? Cameras were only marginally profitable. But Kodak wanted people to have cameras so that it could make money on film and even more money on developing that film.

In fact, Kodak reaped huge profits from the processing of film. The company manufactured all its own photographic chemicals and coated papers, and it owned the processing labs. Eventually, Kodak came to think of itself as being in the 'chemical imaging' business, and it said so to its stock analysts and anyone else who would listen. While Kodak's executives and managers were busy patting one another on the back, new competitors – and new technologies – were sneaking in the back door.

As it turned out, customers weren't exactly interested in chemical images for their own sake. Nobody had a hankering for chemically-coated paper or clamoured for the bulk photographic chemicals that Kodak produced so well. People really wanted memories, that's all. They wanted to capture special moments and save them forever. Kodak was really in the 'memories' business. And new ways of saving memories were evolving.

Then a Japanese firm came along and introduced the video camera to the world. All of a sudden, memories were made of electrons, not chemicals. Sony was soon joined by Hitachi, Matsushita, and Sharp. Given that few railroads were still around, Kodak was left to wonder what kind of train had hit it. Although snapshots haven't gone away, Kodak's exclusive monopoly on 'memories' is over. The company has yet to fully recover.

Analysing Your Industry

No matter what kind of business you're in, the world around you is shaped by forces that you have to recognise, plan for, and deal with to be successful over the long haul. Ivory-tower types often call this process *industry analysis*. You may have the urge to run the other way when anything having to do with analysis pops up. We don't want to sugar-coat this step, but we try to make the process as painless as possible.

Just how much do you already know? Take a moment to complete the Industry Analysis Questionnaire (see Figure 4-1). If you're unsure about an answer, tick the box with the question mark alongside.

Your answers provide a snapshot of what you think you know. The question mark boxes that you have ticked highlight the areas that need a closer look. In any case, it's time to jump right in, roll up your sleeves, and make a serious stab at completing your industry analysis.

The good news is that many smart people have already worked hard at analysing all sorts of industries. Although no two businesses are really the same, basic forces seem to be at work across many industries (see Figure 4-2).

The following sections describe the most important of these forces – those that are likely to be factors in your own industry – and provide some hints on how you can think about these forces in terms of your own business planning.

Industry Analysis Questionnaire

Number of competitors in your industry:	❏ Many	❏ Some	❏ Few	❏ ?
Your industry is dominated by several large firms:	❏ Yes	❏ No		❏ ?
The combined market share of the three largest companies in your industry is:	❏ <40%	❏ In between	❏ >80%	❏ ?
New technologies change the way your industry does business every:	❏ 1 year	❏ 5 years	❏ 10 years	❏ ?
The barriers that stop new competitors from entering your industry are:	❏ High	❏ Medium	❏ Low	❏ ?
The barriers that prevent competitors from getting out of your industry are:	❏ High	❏ Medium	❏ Low	❏ ?
Overall market demand in your industry is:	❏ Growing	❏ Stable	❏ Declining	❏ ?

(continued)

Industry Analysis Questionnaire *Continued*

There's a large, untapped market that your industry can take advantage of:	❑ Yes	❑ Maybe	❑ No	❑ ?
Your industry offers a selection of features and options in its product lines that is:	❑ Extensive	❑ Average	❑ Limited	❑ ?
Customers buy products in your industry based almost entirely on price:	❑ Yes	❑ No		❑ ?
Customers can find other alternatives to take the place of your industry's products:	❑ Easily	❑ With difficulty	❑ No	❑ ?
Suppliers to your industry have a lot of influence when it comes to setting terms:	❑ Yes	❑ No		❑ ?
Customers have a lot of bargaining power when buying your industry's products:	❑ Yes	❑ No		❑ ?
Distributors have a lot of power and play a major role in your industry:	❑ Yes	❑ No		❑ ?
Overall costs in your industry have been:	❑ Declining	❑ Stable	❑ Rising	❑ ?
Profit margins in your industry are:	❑ Strong	❑ Average	❑ Weak	❑ ?

Figure 4-1:
The Industry Analysis Questionnaire.

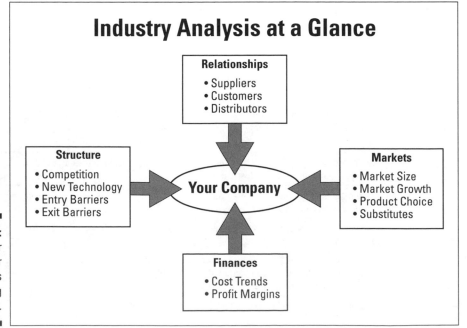

Figure 4-2:
The four major components of analysing an industry.

Structure

Every industry, from flower shops to antique dealers, has its own shape and structure. Following are a few tips on what to look for.

The arrangement of rivals

The number of competitors, taken by itself, has a major impact on the shape of an industry. An industry can be a *monopoly* (one monster company with no competitors), an *oligopoly* (a small number of strong competitors), or a *multiopoly* (many viable competitors). Actually, we made up the word *multiopoly* because we figured that there should be a word to represent the vast majority of industries in this competitive world. In addition to the number of competitors, you want to check out how many of the companies are big and how many are small, as well as how they carve up the various markets that they compete in.

Make a list of all the major competitors in your industry. Find out their sizes, based on revenue, profits, or some other readily available measure, and estimate their relative market shares for the markets that you're most interested in.

New technologies

Many industries are driven by changing technology. Look both at how much and how fast things are changing in your own business. Although you don't need to be a rocket scientist, it's important that you feel comfortable with the underlying technological issues that fuel the change around you. You should also find out who controls the technologies and how easily the technologies can be obtained.

Identify obsolete technologies, current technology, and a future technology in your own industry. How long were old technologies around before they were replaced? Try to predict when new technology may become important to your business. At the same time, try to keep track of any copyrights, patent protection, or special expertise that could influence the adoption of a new technology.

Can anybody play?

The cover charges that make it more or less difficult for new competitors to join the party are referred to as *entry barriers*. Some of these barriers are obvious – high capital costs (lots of money needed up-front), for example, or complex distribution systems that make it hard to reach customers. Other barriers are easy to miss. *Economies of scale,* in which the bigger you are, the more money you make, often discourage brand-new competitors. Strong customer loyalty or high customer costs associated with changing products can also create formidable barriers for new kids on the block.

As you think about your own business, list the entry barriers that you see as being obstacles to new competitors: capital costs, distribution, organisation, raw materials, new technology, scale economies, regulation, patents, and customer-switching costs, for example. Then rank these barriers based on how impenetrable they really are. On which side of each barrier do you stand?

Cashing out

Sometimes, it's hard to leave a party, even when you really want to. How difficult is it for companies in an industry to get out of the market if they want to? The ties and attachments that keep competitors around are called *exit barriers*. Exit barriers can include everything from expensive factories or specialised equipment that can't be easily sold to long-term labour contracts, extended customer leases, service agreements, and government regulations.

Ask yourself how many companies have left your industry over the past five years. Try to figure out why they got out of the market and what sort of difficulties they ran into as they made their way to the exits. How many of them left voluntarily, and how many were asked to leave, penniless and in tatters?

Markets

Competition comes down to customers, and customers create markets. Ideally, the customers whom you're going after represent a market that's ripe for new goods or services. The following tips help you judge for yourself.

Just how big is big?

The size of a market tells you a lot about what's likely to happen to it over time, especially when it comes to competition. Large markets, for example, are always big news and can't help but attract competitors. Smaller markets don't get the same attention, however, and because they're easily overlooked, they often represent business opportunities. You hit the real jackpot if you can turn a small market into a bigger market by discovering some sort of *usage gap* – finding a use for your product or service that no one else has thought of before.

Try to work out some estimates of the overall size of your market, based on current usage patterns. Then, while you're on this subject, try your luck at coming up with novel approaches or applications that have the potential to redefine your market. Just for fun, make some market projections based on the new uses that you're thinking about.

Growing or shrinking?

If large markets are good news, rapidly growing markets are great news, and competitors will come crawling out of the woodwork. A growing market offers the best odds for new players to gain a foothold and unseat the existing competition. As for markets that are shrinking, you can bet that the old competitors will get leaner, meaner, and more fierce. So as markets change size in either direction, the competition is likely to heat up.

Identify changes in the size of your own market over the past five years, in terms of both units sold and revenue generated. If the market is changing rapidly in either direction, look for opportunities and predict the likely effect on both the numbers and the intensity of the competition.

Choices

A quick survey of the similarities and differences among products or services in a market measures something called *product differentiation*. If each product looks pretty much like every other product (think sugar or cement), you can bet that price is important to customers in what is known as a *commodities marketplace*. On the other hand, if each product is different and offers customers something unique or special – from laptop computers to hot little sports cars – product features are likely to determine long-term success or failure in the market.

Take a hard look at the products or services offered by the top three competitors in your market. How similar are they? In what ways are they unique? Think about what you can do to differentiate your own product so that you can compete in ways beyond simply raising or lowering price.

Something altogether different

Every once in a while, a completely new type of product or service suddenly makes its debut in a market, crashing the party, so to speak. The product usually comes out of another industry and may even be based on a different technology. The new product becomes an overnight rival for the affections of existing customers – the rise of fax machines and e-mail to challenge overnight delivery, for example, or the appearance of video cameras to challenge still photography. The threat of *product substitution* – new products taking over existing ones – is real, especially in fast-changing, highly competitive markets.

Think about what your customers did five, ten, or even 20 years ago. Did they use your product or a similar one back then, or did a completely different kind of product serve their needs? What about one, five, or ten years from now? What types of products or services may satisfy your customers' needs? Although you can't predict the future, you can envision the possibilities.

Relationships

Business is all about connections. Connections aren't just a matter of who you know – they're about who supplies your raw materials and who distributes your product or touts your services. Connections are about who your customers are and what kind of relationships you have with them. A few tips can help you spot the key connections on which your business depends.

Supply and demand

One obvious way to think about products and services is how they're finally put together. Every company relies on outside suppliers at some stage of the assembly process, whether for basic supplies and raw materials or for entire finished components of the product itself. When outside suppliers enter the picture, the nature of what they supply – the availability, complexity, and importance of that product or service to the company – often determines how much control they have over the terms of their relationship with a company. That means everything from prices and credit terms to delivery schedules.

Think about your own suppliers. Are any of them in a position to limit your access to critical components or to raise prices on you? Can you form alliances with key suppliers or enter into long-term contracts? Can you turn to alternative sources? Are any of your suppliers capable of doing what you do, transforming themselves into competitors? How can you protect yourself?

Keeping customers happy

You've probably heard the expression 'It's a buyers' market'. As an industry becomes more competitive, the balance of power naturally tends to shift toward the customer. Because they have a growing number of products to choose among, customers can afford to be finicky. As they shop around, they make demands that often include pressure to lower prices, expand service, and develop new product features. A few large customers have even greater leverage as they negotiate favourable terms.

The last time that you or your competitors adjusted prices, did you raise or lower them? If you lowered prices, competitive pressures will no doubt force you to lower them again at some point. So think about other ways in which you can compete. If you raised prices, how much resistance did you encounter? Given higher prices, how easy is it for customers to do what you do for themselves, eliminating the need for your product or service altogether?

Delivering the sale

No matter how excited customers are about a product or service, they can't buy it unless they can find it in a shop, through a catalogue, on the Internet, or at their front doors. *Distribution systems* see to it that products get where the customers are. A *distribution channel* refers to the particular path that a product takes – including wholesalers and anyone else in the middle – before it arrives in the hands of the final customer. The longer this chain, the more power the channel has when it comes to controlling prices and terms. The companies at the end of the chain have the greatest control because they have direct access to the customer.

Think about what alternatives you have in distributing your own product or service. What distribution channels seem to be most effective? Who has the power in these channels, and how is that power likely to shift? Are there ways in which you can get closer to your customers – perhaps through direct-mail campaigns or marketing through the Internet?

Finance

Finally, successful business planning depends on making sense of pounds-and-pence issues. What are the costs of doing business? What is the potential for profit? A few tips can help get you started.

The cost side

With a little effort, you can break down the overall cost of doing business into the various stages of producing a product or service, from raw material and fabrication costs to product assembly, distribution, marketing, and service expenses. This cost profile often is quite similar for companies that are in the same industry. You can get a handle on how one firm can gain a cost advantage by identifying where the bulk of the costs occur in the business and then looking at ways to reduce them.

Economies of scale come into play, for example, when major costs are fixed up-front; increasing the number of products sold automatically reduces the individual cost of each unit. (For more information on economies of scale, refer to the section 'Can anybody play?' earlier in this chapter.) *Experience curves* refer to lower costs that result from the use of new technologies, methods, or materials somewhere during the production process. (For more information on experience curves, see Chapter 13.)

Separate your business into its various stages, and ask yourself where the bulk of the costs occur in your own company. Can you take any obvious actions to reduce these costs immediately or over time? How does the doubling of sales affect your unit costs? How are your competitors toying with new cost-saving ideas?

The profit motive

Industries traditionally have their own rules of thumb when it comes to expected *profit margins* – how much money they expect to end up with after all the costs have been added up, divided by all the money that they take in. In certain industries, these profit margins remain fairly constant year after year. A look at the history of other industries, however, points to cycles of changing profitability. These cycles often reflect changing *capacity levels* – how much of a product or service an industry can actually produce and deliver. A little insight into where an industry stands along the cycles of profit margin and capacity, as well as a little insight into the direction in which the industry is heading, says a lot about the competitive pressures that may lie ahead.

- ✔ Is your own industry one that has well-known business cycles?
- ✔ Traditionally, how long are the business cycles?
- ✔ If you've been in business for a while, have your own profit margins changed significantly over the past one, two, or five years?
- ✔ What direction do profits appear to be heading in?
- ✔ Do you think that these changes in profitability will affect the number of your competitors or the intensity of the competition over the next one to five years?

Don't stop with our list here. No doubt we've missed one or two industry forces that are important and perhaps even unique to your own business situation. Spend a little extra time and creative effort on coming up with other forces as you work on your own industry analysis.

After giving some thought to your industry in terms of the many forces that are at work, put together a written portrait. If you're stuck, imagine that someone who has no experience in your industry has come to you for advice, asking whether you can recommend a substantial investment in your industry. How would you respond? Get those arguments down on paper, and you've made real progress in assembling a serious industry analysis.

Data

In many cases, you may need a little outside help as well as some hard data to support your take on how various industry forces are shaping your own business environment. Unfortunately, it's not always easy to get your hands on the right pieces of information to explain what makes your industry tick.

Sometimes, you just can't get the data. Maybe no one's bothered to collect and look at it, or perhaps companies aren't willing to part with it because they don't want outsiders (including potential competitors) to analyse the industry too carefully. Most of the time, however, too much data is available, and the problem becomes knowing where to turn for the information that you need.

The good news is that technology can help rescue you from information overload. You can control the recent explosion of business- and industry-related data by taking advantage of Internet-based services and online systems that are designed to search for information that you can actually use.

Following are a few suggestions on places where you can turn for help on industry analysis. Many of the sources listed are accessible through your computer; new ones come online every day. If you have access to the Internet, start your search there.

Government sources: UK government agencies at all levels provide a wealth of data free for the asking. Start with the Business Link website at www. businesslink.org which should put you on the right track. Check out Companies House (www.companieshouse.co.uk), the Patent Office (www. patent.gov.uk), and National Statistics (www.statistics.gov.uk). The National Statistics website contains a vast range of official UK statistics and information about statistics, which can be accessed and downloaded for free.

Trade associations: There are two ways in which you can find out more about trade associations and the information they provide:

From your computer via www.brainstorm.co.uk/TANC/Directory/ Welcome.html, where you can search the Directory of Trade Associations alphabetically, or browse through to see which best suits your purposes. Alternatively you can visit www.martex.co.uk/trade-associations/ index.htm, run by the UK Trade Associations Forum, which provides an online directory. The second route is to visit your local reference library and look at a hard copy of one of these directories.

Libraries: There are thousands of libraries in the UK and tens of thousands elsewhere in the world, that between them contain more desk research data that any entrepreneur could ever require.

Apart from public libraries, there are hundreds of university libraries, specialist science and technology libraries and government collections of data, which can be accessed with little difficulty.

Librarians are trained, amongst other things, to archive and retrieve information and data from their own libraries and increasingly from Internet data sources. As such, they represent an invaluable resource that entrepreneurs should tap into early in the research process.

Start with The Business Information Service (BIS) (www.bl.uk/services/ information/business.html) of the British Library located at 96 Euston Road, London NW1 2DB; phone: 020 7412 7454, fax: 020 7412 7453; email: business-information@bl.uk

The information is practical rather than theoretical in nature. It is particularly useful for company news and financials, competitor information, and market research including trends and statistics.

Colleges and universities: In addition to offering library resources, business schools often offer flesh-and-blood business experts. These people are paid to analyse things, and every once in a while they come up with a valuable insight or a really good idea. If you run across an expert in your own industry, paying him or her a visit may be worthwhile. You might even be able to get students on business degree programmes to carry out some of this research for you at a fairly nominal cost.

Online data providers: A growing number of companies specialise in providing business- and industry-related data at your fingertips. Kelly's (www.kellys.co.uk), Dun & Bradstreet (www.dnb.com), Kompass (www.kompass.com), Key Note (www.keynote.co.uk), Mintel (www.mintel.com), and Jordan's (www.jordans.co.uk) have all been in this business for some time, and growth of the Internet has expanded their ranks. The information usually isn't free, but it can be worth the investment. Look for first-time user offers or special promotions.

Direct industry contacts: Go right to the source, if you can. Useful information can come from anywhere, including companies' public relations departments, industry suppliers, distributors, and salespeople. You can also find information at industry conventions, trade shows, and even factory tours.

- ✔ Your business plan must take into account the major forces that are at work in your industry.

- ✔ The number and size of your competitors shape the structure of your industry.

- ✔ How big your market is and how fast it's growing determine how fierce your competition will be.

- ✔ How well your business works depends on your relationships with suppliers, customers, and distributors.

- ✔ If you want your company to be successful, you have to keep costs down and profits up.

- ✔ You can find loads of good industry data on the Internet.

Recognising Critical Success Factors

If you spend some quality time working on an industry analysis, the time spent should reward you with a fairly complete picture of the major forces that are at work in your business: the basic structure of your industry; your core markets; key relationships with suppliers, customers, and distributors;

costs and changing profit margins. The analysis can also point out trends in your industry and show you where your company is in terms of general industry and business cycles.

This is all well and good. But how do you go about interpreting this industry landscape so that you can use it to improve your own business planning? Just for fun, take a moment to think about your industry as a great whitewater river. Imagine the many forces that you've listed as being the swift currents, dangerous rapids, and even whirlpools in that river. You're in the company canoe. You have to do more than just point out these features and paddle merrily along; it's your job to navigate the hazards. As any whitewater expert will tell you, this means figuring out what needs to be done at every turn – what special skills, resources, and lines of communication need to be in place for you to survive and conquer each stretch of river.

Back on dry land, take a fresh look at your industry analysis. Ask yourself what your company must do to succeed in the face of each powerful force that you identify. Again, what special skills, organisation, and resources need to be in place for you to survive and conquer? In the business world, these assets are known as *critical success factors* (*CSFs*). Critical success factors are the fundamental conditions that absolutely, positively have to be satisfied if a company's going to win in the marketplace. These factors are different for every industry because they depend so directly on the particular forces that are at work in each industry.

The critical success factors for your company are going to be rather specific – a one-of-a-kind set of conditions based on your industry analysis and the forces that you see shaping your business. You probably don't want to juggle more than three or four CSFs at any one time. But no matter how many factors you identify as being important, odds are that your CSFs fall into several general categories that you can identify ahead of time. Below, we provide a starting point for creating your own CSF list.

Technology

When jet engines became available in the late 1950s, it quickly became apparent that commercial airlines had to adopt this technology if they were to remain competitive. Jet-engine technology became a CSF for players in the industry. If you (or your children) fly jets by using computer simulators, you already know that the adoption of faster processors and speedier algorithms is just as important for success in the game-software industry. Small businesses can also leverage a new technology such as the Internet as a CSF by creating snazzy home pages.

Manufacturing

For commodity products such as steel or oil, large-scale mills or refineries are often the critical factors that lead to low-cost production and the capability to compete on price. In high-tech industries, on the other hand, automation and efficient 'clean rooms' may be the critical ingredients that allow the production of competitively priced consumer electronics products: CD players, video cameras, mobile phones, and so on.

Human resources

Consulting firms usually recruit only at the top business schools, because what they are selling is the expertise of their consultants, and clients often equate skill with educational background. In the same way, software companies really are nothing more than the total of the creativity and expertise of their programmers. In each case, people themselves are the CSF.

Organisation

The long-term success of film companies that consistently produce hits and make money often hinges on logistics – the capability to evaluate, organise, and manage independent writers, actors, site scouts, and production companies, as well as the media and distribution outlets. In the health care industry, health care trusts are often successful because they are good at record-keeping, efficiently steering doctors, patients, medical supplies, drugs, and insurance claims through the system. Even a family-run video rental shop can gain an advantage by offering a quick, easy-to-use inventory of what's available and a system for reserving the hottest new films.

Services

Businesses that offer services of one kind or another sell rather abstract products which can't be held or touched and are difficult to copyright or patent. Success often goes to those service companies that are first in the market and work hard to cultivate a following of loyal customers. ACAs (Associates of the Institute of Chartered Accountants) and accounting firms, for example, build impeccable reputations one step at a time. A major reason why clients come to them for financial advice in the first place is simply that they are known to be trustworthy.

Location

It's no coincidence that profitable mills tend to be located in agricultural areas and that brickworks crop up near rock quarries because transportation of the raw materials is so costly. But transportation costs are not the only reason why location matters. At the other end of the spectrum, fast-food restaurants and petrol stations also live or die based on their locations. By far the most important success factor for these businesses is nabbing just the right spot along a heavily travelled route.

Marketing

Manufacturers of cosmetics, clothing, perfume, and certainly trainers all sell hype as much as they do the physical products themselves. In these cases, critical success factors have most to do with the ability of companies to create and maintain strong brand images. Their customers are buying the name, the logo, or the label first and only then the lipstick, jeans, or trainers that are attached.

Distribution

Packaged foods, household products, snacks, and beverages often sink or swim depending on how much shelf space they're allotted at the supermarket or local grocery shop. A successful packaged-goods company works hard to create incentives for everyone in the delivery chain, from the driver to the grocer, to make sure that the shelves have plenty of room for its own brands, even squeezing out competing products. Speed of delivery can also be a critical success factor sometimes, especially when freshness matters.

Government regulation

Companies that contract directly with public agencies, such as waste-management firms and construction companies, often succeed because of their unique ability to deal directly with bureaucrats and elected officials. But government regulation plays a role in many industries, and the ability to navigate a regulatory sea is often the critical factor in a company's success. Pharmaceutical companies, for example, invest huge amounts of money in developing new drugs, and they stake all their potential profits and success on their skill in shepherding those drugs through the Licensing Authority's complex regulatory approval process.

One last thing before you start preparing your own CSF list: critical success factors determine which companies are likely to succeed over the long haul in a given industry and marketplace. Unfortunately, CSFs are not always the same as your company's current capabilities. Chapter 8 talks more about your company's specific capabilities and how you can make sure that they reflect the CSFs that you come up with.

- ✔ Critical success factors (CSFs) are the skills and resources that you absolutely, positively must have to win.
- ✔ CSFs may include the coolest technology, the friendliest service, dynamite marketing, or location, location, location.
- ✔ Keep your own list of CSFs manageable; aim for no more than four.

Preparing for Opportunities and Threats

When you have a handle on the major forces that shape your industry and can point out the critical success factors that really determine what kind of company has the best shot at coming out on top, you can look ahead. Using everything that you've discovered about how your industry works, what possibilities do you see for your company, and where do the obstacles lie?

These kinds of questions often come under the umbrella of something called *situation analysis*. When you think about it, your company's situation depends partly on things that are inside your organisation (call them your strengths and weaknesses) and partly on things that happen outside (opportunities and threats).

For the moment, we're going to concentrate on the opportunities and threats that you face. (Turn to Chapter 8 to work on your own strengths and weaknesses.) Opportunities and threats come from the forces, issues, trends, and events that are beyond your control as a manager. But they represent the challenges that your company has to tackle if you want to beat the competition.

It's a beautiful morning

Opportunities don't always knock, sometimes, you have to find the door yourself and know when to open it. Consider the following situations. They can all lead to opportunities, so see whether any of them generate new possibilities in your own industry.

Major shifts in technology. When technologies change, companies are often slow to pick up on what's new because they have so much invested in what's old. From better software products based on new operating systems to more efficient steel production using new blast-furnace technology, business opportunities present themselves.

Availability of new materials. New-materials science can lead to innovative products and expanded market opportunities. The DuPont Corporation, for example, developed a chemical treatment that protects fibres from discoloration; then it created a new kind of carpet and its own StainMaster line.

New customer categories. New market opportunities are born when you identify groups of customers who aren't satisfied with what's available. Renault discovered that young families following a more active lifestyle want something bigger and more comfortable than a basic saloon car, and the people-carrier market was born. In the agriculture industry, small, innovative growers around the country are rushing to fill the growing demand for organic produce.

Sudden spurts in market growth. When a market suddenly takes off, opportunity passes to the companies that are first to gear up production to satisfy the growing demand. Nike, for example, has been able to sprint out in front by meeting the phenomenal jump in demand for every type of athletic shoe imaginable.

New uses for old products. Growth markets also spring up when new uses are found for old products. Mobile phones used to be for top executives and emergency purposes only; now they're accessories for teenagers. Teenagers can't afford lots of mobile phone calls but can't bear to be out of touch, so they text one another by the minute. Texting has become a major new use for the mobile phone, opening up major new markets – teenagers and sub-teenagers.

Access to highly skilled people. In many industries, skills are scarce and valuable resources. Business opportunities often arise when skilled workers become available. From aerospace engineers in Southern California to programmers in India and scientists in Russia, companies take advantage of any sudden expansion of the talent pool.

Additional locations. Location means business. Once shunned by shopping centres, cinemas are being sought out as important magnets to attract additional shoppers. Entertainment complexes in shopping centres now represent a major percentage of the cinema screens across the country.

Fresh organisation models. New ways of doing business represent business opportunities in themselves. The urge to downsize, for example, has led to the outsourcing of all sorts of functions to other companies that now do nothing but manage computer systems, supply training programmes, or produce corporate newsletters for their clients.

New distribution channels. There's really nothing more exciting in the business world than finding a new way to get to customers. Distribution creates a market, whether it's a mega-discount store or a direct telephone marketing campaign. The phenomenal growth of the Internet is based on its promise of being an efficient, effective way to reach customers with all sorts of products and services.

Changing laws or regulations. The government has had a great deal to do with the way that UK companies operate and make money in all sorts of industries. In particular, deregulation has provided tremendous opportunities for rail operators, utilities such as water and gas, airlines, telephone companies, and television and radio stations.

Dark clouds on the horizon

Business is risk. We can't take credit for recognising that fact, but it's certainly worth repeating. For every big opportunity in an industry, there's an equally powerful threat to challenge the way in which things are currently done. Consider the following examples, all of which resulted in major problems for companies that either didn't see the threat or didn't heed the warning signs. See whether any of these lessons apply to your own industry.

Market slowdowns. A shrinking market, either predicted or unforeseen, takes its toll. Excess capacity can bring a company to its knees, whether the cause is a sudden slowdown in the sales of home computers or a projected decrease in the number of passenger jets ordered by international carriers. Often, the trick is to reduce near-term production without losing the capability to react quickly when markets finally turn around.

Costly legislation. Government programmes, rules, and regulations often affect the bottom line. UK businesses, large and small, must plan to comply with all sorts of agency demands, from the Health and Safety Executive (HSE) to the Office of Fair Trading (OFT) and the Inland Revenue (IR). As the saying goes, ignorance of the law is no excuse, and failure to comply can be extremely expensive in terms of both time and money.

Changing trends. General population trends can have profound effects on certain marketplaces. The inevitable aging of the Baby Boomers, for example, was bound to put a damper on the growth of tropical resorts and the lifestyle popularised by Club 18-30. Club 18-30 responded with new family resorts to compete with Disney Land, Paris, as a wholesome destination.

New and aggressive competition. Although new competitors usually have an uphill battle on their hands, they almost always come into a market with the advantages of energy, fresh talent, and a burning desire to win. After the oil shortages of the 1970s, Japanese car companies came into the UK and US market with small, fuel-efficient cars, a serious marketing strategy, and a commitment to succeed over the long haul. The rest is history.

Substitute products. What happens when a gizmo comes along to replace a widget? Often, the widget company is in big trouble. The danger with substitute products is that they often seem to come out of nowhere. Videotapes have given holiday photos a run for their money, CDs have turned vinyl LPs into collectors' items, and the new digital video discs (DVDs) are already making videocassettes seem quaint.

Exchange-rate volatility. Today, even a local business can be affected by global economic forces, including exchange rates. For example, when the pound is strong, it can be cheaper to buy products from abroad than from the UK. This has a direct effect on the competitive position of UK businesses.

Shortages of raw materials. From an oil crisis to the shortage of memory chips, supply problems can threaten a business. Companies often enter into long-term contracts with their suppliers to minimise these kinds of disruptions, but extended agreements pose their own set of risks and must be carefully managed.

Loss of patent protection. Creativity and intellectual property are usually protected by copyrights and patents. But patents expire, and companies have to prepare for the competition that inevitably follows. Pharmaceutical firms, for example, have had to learn to compete with the cheaper generic drugs that become available soon after successful prescription brands lose their patent protection.

Labour agreements. Unions have a significant impact on the cost of doing business, and companies in various industries have learned how to factor in their particular relationships with organised labour. Although union activity in general has been on the wane for many years, companies that have no union histories may have to come to terms with organised workers in the future – especially in service industries, in which long hours and few benefits are becoming the norm.

Laziness and complacency. It's easy to get lazy when the money starts rolling in, and the list of companies that have fallen into the complacency trap is much too long for comfort. Rover, Ford, and Vauxhall fell into the trap, of course, and were beaten up by Honda, Toyota, and Nissan. Likewise, Sainsbury's was dislodged from pole position by Tesco when they failed to respond to Tesco's aggressive discounting strategy.

There's no end to the number of potential opportunities and threats in an industry. A winning business plan should include a situation analysis that points out both the biggest opportunities and the clearest threats to your company, so that you can anticipate ways to deal with both as part of your planning process.

- ✔ Good business planners keep a sharp eye out for opportunities and threats.

- ✔ Big leaps in technology, new uses for old products, and innovative ways to reach customers open opportunities for your company.

- ✔ Changing lifestyles, shrinking markets, and new competitors can threaten your business.

- ✔ You can turn threats into opportunities.

Chapter 5

Taking a Closer Look at Customers

. . . .

In This Chapter

▶ Checking out who your customers are

▶ Discovering why your customers buy

▶ Finding out how your customers make choices

▶ Remembering the big picture

▶ Dealing with business customers

. . . .

*T*he most crucial part of business planning involves taking a long, hard look at customers – those you enjoy having, those you would love to land, and those you would just as soon give away to some unsuspecting competitor. The stakes are high. How well you know your customers ultimately determines how successful you are. But figuring out what makes customers tick can be downright frustrating. If you've tried it before, you may be tempted to throw up your hands and leave the entire mess to the so-called experts – marketing gurus, consultants, or perhaps astrologers. Don't. This chapter shows you how to better acquaint yourself with your customers so that you can offer them more value and serve them more profitably than anyone else out there.

In this chapter, we take a closer look at why customers buy your products and services in the first place by exploring their needs and motives. And we investigate how they make choices in the marketplace by examining customer perceptions and their decision-making process. Finally, we take a quick look at your customers that are actually other businesses.

Checking Out Who Your Customers Are

A fresh look at customers starts with the ones you enjoy seeing – those who regularly purchase goods or services from you. But sometimes, knowing what something is *not* can be just as important as knowing what it *is*. You can learn as much about your own business and best customers by observing the other kinds of customers out there – the customers who are difficult, the customers who are gone, and the customers whom you never had.

The good customer

Good customers are the ones who bring a smile to your face, the ones you like serving, the ones who appreciate you, the ones who keep you in business. They are the customers you want to keep coming back time and again. To keep all those good customers happy, however, you may need to know more than the fact that Tom likes Chinese food, Mary has a weakness for chocolates, and Harry loves red ties.

Why? Isn't simply knowing individual customers on some personal basis enough? Well, not quite. What happens if you have hundreds or even thousands of small customers, such as a shop, or if your staff turnover is high as in most parts of the catering industry?

In such cases there is no substitute for a good database sytem for tracking your relationship with clients and then making appropriate product or sevice offers. For example supermarkets now analyse customer purchases and make targeted special offers based on their understanding of the customer profile. This all helps to make customers feel special and loved.Your business can measure and describe its customers in several ways:

- ✔ Track *where* your customers are, breaking them down by country, region, city, or postcode.

- ✔ Figure out *who* your customers are, including their age, gender, occupation, income, and ethnic origin.

- ✔ Learn more about *how* they live – their hobbies, favourite sports teams, restaurant choices, and holiday destinations, for example.

You're probably a step ahead of us here and have already noticed that many of these criteria result in groups of customers that look alike. When marketing gurus divide customers into specific groups, they call them *market segments*. If you'd like to get a better handle on how to separate your own customers into market segments, check out Chapter 6.

When it comes to understanding customers, one good strategy is to find out what other businesses try to learn about their customers. Keep track of the questions that other companies ask you. Richer Sounds stores (a chain of hi-fi and home cinema retailers), for example, routinely ask for your postcode when you step up to the till. And you often find a list of personal questions on product registration forms, warranty cards, and customer service mailings. Some companies even offer a small reward if you tell them something – anything – about yourself. But go easy here. Radio Shack, an American electronics retailer, began to lose a lot of goodwill when customers grew suspicious about – or just annoyed by – all the questions that their shop assistants were asking.

The bad customer

'A bad customer? Isn't that a contradiction in terms?' you ask. 'How can there be such a thing as a bad customer, especially for a customer-orientated company?' Keep in mind that your initial reaction doesn't always tell the whole story. Remember that *you* don't really define the business that you're in, your *customers* do. They place a series of demands on your company and then evaluate how well it performs against those demands.

Good customers do the following:

- ✔ Ask you to do things that you do well
- ✔ Place value on the things that you do and are willing to pay for them
- ✔ Challenge you to improve your skills, expand your knowledge, and focus your resources
- ✔ Take you in new directions that are consistent with your strategy and planning

Bad customers represent the flip side. They do the following:

- ✔ Ask you to do things that you aren't equipped to do well
- ✔ Distract you, causing you to veer away from your strategy and your business plan
- ✔ Purchase in such small quantities that the cost of doing business with them far outweighs any revenue that they generate
- ✔ Require so much service and attention that you can't focus your efforts on more valuable (and profitable) customers
- ✔ Remain dissatisfied with what you do, despite all your best efforts
- ✔ Fail to pay on time – or to pay at all!

The pundits have come up with a principle that we can apply here: the *80/20 principle*. In this case, the rule says that if you survey all your customers, 20 per cent of them account for about 80 per cent of your business. These 20 per cent are your good customers. You obviously want to keep them – and keep them happy! But look at the other 80 per cent of your customers, and you'll probably discover a few whom you'd rather hand over to the competition.

Bank accounts and the 80/20 principle

A large retail bank recently undertook a comprehensive study of those customers using chequebooks. The results presented a classic 80/20 situation: About 19 per cent of the bank's customers were generating 90 per cent of the total profits. What was the chief characteristic of the other 81 per cent? Most of those customers had accounts with average balances of less than £250, yet they wrote lots of cheques. As a consequence, the bank was losing serious money on this customer group; internal processing costs were simply greater than the revenue generated from the use of their deposited funds.

The bank conducted further research. Obviously, not all of these account-holders were bad customers. Some of them were senior citizens, for example, and a percentage of them were new and would go on to become profitable customers over time. The bank wanted to nourish developing relationships, so it set up incentives to encourage new customers to accumulate savings in related savings accounts. But the bank also knew that many of its customers would never change and would simply remain a drain on profits. So it created hurdles to 'de-market' its less profitable customers, using a new fee structure that penalised accounts when monthly average balances fell below certain levels, unless customers maintained certain balances in savings accounts.

When you analyse what you do for that 80 per cent of customers and what they do for you, these customers are often more trouble than they're worth. Their shoe styles are never in stock, and their special orders are always returned. Maybe their finances are a mess, which makes them late in paying. Still, the lure of additional revenue and more customers – or the belief that you should never say no to any customer – often keeps you involved with this group. You would be better off without these customers, though, and leaving your competitors to handle such bad business impairs their ability to compete with you for good business.

To handle bad customers, follow these steps:

1. **Figure out who they are, by establishing if you can make a profit out of doing business with them.**

2. **Convert them into good customers, by exploring ways of turning loss-making customers into profitable ones. For example, by putting up prices, introducing minimum order sizes or minimum drop quantities or by encouraging them to order online.**

3. **Alternatively, hand them over to someone else. If they don't accept the changes to your service that you introduce to ensure they make you money, they will soon move on to other suppliers.**

A note of caution: some of this year's bad customers may become next year's good customers. Ensure you only divest yourself of *permanently* bad customers.

The other guy's customer

You may think that focusing on customers whom you've never had points to another sort of failure on your part, but actually, these people present an opportunity. The fact that you haven't been able to serve this group gives you a challenge: to find out what your market really thinks is important. Your competitors' customers are telling you what you are not. This information is extremely useful, especially when you are working on the big picture in the early stages of business planning, defining who you are and who you want to serve.

Unfortunately, getting information out of your competitors' customers is often an expensive proposition. You don't know them, and you don't have an ongoing relationship with them. Market research firms, of course, are always eager to work with you. These companies are willing to bring together focus groups and talk to consumers about all sorts of things that relate to your products in comparison to the competition. The catch, of course, is that their services don't come cheap.

Fortunately, you don't have to be quite this formal about the information-gathering process, at least in the initial stages. As long as you can get selected people to provide sincere answers, you probably can approximate the results of a focus-group study on your own.

An acquaintance of ours used to go into supermarkets and hang around the aisles in which her company's goods were displayed. When a customer came along and picked out a competing product, she offered to buy that product from the startled shopper for more than the listed price! She would offer a minimal amount (a penny, say) and then work her way up, trying to determine the shopper's degree of loyalty to the competing brand. Finally, she would ask questions to find out why. As a reward, she paid the shopper for the price of the product when the conversation was over.

Getting to know your competitors' customers is often difficult, but not impossible.

- ✔ Spend some time where customers gather. Use trade shows, user groups, and industry conferences to make informal contacts and begin a dialogue with your non-customers.

- ✔ Ask pointed questions of people who choose competing products. Did they take the time to see what was available on the market? Have they even heard of your product or service? If they have, did they actually take the time to look at it? If not, why not? If so, what were their impressions?

✔ Really listen to what they have to say, no matter how painful it is. Don't get defensive when people say negative things about your company or your products.

Information about your customers is valuable, if not priceless. A consultant will charge you thousands of pounds for the same information.

✔ To plan effectively, learn as much about your customers as you can.

✔ Of all your customers, 20 per cent are likely to account for 80 per cent of your business.

✔ Some of your customers may actually cost you money.

✔ Your competitors' customers can tip you off to new opportunities.

Discovering Why Your Customers Buy

Perhaps the most difficult – and useful – question that you can answer about your customers is why they buy what they buy. What actually compels them to seek out your products or services in the marketplace? What's important to them? What are they really looking for?

Understanding needs

Why do people buy things in the first place? Psychologist types tell us that *needs fulfilment* is really at the heart of all consumer behaviour (see Figure 5-1, based on the social psychologist Abraham Maslow's famous 'Hierarchy of Needs' model). Everybody has needs and wants. When a need is discovered, it creates the motivation that drives human activity.

✔ Survival, at the most basic level, results in the universal need for grocery shops, carpenters, and tailors.

✔ The urge for safety, security, and stability generates the need for bank accounts, disability health insurance, and home alarm systems.

✔ The desire for belonging and acceptance creates the need for designer-label polo shirts, members-only clubs, and participation in expensive diet programmes.

✔ The urge to be recognised and held in esteem establishes the need for company banquets, fast cars, and award plaques.

✔ The desire for self-achievement and fulfilment results in the need for adventure holidays, quiz shows, and correspondence courses.

Hierarchy of Needs

Highest Level

Self-Achievement

Recognition and Self-Esteem

Belonging and Acceptance

Safety, Security, and Stability

Survival and Physiological Need

Highest Level

Basic

Basic

Figure 5-1:
A basic
overview
of people's
needs.

DHL, for example, is really in the reliability business. Many of its customers are businesses that want the assurance – absolutely, positively – that their precious shipments will be delivered early the next day or even the same day. These customers are so motivated by this need that they are willing to pay a substantial premium over other alternatives, simply for absolute reliability and their own peace of mind.

Determining motives

Motives are needs that have been awakened and activated, so to speak. Motives send people scurrying into the marketplace, searching for products or services that can fulfil a particular need. Motives aren't always what they seem to be.

✔ Greeting card companies, for example, don't just sell cute little jingles printed on glossy paper at exorbitant prices. The prices are justified because the companies are actually selling small insurance policies against their customers' fear of feeling guilty. Perhaps fear of guilt (over a missed birthday or a forgotten anniversary) is really what propels the buyer into the greeting card market.

✔ Recent MBA graduates have been asked to rank the things that are most important to them when they decide among various job offers. When asked point-blank, a substantial majority rank quality of life, community, and schools at the top of the list and place starting salary somewhere in the middle. A more careful survey and analysis of the MBA selection criteria, however, usually settles upon compensation as being the single most important variable in accepting a new position fresh out of university.

✔ Most of us have a need to be accepted and liked by other people. This powerful motivation creates great market opportunities for the likes of beauty salons, gyms, and breath-mint companies.

Although motives obviously apply to individual consumers, they work equally well in the context of business or corporate behaviour. When a particular manufacturing company contracts with a private health and medical insurance company, such as Bupa, for example, is the company motivated to improve the health of its employees? Or is it motivated to reduce the cost of its health insurance premiums so that it can better compete with foreign companies (fulfilling its own need to survive)? If you run Bupa, how you answer this question has a major impact on your internal management of costs versus the overall quality of the health care that you provide.

Your job, of course, is to dig beneath the obvious customer responses and consumption patterns to determine what the buyers' real motives are in purchasing goods and services in your own market. When you understand what's actually driving customer behaviour, you're in a much better position to talk about your own product in terms that customers will respond to.

✔ The most important question to ask about your customers is why they buy what they buy.

✔ Customer needs range from basic survival and security to the urge for self-improvement.

✔ Motives such as vanity, status-seeking, and guilt are the hot buttons that can *really* get customers to buy.

Finding Out How Your Customers Make Choices

How do customers make choices in the marketplace? The most important thing to remember is that customers decide to buy things based on their own view of the world – their own perceptions of reality. Few customers buy without thinking. Instead, they bring their perceptions of the world into a decision-making process that (ideally) leads them to purchase your product or service instead of other options.

Perceptions are reality

Customer perceptions represent the market's world view and include not only what your customers think of your products and services, but also how they see your company and view your competitors.

As customers turn to the marketplace, they confront a mind-boggling array of competing products. Many variables influence your customers as they evaluate their choices: advertising, endorsements, reviews, and salesmanship, not to mention their own gut reactions. You need to know how customers respond to all these stimuli if you ultimately want to earn and keep their business.

Have you ever wondered, for example, why so few yellow jumpers are available in the men's departments of clothing shops? Market research consistently shows that a majority of men believe that the colour yellow suggests weakness. Subconsciously, men feel that they may be perceived as being wimps if they have anything to do with the colour. So the yellow-jumper option isn't too popular.

Or have you noticed that Madonna doesn't do many endorsements? Okay, it's not as though she needs the extra income. But companies may feel that her image is just too controversial, resulting in negative perceptions and the risk that potential buyers will be driven away.

Never lose sight of the marketer's motto:

Customer perceptions are the market reality.

People buy goods and services based on what they perceive to be true, not necessarily on what you know to be the facts. To be successful in the marketplace, you have to develop a clear insight into customers' perceptions, understanding how buyers react to products and services in your market before you complete your own business plans.

The five steps to adoption

Marketing gurus often refer to the customer's *decision-making process* as the *DMP* (the acronym makes the term sound more official). In many markets, the DMP involves a series of well-defined steps that are dubbed the *consumer adoption process*. (Okay, we'll call it the *CAP*.) In this case, of course, *adoption* refers to a newly formed relationship with a product, not a child.

By understanding the steps that consumers often go through, you are better able to take advantage of customers' behaviour and build strategies that help them complete the adoption process. The process involves five major steps, which are described in Table 5-1.

Suppose that you're in a startup firm with a top-notch consumer-software title. You are afraid, however, that customers are reluctant to give the program a try, for fear the software will be difficult to learn or incompatible with their computers. (Keep in mind that people act on their perceptions of reality rather than on the reality itself!) To move potential customers past the evaluation and into the trial step of the adoption process, you may want to consider setting up a free new-user hotline and offering a money-back, no-questions-asked guarantee.

Table 5-1	The Consumer's Five-step Adoption Process	
Primary steps	*Description of consumer*	*Your task*
Awareness	Aware of a product or service, but lacking detailed knowledge	Develop a strategy that educates and excites potential customers
Interest	Curious because of publicity and seeking more information	Provide more detailed product information and continue to build momentum
Evaluation	Deciding whether to test the product or service	Make the product-evaluation process as easy and rewarding as possible
Trial	Using the product or service on a test basis	Make the trial as simple and risk-free as you can
Adoption	Deciding to become a regular user	Develop strategies to retain good customers

✔ Customers make choices based on their perceptions, not necessarily on the facts.

✔ Before they buy, customers go through a distinct decision-making process.

✔ The five steps in making a purchase are awareness, interest, evaluation, trial, and adoption.

✔ If you understand how customers make choices, you have a better shot at getting their business.

Remembering the Big Picture

Remember that old saying about not seeing the forest for the trees? Well, when you first start to think about your customers, you don't want to fall into a similar trap. Seeing only the small number of individual customers whom you know, and focusing on their personal habits, likes, and dislikes, is tempting sometimes. Even when you begin to look at more general customer trends, including why your customers buy and how they make choices, getting buried in the details still is awfully easy.

Don't take the bait! Don't view your customers and your own business activities too narrowly. Look instead at the larger forest – those general customer behaviours and basic needs that define your market.

If you think about your business only in terms of your existing products, for example, you risk losing sight of customer needs that you've overlooked – needs that a competitor is no doubt going to satisfy at some point. You also create a short-sighted view of your own strategic choices that can result in missed market opportunities and woefully inadequate business plans.

Unfortunately, companies (and even entire industries) still lose sight of the big picture all the time. Markets are viewed too narrowly, and customer needs are neglected – a classic management blunder. Check out these examples:

- ✔ Companies that make home-improvement tools often view their business in terms of product components – the making and selling of 6mm drill bits, for example. But when you think about it, nobody really wants or needs 6mm drill bits (not even your dentist). What customers are *really* looking for are 6mm holes. That basic need creates the potential opportunity for any number of possible solutions.

- ✔ Glasses manufacturers – the companies that make the frames and lenses – continue to see themselves as being in the glasses-fashion business. But the customers, frustrated by not being able to read a menu closer than three feet away when they've forgotten their glasses, simply want to see better. The manufacturers are now learning a hard lesson with the advent of laser technologies that promise to improve vision by reshaping the cornea – no vision problems, no need for glasses, no more business.

- ✔ Charles Revson revolutionised the cosmetics industry when he quipped, 'In the factory, we make cosmetics; in the store, we sell hope.' As the founder of Revlon, he understood that he was offering his customers something far more important than simple chemistry: the prospect of youth, beauty, and sex appeal.

The key point here is simple: If you don't know what your customers really want, you can't possibly fulfil their needs in an effective way.

Politics and the marketplace

Bill Clinton had a little sign tacked up on the back wall of his 1992 US presidential campaign headquarters that read:

It's the economy, Stupid!

Campaign manager James Carville posted the sign because he wanted everyone to focus not so much on the product – Mr Clinton – as on the marketplace and customer needs.

In this case, of course, the marketplace was the election itself, and the customers were the voting public. At the time, workers in the United States were suffering through a steep recession, worried about foreign competition and petrified about the 'new world economy'. As a shrewd campaign strategist, Carville knew that the road to success lay in getting beyond the candidates themselves and appealing to the voters' innermost needs – those universal, underlying issues that would ultimately sway decision making in the polling booth.

As a business planner, you have to do the same thing: focus on being market-driven when you approach your customers.

Put yourself in your customer's shoes:

- Take a hard look at one of your own products or services, and honestly ask yourself, 'Why would *I* need this thing?'
- Ask the same question of several people who also use your product or service.
- Try to imagine a world without your product or service. What would you substitute for it?

Answering questions such as these goes a long way toward fostering creativity, generating new strategies, and providing expanded market opportunities.

Dealing with Business Customers

Although we've mentioned companies that sell principally to other companies (as opposed to those that sell primarily to individual consumers), some of you in this so-called *business-to-business market* may think that we're ignoring you. We aren't – honest! In this section, you find details on how companies, institutions, and government agencies act when they themselves are the customers. What makes the business buyer different? Many things.

Secondhand demand

Demand for goods and services in business-to-business markets is almost always *derived demand.* In other words, businesses purchase only those goods and services that they can use to better serve their own customers.

Steel, for example, is a product that no end-user buys. When was the last time you had the urge to go out and get your hands on some flat-rolled sheeting? Steel purchasers tend to be automobile manufacturers, construction firms, appliance companies, and the like. After these businesses use the steel to make their own products (cars, office blocks, and refrigerators), we come into the picture as potential customers.

What are the implications for the steel sellers? If a steelmaker cuts its prices across the board, for example, should it expect a huge increase in orders? Not necessarily. The steel buyers will increase their purchases only if they think that they can sell more of the things that *they* make, and their own sales may be affected by many factors beyond the underlying price of steel. How many of us dashed out to buy a new car the last time steel prices were reduced by 10 per cent?

Inelastic demand is a term that number crunchers use when they talk about demand for a particular product that doesn't stretch or change automatically when the price of the product changes.

If you offer products or services in the business-to-business market, make sure that you take the time to think through what your planning decisions mean to your business buyers. And that means thinking about your customers' customers as well.

- ✔ Will a price reduction on your part result in increased sales for your customers – and your company?

- ✔ Will your customers (and their customers) benefit if you offer them additional bells and whistles while raising their costs?

- ✔ Are your customers looking for continuity and price stability?

Decision making as a formal affair

Purchase decisions in the business-to-business marketplace tend to be more formal, rational, and professional than in most consumer markets. Many people from different parts of the target company are often involved in the decision-making process (DMP). One division in the company may recommend your product or service, another may acquire it, yet another may pay for it, and all of them do the work for a separate customer centre that actually uses that product. Taken together, these divisions form the *decision-making unit* (or DMU) – another marketing term foisted off on us nice folks by marketing gurus.

Table 5-2 describes three ways in which a business DMU may behave when it's thinking about buying a product or service.

Table 5-2	How Businesses Behave When They Buy
Buying behaviour	*Description of the customer's DMP*
Business as usual	Continues to order more of the product or service, perhaps even automating the process so that inventories don't fall below certain levels.
Yes, but . . .	Asks for changes in the existing sales arrangement, modifying one or more purchase terms (such as pricing, financing, quantities, and options) and including various people who are part of the DMU.
Opportunity knocks	Purchases a product or service for the first time, perhaps after putting out a request for proposal (RFP) to several possible suppliers and making a deliberate, complete decision involving all parties in the DMU.

Forces to be reckoned with

In working with business customers, you most likely have to deal with several powerful customer forces that you rarely encounter in consumer markets. If your business-to-business strategies are going to succeed over time, you must factor these forces into your business plans. Consider the following questions:

✔ What's the state of the customer's business?

- Is the customer's business booming, mature, or dying?

- Is it facing increased competition or enjoying record profits?

- Is it outsourcing business, creating new opportunities?

- Does it threaten to become a competitor?

✔ How does the customer's company operate?

- Does the customer purchase centrally, or does it have buyers scattered around the company?

- Does it require several levels of approval before a decision is made?

- Do senior executives (who may or may not know a lot about the product) make the ultimate purchase decisions?

✔ Who's important to whom?

- Do the customer's key decision-makers tend to be engineers or marketing people?

- Does the customer use both small and large suppliers?

- Does it have a policy of requiring more than one supplier in critical areas?

As you begin to develop strategies for your business customers, take the time to investigate the forces that are unique in business-to-business markets.

✔ Get out into the field and talk to potential business buyers.

✔ Read about customers' organisations and their industries.

✔ Attend the conferences and conventions that your customers attend, and learn about the critical events and forces that shape their thinking.

All these activities take time and resources, of course, but your investment will be rewarded many times over when you incorporate what you learn into your business-to-business planning.

✔ Some of your customers may be other businesses, and the way in which they buy is different from the way that individuals buy.

✔ Several people may be involved in making the decision to buy from you.

✔ Sometimes your business customers aren't the end users, so you need to understand your customers' customers as well.

Chapter 6

Dividing Customers into Groups

• •

• •

*I*t's nice to think of your customers as being flesh-and-blood people – the Tom, Dick, and Mary who regularly walk through your doors. But it's also tempting to think of customers as being everybody out there – hey, shouldn't the whole world want your products and services? Unfortunately, neither of these views is practical when it comes to creating your business plan.

Take a closer look at your customers (a good place to start is Chapter 5). One of the first things that you'll notice is that many of them have a great deal in common – a fact that gives you a golden opportunity to divide customers into specific groups based on their similarities. Eureka! By planning your business around these customer groups, you can serve your customers' particular needs effectively.

In this chapter, we look at your customers in groups, introducing the concept of market segments in detail. We explore various ways to identify market segments based on who is buying, what they buy, and why they buy. Then we show you how to create practical market segments that you can use in your business plan. Finally, we talk about things you can do to figure out more about how market segments are behaving.

Defining Market Segments

Take a moment to think about your customers. You'd no doubt call many of them good customers, for these reasons:

  ✔ They bring in lots of business.

  ✔ They are loyal.

  ✔ They pay on time.

  ✔ They make useful suggestions.

  ✔ They say nice things about you.

These people are good customers because they are satisfied customers. You understand what they are looking for, and you translate their needs and wants into the products and services that you sell them. But let's face it – not every customer is a good customer, and you probably wish that you had a few more of the good ones.

Addressing each customer individually may be effective, but it is rarely efficient in today's markets. How can you make sure that you satisfy as many potential customers as possible? Although each individual customer is unique, groups of customers often look a great deal alike.

Whenever you make sense of your own marketplace by grouping customers for one reason or another, you create *market segments*. To be of any practical use in your business planning, however, market segments should describe groups of customers that you can reach and who respond to your products and services in similar ways – ways that are distinct from those of other customer groups. A successful market segment allows you to satisfy the particular needs and wants of an entire group of customers.

There was a time when trainers were rubber-soled canvas shoes that kids played in and maybe used for school sports. Back then, most of the buyers were parents, and most of the wearers were boys. If you wanted to play in the trainers market (Adidas and Hi Tech, for example, produced trainers that parents bought in droves), you kept your eye on what those boys were looking for.

Look at the market for sports shoes today. The difference is phenomenal. Young males still wear the shoes, of course, but so do toddlers, cool teenagers, serious runners, senior citizens, and everyone else – all demanding trainers in various shapes and colours, with different features and options, in a wide range of prices.

Literally dozens of athletic-shoe segments exist now, each defined in unique ways. For Nike or Reebok to attempt to capture the market today with one universal trainer would be sheer folly and a financial disaster. The athletic-shoe business and the market segments that shape it have changed beyond recognition over the past two decades.

✔ A market segment is a group of customers who have specific needs and wants in common.

✔ By grouping similar customers, you can satisfy their particular needs more efficiently.

✔ The more features and choices that customers demand, the more reason you have to divide customers into groups.

Extra! Extra! Cars to have options!

In the early 1920s, Henry Ford and his famous Model T dominated the growing automobile industry in the United States. As Ford was fond of saying:

You can get the T in any color you like – as long as it's black.

The key to the company's early success was its focus on just one product. Ford believed that if one size could fit all, standardised parts and mass production would lead to lower costs, lower prices, and satisfied customers. He was absolutely right . . . up to a point.

The market reached that point when car buyers began to develop a taste for options. Some buyers wanted to be sporty; others, classy. Some wanted more leg room; others, more room for the kids. Ford continued to improve his cars, of course. The chassis became sturdier, the engine quieter, and the ride smoother. But when customers visited a Ford showroom, all that they saw was the same old Model T – still available in all shades of black.

Then along came Alfred P. Sloan, Jr., the legendary head of General Motors. Sloan's genius was in recognising that car buyers weren't all looking for the same car. He captured this vision when he said:

GM will produce a car for every purpose and a car for every purse.

Sloan soon hired a new kind of employee – the market researcher – to figure out what potential car buyers were really looking for. Although he couldn't produce a unique car for each individual buyer, his market research identified five major groups of buyers with similar tastes and needs. In a bold move, he instructed his designers and engineers to come up with cars that would meet those needs. The result was a new line-up of products tied directly to market segments:

✔ Chevrolet for entry-level buyers

✔ Pontiac for buyers who were moving up

✔ Oldsmobile for the growing middle class

✔ Buick for those who wanted something finer

✔ Cadillac for status-seekers

GM cars soon began to outsell Fords, and market segments took their rightful place as an important business-planning technique – not only for cars, but also for major industries across the nation and the world.

Ways to Make Market Segments

There are several common ways to divide customers into groups. But don't just rely on these. Frankly, the more you can apply your own imagination and creativity in this area, the more successful you're likely to be in coming up with market segments that are unique and effective.

Despite what the marketing gurus tell you, there's really no right or wrong way to divvy up your market. You need to view your customers from various angles and to describe them based on several factors. One dimension won't be enough. As Figure 6-1 shows, you can come up with ways to create market segments by asking three basic questions:

- ✔ Who is buying?
- ✔ What do they buy?
- ✔ Why do they buy?

Figure 6-1:
You can define market segments by asking three basic questions and then answering those questions from different market viewpoints.

Market Segments at a Glance

Who is Buying?
- Geography
- Profile
- Lifestyle
- Personality

What Do They Buy?
- Features
- Packaging
- Pricing
- Delivery

Your Product or Service

Why Do They Buy?
- Benefits
- Traits

Who is buying?

A general description of who is buying your product or service is a good place to start when you begin to put your customers into market segments. If your customers are individual consumers, learn a bit about how they live their lives. If your customers are other companies, find out how they operate their businesses. Think about your customers in these terms:

- ✔ Geography (where do they live?)
- ✔ Profile (what are they like?)
- ✔ Lifestyle (what do they do?)
- ✔ Personality (how do they act?)

Where do they live?

Perhaps the simplest and most widely used way to describe your customers is based on where they are, beginning with a simple geographic breakdown by these factors:

- ✔ Country
- ✔ Region
- ✔ City
- ✔ Postcode

But geography can also lead to more nitpicky groups, describing customers based on these factors:

- ✔ How close their nearest neighbours are
- ✔ How hot or cool their summers are
- ✔ How long their trips to the airport take

Dividing customers into groups based on geography turns out to be a good way to separate them according to regional taste – which often is a significant factor in the distribution and delivery of a product or service.

Arsenal shirts, for example, don't sell that well in Manchester.

UK electricity and gas markets regulator Ofgem reports that more UK customers are taking advantage of the right to change their electricity and gas supplier than ever before. The UK, argues Ofgem, now has the most competitive energy market in the world.

According to Ofgem's latest figures, an average of between 30 per cent and 40 per cent of UK customers have switched their supplier, but there are wide regional variations.

What are they like?

A profile of your customers includes all the attributes that you may expect to find in a national census. Marketing gurus call these attributes *demographic data*. These data include the following:

- Age
- Gender
- Family size
- Education
- Occupation
- Income
- Ethnicity
- Nationality
- Religion

Company profiles, of course, are somewhat different. These profiles can include basic characteristics such as the following:

- Industry
- Size of company by turnover or market valuation
- Number of employees
- Years in business

You can often use customer profiles to spot market trends and take advantage of potential opportunities. Why is the market for health care products booming today? Because the fabled Baby Boom generation – those millions who were born between 1946 and 1964 – is beginning to come face to face with its own mortality. And where can you find a growing market for financial loans? The growing number of families who have university-age children.

What do they do?

Lifestyle is an awfully tired word these days, used to describe anything and everything that we do in the modern world. But when applied to your customers, *lifestyle* has a particular meaning; it's meant to capture characteristics that go deeper than what's available in plain old census data. Customer lifestyle factors include:

- ✓ Hobbies
- ✓ TV viewing habits
- ✓ Social activities
- ✓ Club memberships
- ✓ Holiday preferences

All this information is sometimes called *psychographic data* because it's used to map out the psychology of the customer.

Applied to business customers, lifestyle factors include such things as what companies do when it comes to the following:

- ✓ Protecting the environment
- ✓ Donating to charitable causes
- ✓ Investing in employee training
- ✓ Offering employee benefits
- ✓ Promoting people from inside the company

You can use any of these characteristics to understand how you may better serve a particular segment of your business market.

How do they act?

Your customers are individuals who have their own ways of acting and inter-acting with the world. Wouldn't it be useful, however, if you could create market segments based on general personality types? Luckily, you don't have to start from scratch. Some behavioural scientists (the spooky folks who always have their eyes on us) have come up with five basic personality types, which are described in Table 6-1.

McGovern and the Volvo lifestyle

In the 1972 US Presidential campaign, the Democratic candidate, George McGovern, sent out fund-raising letters specifically to the owners of Volvo cars. Why? His polling showed that people who bought Volvos tended to be well-educated, middle- to upper-middle-class, of above-average income, and liberal in their political beliefs – characteristics that resonated well with the McGovern campaign. Rather than mailing general fund-raising appeals to a wide audience, the campaign found that a targeted mailing to Volvo owners, for example, yielded far better returns when costs were measured against contributions. Unfortunately for McGovern, the Volvo isn't a car that appeals to – or is in the price range of – a majority of Americans.

Table 6-1	Customer Personality Types
Type	*Description*
Innovators	Risk-takers of the world Young and well-educated Comfortable with new ideas and technologies Mobile and networked Informed by outside sources
Early Adopters	Opinion leaders in their communities Careful evaluators Open to well-reasoned arguments Respected by their peers
Early Majority	Risk avoiders whenever possible Deliberate in their actions Unlikely to try new products until those products catch on
Late Majority	Sceptics Extremely cautious Disappointed by other products Reluctant to try new products Respond only to pressure from friends
Laggards	Hold out until the bitter end Wait until products are old-fashioned Still hesitate!

As it turns out, personality type has a great deal to do with how eager people are to try new products and services. (Check out the consumer adoption process in Chapter 5.) Although some of us are adventurous and willing to try new things, others are quite the opposite, never using anything until it has made the rounds. In general, the laggards among us simply take longer to adopt new ideas than the innovators do. Experts make all this stuff sound like rocket science by calling it the *diffusion of innovation* (see Figure 6-2).

In Figure 6-2, the percentage of people who represent each personality type is just an estimate, of course. But still, you get a rough idea of the relative size of each personality group in your own marketplace.

Over the years, marketers have accumulated lots of data on the typical person in each of the five groups. You can use this information in your planning efforts. First, identify which personality types are most likely to have a positive response to your product or service. Then you can begin to assemble a description of your target customers and create a business plan that enables you to reach them efficiently and effectively.

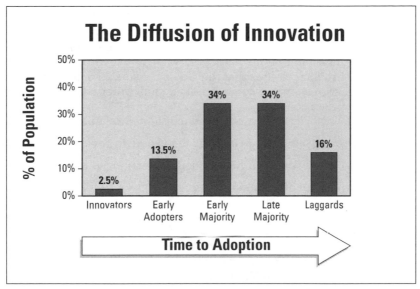

Figure 6-2:
Product adoption occurs at different times for different personality types.

What do they buy?

A description of your customers in terms of their geography, profiles, lifestyles, and personalities gets you only so far. Unfortunately, these basic characteristics don't talk about your customers in terms of your own marketplace and the products and services that you want to sell them. So it's hard to use these kinds of market segments to better serve your customers or provide them superior value. For that kind of help, you're going to have to look at other ways of grouping customers.

A description of customers based on what they buy enables you to view them from a perspective that you're very familiar with: your own products and services. After you come up with market segments based on what your customers purchase, you can address the needs of each group by making changes in the following aspects of your product or service:

✔ Features

✔ Packaging

✔ Pricing

✔ Delivery options

What can it do?

Features refer to all the specifications and characteristics of a product or service – things that you often find listed in a product brochure, users' manual, or the small print on the packaging itself. When you group customers based on the product features that they look for, the customers themselves turn out to have a great deal in common. Their similarities include:

- How much they use the product (light, moderate, heavy)
- How skilled they are in using the product (novice, intermediate, expert)
- What they do with the product (recreation, education, business)
- What kind of customers they are (adviser, reseller, user)

Packard Bell, for example, sells low-end computers primarily to buyers who aren't technology wizards. These buyers probably use their machines at home for a few hours a week to do family finances, finish homework, surf the Internet, or just play games. Packard Bell's customers are completely different from those of Sun Microsystems, a maker of high-end workstations. Sun's customers most likely are technically trained professionals who use their computers at work for many hours each day. All you have to do is compare the features of Packard Bell computers and the Sun workstations to discover that these companies' products target two very different groups of customers.

How is it sold?

Packaging involves much more than cardboard, shrink wrapping, and plastic. *Packaging* really refers to everything that surrounds a product offering, including the following:

- Product advertising (radio/TV, magazines, billboards, T-shirts)
- Promotions (in-store sales, coupons, competitions)
- Marketing (book reviews, telethons, celebrity endorsements)
- Product service (warranties, helplines, service centres)

Again, the market segments that you identify based on packaging criteria often reflect customer attributes similar to the ones based on product features: frequency of use, level of sophistication, product application, and type of user.

Because Packard Bell sells primarily to the home market, for example, it advertises its computers in the mass media, pre-installs all sorts of popular software titles on them, and services them widely. The sophisticated Sun machines, on the other hand, are written up in computer journals, are compatible with sophisticated operating systems, and are mostly serviced through on-site warranty agreements.

What does it cost?

The pricing of a particular kind of product or service is bound to create different groups of customers. Customers who are price-sensitive are in one camp; those who are willing to pay for a certain level of quality are in the other. If you've ever had to endure a course in microeconomics (yuck), you won't ever be able to forget two facts: price is a major market variable, and the price/quality trade-off is a fundamental force in every marketplace. Packard Bell computer buyers are price-sensitive, whereas the techies who buy Sun workstations are more interested in satisfying their own state-of-the-art needs.

In general, the mass market tends to be price-sensitive, and the so-called *class market* buys more on the basis of quality, high-end features, and status. But price isn't the only financial factor that can lead to different market segments. Other criteria include:

- Available financing (offered by home-furnishings companies)
- Leasing options (offered to airlines that are buying planes)
- Money-back guarantees (offered regularly on TV)
- Trade-in arrangements (offered by car dealerships)

Where is it found?

Distribution and delivery determine how customers actually receive your product or service. In this case, market segments are often based on where your customers shop, such as the following:

- Warehouse stores
- Discount centres
- Department stores
- Boutiques
- Catalogues
- The Internet

Packard Bell sells a large percentage of its computers at warehouse stores such as Dixons and PC World. But you won't find Sun workstations at those stores. Those workstations are more than likely purchased through computer resellers that specialise in high-end technology.

The Avon cosmetics company reaches its customers directly at home, using independent sales consultants, and its products aren't available in any shop. The company believes that beauty aids are personal in nature and require highly personalised selling to be successful. With the same aim in mind, other cosmetic companies strategically place consultants (you can easily spot them by their white coats, perfect faces, and expensive aromas) in department stores.

Market segments based on delivery also may rely on additional criteria, including the following:

- ✔ Any-time availability (corner shops)
- ✔ Anywhere availability (petrol stations)
- ✔ Guaranteed availability (video rental outlets)
- ✔ Time sensitivity (flowers, pizza, produce)

Why do they buy?

When it comes down to really satisfying customers' needs over the long haul, you can't forget the big picture (see Chapter 5). Perhaps the most difficult – and useful – questions that you can ask yourself about customers have to do with why they buy in the first place. These questions are:

- ✔ What are customers looking for?
- ✔ What's important to them?
- ✔ What motivates them?
- ✔ How do they perceive things?
- ✔ How do they make choices?

When you group customers by using the answers to these questions, you create market segments based on the benefits that customers are looking for. Because these market segments describe your customers from *their* point of view, rather than your own, they provide the best opportunity for you to satisfy the particular needs of an entire customer group.

What do they get?

As you try to figure out exactly why customers buy products and services in your marketplace, start a list of the benefits that you think they're looking for. We know what you're probably thinking – that product benefits sound an awful lot like product features. But in subtle yet crucial ways, product *benefits* and product *features* are different.

Features are defined in terms of products or services. A car, for example, may have a manual transmission (as opposed to automatic) and may come with accessories such as electric windows, air conditioning, and a CD player. *Benefits,* on the other hand, are defined by the customer. Depending on the customer, the benefits of a manual transmission may be in handling and responsiveness, or in improved fuel consumption. Accessories may represent luxury or may simply be elements of convenience. Again, the benefits are in the eyes of the customer.

It's absolutely critical to understand the difference between benefits and features if you are going to use the market segments that you come up with to create an effective business plan. Take a moment to think about the business situations sketched out in Figure 6-3.

Which of the benefits listed in Figure 6-3 represent genuine benefits to the customers of each company? It's a trick question, of course. *You* don't define benefits – the *customers* do. It's easy to imagine that certain groups of customers in each market seek any and all of these potential benefits.

Choose The Customer Benefits	
Situation	*Potential customer benefits*
A boutique offers upmarket bath and beauty products imported from France, tasteful gift wrapping, and hassle-free delivery anywhere in the world.	❑ A nice place to go after lunch when there's extra time to kill ❑ The opportunity to impress relatives back in Sweden ❑ An alternative to divorce after discovering that today's the anniversary ❑ Aromatherapy after an ugly day at the office
A franchised quick-printing outlet provides self-service copy machines; sells custom-made stationery and business cards; and offers two-hour rush jobs on flyers, posters, and newsletters.	❑ The ability to look like a big company — at least on paper ❑ A money-saving alternative to buying a copier ❑ A threat used to keep the printing and graphics supplier in line ❑ A job-saver when the printed brochures don't arrive at the trade show
A semiconductor manufacturer sells customised chips to high-tech companies for use in brand-name consumer products, including home-electronics gadgets, computers, and games.	❑ An extension of the in-house research and development department ❑ An easy way to expand the product line ❑ A weapon in the cost/price wars ❑ A way to reduce a new product's time to market

Figure 6-3: Consider these business situations.

The benefits of toothpaste

For many years, the toothpaste market defied successful analysis, until a team of market researchers applied the concept of customer benefits. This research resulted in the discovery that four principal benefits – seen by toothpaste users themselves – describe the toothpaste market. Customers seek out one or more of the following benefits when they make their purchase decisions:

✔ **Dental health.** One group of customers seeks perceived dental benefits. Mothers, for example, hope to deny the dentist an opportunity to buy yet another yacht.

✔ **Taste appeal.** Another group is looking for good-tasting toothpaste. Children, of course, don't particularly like to brush.

✔ **Sex appeal.** A third group desperately hopes to appeal to the opposite sex. This group, of course, includes teenagers, who are struggling through the rigours of adolescence.

✔ **Dental hygiene.** The final group seeks basic dental hygiene at a good price. Many men, for example, view all toothpaste as being the same anyway.

As a result of the new research, toothpaste suppliers began to market their offerings around the defined benefit categories. Crest ('recommended by 9 out of 10 dentists!') targeted mothers, for example. Macleans Milk Teeth went after kids, Aquafresh targeted teenagers, and the low-price own-brands appealed to men.

To identify the benefits your products offer, choose one of your products or services and follow these steps:

1. **Draw a mental image of the product or service, based on its features, attributes, and options.**

2. **Put that picture completely aside for a moment.**

3. **Place yourself in your customers' shoes.**

4. **Now create a new description of the product or service from your customers' viewpoint that focuses on the benefits that the customers are after.**

Grouping customers based on the particular benefits that they're looking for when they select a product or service in your market is the key to satisfying individual customers and keeping them happy in the long run.

How do they decide?

Customers are bound to approach your market in different ways, and you can often identify market segments based on certain customer traits as they relate to your own business. Some of the conditions that guide customer buying decisions include the following:

- **Speed of the purchase decision.** The *decision-making process* (DMP) that customers go through before they purchase a product or service varies, depending on the product or service's complexity and on its price tag. People may buy chewing gum at a corner shop without much thought. But car dealerships and estate agents face a completely different DMP in their customers, resulting in a slower decision to buy.

- **The actual decision-maker.** Families of one sort or another represent a common *decision-making unit* (DMU) that's involved in buying various consumer goods. But who in the family has the final word? If you're in the business of selling clothes designed for teenagers, for example, it makes a big difference whether the kids have the final say or whether Mum or Dad is always in the background, giving the thumbs-up or thumbs-down sign. This difference alone may lead to two separate market segments, each of which has unique requirements.

- **Customer loyalty.** The way that companies relate to their own customers can easily define a set of market segments. Supermarkets, for example, have gone out of their way to identify and encourage customers based on their loyalty. You've probably been asked to join more than one loyalty card programme offered by shops that promise to cater to and reward you for being a member of a loyal customer group.

- **Level of product use.** In many industries, a small percentage of consumers account for a large percentage of sales. If you want to sell sherry, for example, you can't ignore the heavy-sherry-drinking population. In the UK 85 per cent of sherry sales are accounted for by the over-50s and only 1 per cent is drunk by the under-24s. Keeping this high-consumption group of customers satisfied can be profitable indeed.

You can group customers in many ways as you go about the creative process of dividing markets up into segments:

- To understand *who* customers are, look at where they live, what they do, and how they play.

- To understand *what* customers are buying, look at the features, packaging, and pricing of the products, and consider where the customers shop.

- To understand *why* customers buy, look at the benefits that they're after and the ways in which they make up their minds.

Finding Useful Market Segments

Simply coming up with a clever way to describe a group of customers isn't good enough, of course. A market segment is useful only if it allows you to deliver something of value to those customers – and to do so profitably. The fact is that not all the market segments that you come up with are going to pan out. What should you look for if you want to find a really useful market segment? In general, you want to make sure that it has the following characteristics:

- A size that you can manage
- Customers you can identify
- Customers you can reach

Is the segment the right size?

Identifying useful market segments requires a delicate balance between defining your markets so broadly that they don't offer you any guidance in planning and defining them so narrowly that they are ultimately impractical and unprofitable. A useful market segment has to be manageable. The right size depends on your particular business situation, including your resources, the competition, and your customers' requirements.

Choosing a manageable group of customers takes you back to the twin business goals of efficiency and effectiveness (covered more extensively in Chapter 3). You want to be effective in serving your market segment, but you also have to be efficient. For British Telecom, Ford, or Unilever, manageable market segments are likely to be rather large and quite different from those of a boutique, a high-tech startup firm, or a small, ecologically-conscious manufacturing company.

A rather obvious trend over the past half-century has been to slice markets into smaller and smaller pieces. Headlines in the business press tell the story:

- 'Mass markets are all the rage' (1950s)
- 'Market segments come of age' (1960s)
- 'Niche markets have arrived' (1970s)
- 'Mass customisation is in' (1980s)
- 'Micromarkets are hot' (1990s)
- 'E-Markets make the running' (2000s)

Clearly, the notion of what a manageable market segment is has changed over the years. Market segments are shrinking. Why? Customers continue to get more sophisticated and demanding in all markets, and companies have found new ways to become more efficient and effective at what they do. How have they done it? In a word: computers.

Did you know, for example, that your credit card company makes a great deal of money by selling information about you to other companies? Each time you make a purchase with your card, you reveal something highly personal and unique about yourself. Sophisticated software programs analyse your revelations (and those of your friends, neighbours, and fellow consumers), using a variety of high-tech tools to place you in a very particular consumer category. Companies – and maybe yours is one of them – pay handsomely for your name, address, and type so that they can target you directly with products and services that are tailored precisely to your identified needs.

You can bet that your own customers, whoever they are, will become more demanding over time and that your competitors are bound to become more adept at serving smaller markets. As you choose the manageable market segments in which you want to compete, make sure that you factor in ways to use information technology in your own business.

Can customers be identified?

As you piece together a complete picture of your customers, you want to take advantage of all the different ways that we've introduced to describe them. In particular, market segments based on why customers buy are often the best, because they define groups of customers who have similar needs. Whenever possible, you want to come up with market segments that take into account your customers' viewpoints – the benefits that they're looking for, as well as their buying behaviour.

But then what? Unfortunately, sometimes it's really hard to detect intimate customer behaviour – motives, wants, needs, preferences – from the outside (unless you're a psychotherapist, of course, or are friends with a behavioural scientist). You may know what these people are really like, but how do you go about tracking them down? If you want to be able to recognise the customers in your market segment, you're going to have to tie their behaviour to characteristics that you can see.

Suppose that you discover a particular employee type based on an attitude about work. Members of this group would like to be more productive on the job, yet they feel neglected and frustrated with their working conditions and office environment. Perhaps you've identified a potential market segment.

But what next? How do you recognise these potential customers? Well, maybe you go on to discover that many of these workers are left-handed and would feel more comfortable with their numeric keypads on the left side of the computer keyboard and with their handsets on the right side of the telephone. Now you've taken a major step toward defining a useful market segment, because the segment is based on customer wants and needs, and is made up of customers who can be described, observed, and identified.

Given this situation, you may have the urge to take a planning shortcut and base your market segment entirely on what you observe: left-handers, who, after all, constitute about 10 per cent of the population. Bingo! You decide to design and produce office equipment exclusively for left-handed customers. But wait, control that urge. Before you identify a really useful market segment, you need to look at one more requirement that needs to be satisfied.

Can the market be reached?

After you define a promising market segment that's based on need and whose customers you can describe, you have to develop ways of communicating with those customers – ways that are both efficient and effective. It's not enough just to know that this group of customers exists somewhere out there in the consumer universe, even if you can describe and recognise them. You have to be able to set up an affordable way to be in contact with them through advertising, promotions, and the delivery of your product or service.

In the case of the left-handers market, for example, you have to devise a plan for marketing and distribution that ties into the common behaviour of this group. Ideally, you'd like to get the full attention of left-handers without incurring the costs of reaching the 90 per cent of people in the right-handed world as well. But just how do you gain the attention of, and access to, left-handed customers? An easy method would be to place ads in *Southpaw Press* or *The Gauche Gazette* and to make your products available at all Lefties Outlet shops. The catch is that none of these companies exist.

Maybe it's too early to give up. But if you can't come up with creative ways to reach out to, and communicate with, left-handed customers, they're really not a useful market segment after all. In addition to having similar needs, common observable traits, and a manageable size, a useful market segment has to present realistic opportunities to get to your customers. Perhaps that's why left-handers are always so frustrated.

> ✔ Useful market segments have to be the right size. If they're too big, they're not effective. If they're too small, they're not efficient.

> ✔ To use a market segment, you need a practical way to identify the customers in the group.
>
> ✔ To be really useful, a market segment must be a group of customers you can actually reach.

Figuring Out How Market Segments Behave

Remember back in school when you were told to check your homework before handing it in – especially if it was going to be marked? Well, the marketplace is a difficult subject to tackle (as difficult as, say, calculus or physics), and the stakes are high. Before you commit to a particular market segment scheme, make sure that you look back over your homework. Pose these review questions to yourself:

> ✔ What benefits are customers in the market segment looking for?
>
> ✔ Will product features, options, and packaging satisfy customers' needs?
>
> ✔ Is the size of the segment manageable?
>
> ✔ Can you describe, observe, and identify your customers?
>
> ✔ Can you reach your customers efficiently through advertising and marketing?
>
> ✔ Will distribution and product service be effective?

At some point, you may want to use a sophisticated approach to answer some of these questions. This approach is called *test marketing*. By testing your ideas on a carefully selected sample of potential customers in your market segment, you can often gauge how well your scheme is likely to work before you spend serious money going forward. The bad news is that like all market research, test marketing can be expensive and time-consuming, especially if you bring in big guns from the outside. So you may want to start by conducting a customer interview.

Customer interviews produce a snapshot of who is buying your product, as well as what they think they're buying. You can conduct interviews on an informal basis. Just follow these steps:

1. **Select customers in your market segment.**

2. **Arrange to meet with them individually or in small groups.**

3. **Get them to talk a bit about themselves.**

4. **Have them tell you what they like and don't like about your product.**

5. **Ask them why they buy your product and what they would do without it.**

Maybe informal customer interviews are already built into your day-to-day routine, and you just don't realise it. If not, figure out ways to come in contact with more of your customers, and think about adding informal customer interviewing to your schedule.

One word of caution: use common sense. These interviews aren't meant to be rigorous pieces of market research, so you're going to have to be careful to confirm what you're seeing when you start drawing conclusions about customer behaviour from them.

Chapter 7

Scoping Out Your Competition

. . . .

In This Chapter

▶ Understanding the value of competition

▶ Identifying your real competitors

▶ Making use of strategic groups

▶ Tracking competitors' actions

▶ Predicting competitors' moves

▶ Organising competitive data

. . . .

Spending time with the competition isn't anyone's idea of fun. Think they're out to get you? You bet they are. But the more you learn about the competition, the better off you'll be when it comes to figuring out what they're up to. The competitor that you're familiar with is much less dangerous than an unknown enemy out there.

If you've neglected to think much about the competition so far, you're in good company; many businesses fail to take this part of planning seriously. Here are the typical excuses:

> *There's no way to know who all of our competitors really are or what they're up to anyway.*

or

> *We already know everything that there is to know about them.*
> *We compete with them every day.*

Business owners or managers in the first group wring their hands because trying to find out about the competition is tough. Those in the second group cover their eyes, assuming that if they don't look too hard, nothing bad will happen. Both groups are making a big mistake.

When the Japanese decided to become global players in the car industry in the late 1960s, they planned carefully. They knew what they had to do, because they'd been taught by American business experts. First, they had to understand the consumer markets in the United States and Europe; second, they had to know everything about the worldwide competition.

So Japanese car makers went to America and Europe to analyse and learn from their competitors-to-be. They visited Fiat, Volvo, General Motors, Ford, Chrysler, and American Motors. They asked questions, taped meetings, took pictures, measured, sketched, and studied. Through it all, they were amazed by American and European hospitality. When they got back home, of course, their plans were hatched. And the European and US car companies never knew what hit them, even though the blow was a decade or more in coming.

In this chapter, we show you why it's so important to have competitors in the first place. Then we help you identify your current competitors and your potential competitors. We look at competition from the viewpoint of customers and choices made in the marketplace. And we explore your competitors in relation to their own strategies and company structure, introducing the idea of strategic groups. After identifying your competitors, we help you understand them better by looking at what they are doing and where they are going by checking out their capabilities, strategies, goals, and assumptions.

Understanding the Value of Competitors

Your competitors are almost always portrayed as being the bad guys. At best, they're nuisances. At worst, they steal customers away and take money from the till. In short, they make your business life miserable. Is this picture unfair? You bet.

Look up from the fray, and we'll point out another side to your competitors: They're the ones who invent new technologies, expand market opportunities, and sometimes create entire industries . . . and believe it or not, they also bring out the best in you. Competitors force you to sharpen your strategies, hone your business plans, and go that extra mile when it comes to satisfying customers.

The power of competition as a force for good has persuaded regulators around the world to loosen their grip on one major industry after another, including these:

✔ Airlines

✔ Banking

✔ Railways

✔ Telecommunications

✔ Utilities

In each of these industries, a newly competitive marketplace has resulted in more products, more services, more customers – and more choices for those customers. Well-run companies have grown stronger, and market expansion has made room for many new players. The biggest beneficiaries of all are those of us who travel, use cash machines, phone home, and turn on the lights at night.

Competition is a force to be reckoned with because of the power of customers. (If you need a refresher on customers' needs, benefits, and buying behaviour, turn to Chapters 5 and 6.) Customers are out there making market choices, deciding what to buy and where to spend money based on their needs and willingness to pay. How do they do it? The process that they go through is based on a *value equation,* which looks like this:

Customer value = Benefits ÷ Price

Figure 7-1 illustrates this equation.

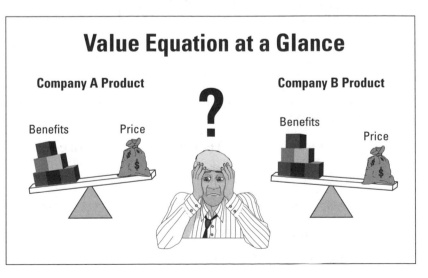

Figure 7-1:
Customers make choices in the marketplace by using the value equation to weigh the value of competing products.

The equation looks complicated, but today's consumers are good at making choices. Think about the last time you went shopping. Chances are that you stopped by the supermarket, where you used the value equation to make all sorts of trade-offs. Maybe you chose a cut of meat, weighing what you were in the mood for and what looked fresh against the price per pound. Maybe you decided that you didn't have time to drive to the discount shop, so you bought cereal in the more expensive 16-ounce box. On your way out, you picked up organic tomatoes for the salad at three times the conventional price. Driving home, you put petrol in the car, opting for the most convenient but more expensive petrol station, which added several pounds to the bill.

Competition encourages each player in your industry to figure out how to provide customers with the best value possible. Competition creates a win–win situation, so don't try to avoid it simply by ignoring your competitors. Don't ever think that you're immune to it, either. Instead, take advantage of competition and what it can do for your company. Learn to thrive on competition.

- ✔ Competition isn't all bad. New competitors mean more products, services, and customers in your market.
- ✔ Customers weigh the benefits of a product or service against the price to measure value.
- ✔ Competition creates a win–win situation.

Identifying Your Real Competitors

Two men are backpacking in Africa. All of a sudden, they come across a lion. One of the men immediately sits down and tightens his shoelaces. The other chap looks down at him and says, 'There's no way we can outrun that lion.' The first man replies, 'I'm not interested in outrunning the lion. I just want to outrun you!' The point is that it's in your best interest to know who you're really competing against.

You can come up with lists of possible competitors based on any number of factors. The problem becomes one of sorting out which method is most successful in identifying competitors that have an impact on your company.

To understand your competition, you need to know the following things:

- ✔ How customers make choices
- ✔ How customers use products

> ✔ The capabilities of your competitors
>
> ✔ Your competitors' strategies
>
> ✔ Where future competition will come from

Competition based on customer choice

Customers choose to buy certain products based on some sort of value equation, weighing the benefits of several products against their relative prices. But which products do customers actually compare? If you want to know who your real competitors are, you need to know how many products – and which products – your customers typically look at before they decide to buy.

Is Coke it?

The Coca-Cola Company produces almost half the soft drinks consumed in the world today, but it still has competition. It's probably safe to say, for example, that most Coke drinkers have tried a Pepsi at least once. PepsiCo accounts for about a quarter of the world soft-drink market. But what other beverages compete with Coke? The following list of competitors starts with the most obvious:

✔ Other colas

✔ Other soft drinks

✔ Juices and juice drinks

✔ Flavoured iced teas

✔ Iced coffees

✔ Mineral waters

✔ Beer and wine

✔ Tap water

Does Coke really compete with tap water? Probably. And it may even compete with bottled water, which was the reasoning behind the launch of Dasani. But Coca-Cola has to draw the line somewhere when it comes to identifying its major competitors – the ones that are going to have a real impact on its business over time. Knowing where and how that line should be drawn largely depends on understanding what customers are looking for. For Coca-Cola, that understanding involves customer choices based on the following factors:

✔ Cola versus non-cola

✔ Diet versus non-diet

✔ High-calorie versus low-calorie

✔ Caffeinated versus caffeine-free

✔ Alcoholic versus non-alcoholic

The importance of these criteria differs in different markets and may change over time. Accordingly, Coca-Cola has to continually assess and reassess its competition.

If you know who your customers are and what their *selection criteria* are – that is, what they're looking for in a product or service – you can divide a list of competitors into groups based on how intensely they compete with you.

✔ **Head-to-head competitors.** Together, these companies represent your most intense competition. Their products always seem to be on customers' shortlists, and customers may ask you to compare your features, benefits, and pricing with theirs. You want to know as much as you can about these competitors.

✔ **First-tier competitors.** These companies are direct competitors, but perhaps not quite as fierce as the head-to-head kind. You may run up against one of these companies only in certain areas and among particular kinds of customers. You don't want to ignore this group too long, however, because any of these companies may have the desire and capability to come after you and become a head-to-head competitor.

✔ **Indirect competitors.** These competitors are the ones that you don't often think about. Their products surface as alternatives to your own only occasionally, and you usually have more important competition to worry about. Again, this group deserves a periodic review, because indirect competitors always have the potential to surprise you with competing products out of the blue.

You should be able to count your head-to-head competitors on one hand. You may have twice as many first-tier competitors to track and an equal number of indirect competitors. Be careful to keep the number of competitors that you're tracking manageable. Your head-to-head competition deserves much more attention than your indirect competitors, obviously, but you may want to set up a schedule for reviewing companies in each of the three competitor groups. Start with a weekly analysis of your head-to-head competition, a monthly review of first-tier competitors, and a quarterly review of your indirect competitors, adjusting the schedule to fit the pace of change in your industry.

One way to come up with levels of competition in your own business is to ask potential customers to consider playing their product-selection process backward for you, as described below. Sometimes, you can also get this kind of information through your salespeople or customer service representatives (if you have any).

1. **Ask customers for the shortlist of products that they are seriously evaluating.**

   These products probably are offered by your head-to-head competitors.

2. **Ask customers for the larger list that they came up with when they started investigating what was available in the market.**

   These products are likely to be offered by your first-tier competitors.

3. **Ask customers for the names of products that popped into their heads when they first decided to go shopping.**

   These products may include those offered by your indirect competitors.

Competition based on product use

Looking at products and services in the context of how they're going to be used by customers gives you another viewpoint from which to eye the competition. In this case, you have different steps to take:

1. **Ask customers to think about situations, applications, or occasions in which they would be likely to use your product.**

2. **Ask customers to come up with other kinds of products or services that would also be appropriate and may be just as satisfying in the same situations.**

Coca-Cola drinkers, for example, may associate outdoor sports (such as tennis and football) with enjoying a Coke. They also may single out other fizzy drinks and maybe mineral water as other possibilities to help them cool off and relax after a game. In this context, Coke has a well-defined set of competitors that may be quite different from its competition in other settings.

By viewing your competitors from a marketplace perspective – how customers choose and then use alternative products – you're rewarded with a fairly complete picture of the competitive landscape that you're facing.

Competition based on strategy

Sometimes, if you step back and look at the competitors around you, you're amazed by how different they can be. In certain industries, for example, companies that have a full product line compete with companies that offer a single product. In other industries, companies that are known for their innovative research and development compete with companies that don't develop anything on their own.

But how can this be? How can competitors in the same industry be so different? Over time, doesn't every company figure out the best strategies, as well as the most efficient and effective ways to do business? Shouldn't all companies end up looking pretty much alike? These are good questions. Here are two answers:

> ✔ There isn't always a best way to do things. Markets and industries are complex, and different ways of doing business can exist side by side and be equally successful.
>
> ✔ It's not always easy for a company that does business one way to change and start doing business another way.

Identifying competitors based on their unique capabilities and strategies has a great deal in common with some of the industry analysis discussed in Chapter 4. Sometimes, you can take that analysis one step further and divide companies in your industry into groups based on what they do and how they operate – sort of like the market segments that we talk about in Chapter 6, but this time applied to companies rather than individual customers.

A *strategic group* is a set of companies in a particular industry that look a lot alike and tend to behave in similar ways. In particular, firms in the same strategic group have the following traits:

> ✔ They display similar characteristics (size, geography, rate of growth)
>
> ✔ They operate in similar ways (degree of risk-taking, level of aggressiveness)
>
> ✔ They demonstrate similar capabilities (people, skills, image, money in the bank)
>
> ✔ They pursue related strategies (distribution, marketing, and product-line decisions)

You can apply all sorts of business criteria to identify the most useful strategic groups. Although every industry is different, you'll want to consider these general variables:

> ✔ Companies that manufacture most of their product components versus those that assemble or resell products
>
> ✔ Companies that produce name-brand products versus those that produce generic or private-label brands
>
> ✔ Companies that rely on their own R&D (research and development) versus those that license or buy technology
>
> ✔ Companies that have a full product line versus those that have limited or specialised products
>
> ✔ Companies that emphasise marketing versus those that focus on production
>
> ✔ Companies that are diversified versus those that are in only one industry

Strategic groups fall somewhere between an individual company and the entire industry. Lumping your competition into groups is helpful, because all the companies in a strategic group tend to be affected by, and react to, changes in the marketplace in the same ways. But grouping works only if those companies stay put in their assigned group long enough to be analysed. Fortunately, they usually do.

As part of your own industry analysis, you may have already discovered a few *entry barriers* – things that make it tough to get into your business, such as high capital costs, expensive distribution systems, new technology, and regulation. You also may have come up with some *exit barriers* – things that keep competitors from getting out of the business, such as expensive factories, specialised equipment, and long-term agreements. Strategic groups can have the same kind of *mobility barriers,* which tend to keep competitors where they are, in one group or another.

Strategic groups can be a great time-saver in business planning, because when you put all your competitors in one, you know where to focus your energies. You can spend most of your time analysing the companies in your own strategic group and deal with the rest of the companies in clusters, rather than track each of them separately.

A strategic circle of friends

The worldwide motor industry is so large and complex that keeping track of competitors would be tough without the help of strategic groups. Fortunately, car makers can use several criteria to break the automotive world into more manageable industry segments.

When Ford looks out over the competitive landscape, the competitors that loom the largest are likely to be Toyota, Nissan, Fiat, and Volkswagen. What do these companies have in common that places them in the same strategic group? Well, for starters, all of them have these traits:

✔ They are extremely large companies.

✔ They are involved in almost all aspects of the car-making process.

✔ They have a full line of cars with many sizes, models, and prices.

✔ They distribute vehicles on a global scale.

These companies don't have much choice but to know as much as there is to know about one another in terms of resources, capabilities, goals, and strategies. Although Ford is going to keep its eye on BMW, Volvo, and Mercedes-Benz (after all, Ford owns Jaguar), the company isn't going to put as much effort into tracking those luxury car makers as it does into tracking Volkswagen and Toyota. By identifying the members of its own strategic group, Ford focuses on the competitors that are likely to have the greatest impact on its business.

To divide your own list of competitors into strategic groups, follow these steps:

1. **Put your competitors in a small number of groups, based on how similar you think they are to one another.**

2. **Add your own company to one of the groups.**

3. **Looking at each group carefully, try to come up with the basic criteria that you used to make your selections.**

4. **Take a hard look at the group in which you put your own company.**

    Are these competitors really closest to you in terms of their characteristics and the criteria that you've identified?

5. **Adjust the groups, if necessary, and work on additional criteria that may point to other strategic groupings.**

Strategic groups are relevant and useful in many industries; they often provide a means of organising competitors in ways that can simplify the competitive landscape. But keep in mind that all industries don't play by the same rules. If the mobility barriers aren't very high, for example, companies are free to adjust their capabilities and change strategies quickly, limiting the usefulness of long-term strategic groups. Make sure that the groups you identify in your own industry are real and won't dissolve before you've had a chance to analyse them.

Competition in the future

Always remember that competitors can come out of nowhere. Keep at least one eye on your potential competitors. Who are they? Following are the most likely sources of new competition:

- ✔ **Market expansion.** A company that's operated successfully for years outside your geographic region decides to expand into your territory, becoming an overnight competitor. Alternatively, a company that has a product that dominates another market segment sees an opportunity to target your customers as well.

- ✔ **Product expansion.** A company decides to take advantage of its brand name, its technology, or its distribution system and creates a new product line in direct competition with your own.

- ✔ **Backward integration.** One of your major customers decides that it can do what you do – and do it better and cheaper. So the former customer sets up shop and hands the business that it once gave you to its in-house group. All of a sudden, your old customer is a new competitor.

✔ **Forward integration.** Your company buys many things from many suppliers. One day, one of those suppliers decides that it can bring all the pieces together as well as you can. So it creates a new business and a product line that suddenly competes with yours.

✔ **Change in fortune.** Out of the blue, a minor competitor is suddenly purchased by a major company. With access to new resources (financing, marketing, and distribution), the minor competitor becomes a major player. You really have to watch out for these competitors; when they do come out of nowhere, they are likely to catch you off guard and be all the more dangerous.

Keeping track of your future competitors is as important as tracking your current ones. Just keep your eyes and ears open.

✔ To find out who your competitors are, ask customers what other companies' products they consider buying.

✔ Examine how your products are used if you want to identify alternative products that your customers may turn to.

✔ Your capabilities and strategy determine who you compete with in the marketplace.

✔ New competitors arise whenever markets expand, new products appear, or the rules of your industry change.

Tracking Your Competitors' Actions

Suppose that you're armed with a fresh, up-to-date list of competitors. Perhaps you've already ranked which of those competitors you have to watch most carefully, tagging them as head-to-head competitors, first-tier competitors, or indirect competitors. Maybe you've even gone as far as to put them into strategic groups, singling out the competitors in your own group for special attention.

So what's next? You should decide which of the competitors in your list you want to spend more time with. Remember – you're probably not going to be able to know all there is to know about each competitor. Keeping track of a competitor's actions involves looking at both what that company is capable of doing and what it plans to do.

Determining their capabilities

The things that you'd really like to find out about your competitors are the same things that you need to know about your own company. Not surprisingly, you want to ask the same kinds of questions about your competitors that you ask yourself when you complete a company checkup in Chapters 8 and 9. We introduce the basics here, but turn to those chapters for all the nitty-gritty details.

The capabilities that you're most interested in tell you something about your competitors' ability to react as your industry changes. How quickly they can react – and how much they can do to change themselves – say a great deal about how dangerous they are as competitors.

To determine your competitors' capabilities, start with this list of important business functions and areas. The following questions should get you going, but check out Chapter 8 if you need more help.

- **Management.** What do you know about the background and experience of the company's chief honchos? What functional areas (marketing, finance, engineering) do they come from? What about the board of directors? How many good people are at or near the top? Do any of them hail from another industry? If so, what are their track records with those companies?

- **Organisation.** How structured and centralised is the company's organisation? Does it have tight controls in place, or does it delegate authority down through the organisation levels? Does it promote from within or hire from the outside? How would you describe the corporate culture?

- **Customer base.** What is the company's share of the market? Is it growing? How loyal are its customers? Are customers concentrated in one segment, or do the company's products appeal to several segments?

- **Research and development.** Is the company known for innovation and technology? Is it even involved in R&D? How often does it come out with new products? Does it have patents and copyrights to rely on? How stable and committed are the members of its technical staff? Does the company have sources of outside expertise to draw upon?

- **Operations.** How modern are the company's facilities? How has automation affected operations? If the company is a manufacturer, does it have flexible production facilities? What about capacity? Can the company count on its suppliers? What's the general attitude of the work force? Does the company have a history of labour disputes?

- **Marketing and sales.** How strong are the company's products? How broad is the product line? Does the company have a reputation for quality? How about brand-name recognition? Does the company put a large amount of its resources into advertising and promotion? Is it known for its customer service? Are the salespeople aggressive, and are they well trained?

- **Distribution and delivery.** How many distribution channels does the company sell through? Does it have a good relationship with its distributors? Is it quick to take advantage of new distribution opportunities?

- **Financial condition.** Is the company's sales revenue growing? How about profits? Does the company manage costs well? Are profit margins steady or growing? What is the cash-flow situation? Is long-term debt manageable? Does the company have ready access to cash?

Jot down a half-page corporate bio on each competitor. Each bio should capture the company's defining traits, including the following:

- Capability to respond quickly

- Willingness to change

- Determination to compete

- Capacity to grow

Assessing their strategies

Your competitors' capabilities tell you something important about their capacity to get things done in your business. But what are they planning to do? Your off-the-cuff response may be:

> *How the heck should I know?*

We hope to help you do a little better than simply shrug your shoulders and guess. We talk a lot more about how to think strategically in Chapter 13, so turn there for the details. For now, we discuss three basic kinds of strategy that should shed some light on what the competition may be planning. The following three strategies are sometimes called *generic strategies,* because they've been tried and because they work well in almost any market or industry.

Low cost. The first generic strategy comes from a basic economic principle: if you can offer a product or service at the lowest price in the market, customers are naturally going to buy from you. This strategy assumes, of course, that you can also produce your product at a low-enough cost so that the company makes a profit over time. The strategy also assumes that your product or service is similar enough to the competition's that a lower price is going to entice customers and clinch the sale.

Something different. This strategy is based on the simple notion that if you can come up with something different or unique in the products you offer or the services you provide, chances are that customers will beat a path to your company door. These customers are likely to become good customers, loyal customers, and customers that maybe aren't terribly sensitive to price, because you offer them special benefits that they can't find anywhere else.

Focus. The last generic strategy is about the kinds of customers you decide to serve. Rather than position yourself everywhere in the market, trying to sell products and services to everyone, carefully choose your customers instead. You then win these customers over as a group by focusing on understanding their needs better than the competition does and by providing them with just the benefits that they're looking for, be it price savings or something unique.

A competitor doesn't have to go with just one of these generic strategies; Chapter 13 shows that the strategies are often combined. A company that follows a focused strategy may find success in serving a particular market segment simply because its products are different from those of the competition.

Put together a short summary of what you think your competitors may be up to when it comes to a strategy. Review their capabilities and what they've done in the past, considering the following questions:

- ✔ What generic strategies has each competitor adopted in the past?
- ✔ Have the strategies generally been successful?
- ✔ Are changes in the industry forcing competitors to change their strategies?
- ✔ What kinds of change is each competitor capable of making?
- ✔ How fast can each competitor change?

Usually, you find that a long-term strategy requires time and the total commitment of the company. So it turns out that knowing a little about your competitors' history is very useful in understanding their strategies. It also helps you keep in mind what you think your competitors are really capable of in the future.

- ✔ Get to know your competitors as well as you know your own company.
- ✔ Pay special attention to capabilities that enable your competition to react quickly to changes in your industry.
- ✔ Identify the key strategies that each of your competitors relies on to win.

Predicting Your Competitors' Moves

Trying to predict where your competitors are headed isn't easy, of course; looking into the future never is. But where your competitors plan to be in the future certainly depends on where they are today, as well as on their capabilities and the strategies that they've set in motion. Predicting your competitors' actions also requires a little insight into what they think and how they think – the goals that they aim for, as well as the assumptions that they make about the industry.

Figuring out their goals

Your competitors' mission, vision, and values statements tell you a great deal about what they expect of themselves in the future. These documents aren't top secret; they're meant to communicate a company's intentions to all its stakeholders, and you should take advantage of them. You don't have to read your competitors' minds. All you have to do is read what they say about themselves and what they're going to do.

When Jack Welch took over as CEO of General Electric in 1981, he rather quickly spelled out the giant company's new goals to his senior managers: market share, market share, and market share. GE would become either first or second in each of its businesses – or else. No one misunderstood what the 'or else' meant. GE's competitors could (and should) have listened to Welch, because the company was sending a clear signal about how it intended to compete in the future. Any company that was going head-to-head with GE for market share was going to have a battle on its hands. The companies that understood this fact early had a warning and the opportunity to adjust their own strategies to meet a changed competitive landscape.

To discover your competitors' mission, vision, and value statements, try the following steps:

1. **Select a shortlist of competitors.**

2. **Dig up as much information as you can find on each competitor's values, vision, and mission statements, as well as any stated business goals and objectives.**

   If the companies are public, a good place to start is with their annual reports to shareholders.

3. **Write down your competitors' financial and strategic goals.**

Don't forget to read between the lines. In particular, look for the following:

- Market-share goals
- Revenue targets
- Profitability targets
- Technology milestones
- Customer-service goals
- Distribution targets

Uncovering their assumptions

What your competitors plan to do is usually related to their assumptions about themselves and your industry – how they think and the way in which they see the world. Sometimes you can get important clues about your competitors' assumptions by going back over their goals and objectives. It's hard for your competitors to make a statement about where they want to go without giving something away about where they think they are today. You can often come up with valuable insights by comparing your competitors' assumptions about the industry with what you know to be true.

In the 1950s, for example, British and American businesses operated under the broad assumption that all that Japanese companies could ever produce were cheap, poorly-made products that were meant to be thrown away. During that decade, products from Japan were collectively referred to as 'Japanese junk'. When British and American companies finally realised that their assumption couldn't be farther from the truth, the competitive damage had already been done. This monumental misconception altered the balance of global competition and trade for a generation. With the 1995 sale of Zenith Corporation to a Korean conglomerate, for example, the US was no longer a serious television manufacturer. Today, British and American companies often make the equally broad and misguided assumption that it's simply impossible to compete against aggressive Asian firms.

So assumptions aren't always true – that's why they're called assumptions in the first place. False assumptions can be very dangerous for companies, especially when they lead to so-called conventional wisdom or result in competitive blind spots.

Conventional wisdom: Prevailing assumptions in an industry often become so ingrained that they are mistaken for the gospel truth. Conventional wisdom is almost always proved wrong when an unconventional competitor comes along. Watch your competitors for signs that they are taking their own assumptions too seriously and are forgetting the importance of always asking 'Why?'

Blind spots: It's all too easy to miss the significance of events or trends in an industry, especially if they run counter to prevailing notions and conventional wisdom. A competitor's world view often dictates what that company is going to see and not see. As you track your competitors, look closely for actions and reactions that may point to blind spots and a misreading of what's happening in the marketplace.

- ✔ Your competitors' mission, values, and vision statements are a great way to discover their goals for the future.
- ✔ Competitors sometimes signal their intentions by the way they behave in the marketplace.
- ✔ Your competitors' assumptions about the industry – right or wrong – offer important clues about how they will act.

Competing to Win

The more you learn about competitors, the better off you are when it comes to understanding their actions and anticipating their moves.

But remember – the more you learn about your competitors, the more they're probably learning about you. It's safe to say that your company probably is putting out as much information about itself and its intentions as your competitors are, so it's just as important to listen to yourself as to your competition. Put yourself on your own list of competitors. Interpret your own actions from a competitor's point of view. That way, you understand the implications of your own competitive behaviour in the industry as well as you understand your competitors' behaviour.

If you're serious about the competition, you can't do all of this analysis one time, wash your hands, and be finished with it. You're going to have to monitor your competitors in a systematic way. If you observe them well, you are in the enviable position of choosing the competitive battles that you want to win, rather than being ambushed in competitive situations that you're bound to lose.

Organising facts and figures

To learn what really makes your competitors tick, you need to take advantage of data from all sorts of places. (Refer to Chapter 4 for a list of resources.) You can find facts and figures on the competition almost anywhere, including the following sources:

- ✔ Business, trade, and technical publications
- ✔ Trade shows
- ✔ Company documents
- ✔ Filed accounts
- ✔ Stock-market analysts
- ✔ Management speeches
- ✔ Suppliers and distributors
- ✔ Customer feedback
- ✔ Your own employees

The last item in the list deserves a special note. Your own employees are an invaluable source of data when it comes to the competition. As you look inside your company, start with your salespeople, who are slap-bang in the middle of the information stream, talking with customers, dealing with distributors, and occasionally running into competitors. They're privy to all the gossip, rumours, and news flashes that flow through your industry. Take advantage of their position, and figure out how to capture what they know.

You have to be a little careful about gathering information from employees other than your salespeople. In many industries, people move from job to job and company to company. There's nothing wrong with brainstorming about what a competitor may be up to, but warning flags should go up if someone pulls out documents marked 'Top Secret'. It's not only wrong, but it's illegal for you to use certain kinds of knowledge that a former employee may have about a competitor – anything that may be construed as proprietary information or trade secrets. There was plenty of bitterness between General Motors and Volkswagen over a vice president who changed sides, not to mention the lawsuits and criminal charges. If you feel that you're on shaky ground, check out Chapter 2 and your company's values statement, and talk to your company's lawyer.

You need a way to organise the facts and figures that you collect from many sources to turn them into competitive information that you can really use. Filing cabinets and file folders do the trick, but you may want to think about setting up a computer system to keep track of the data. As you set up the system, keep in mind that information about your competitors will not fall in your lap in the next two days – instead, it will trickle in over weeks, months, and years.

More than likely, you already have bits and pieces of data on your key competitors stashed away. You just need to develop a procedure that keeps the bits and pieces coming in and then brings them together to create a useful, up-to-date profile of the competition. The following steps should help you develop that procedure:

1. **Start with a pilot procedure for tracking competitors.**

   Beginning with your sales force (or yourself, if you're self-employed), set up a trial system to capture competitive data from the sales channel. Create periodic paper reports in a standard format, or computerise the process, if you can.

2. **Set up a company-wide system for tracking competitors.**

   Formalise the process of identifying and tracking competitors throughout the company, so that you have accurate information on the competition when and where you need it. Competitor analysis is too important to do haphazardly or only when a crisis hits.

3. **Make someone responsible for competitor analysis.**

   Put a manager (or yourself) in charge of competitor analysis for your company. That way, everyone understands that competitive analysis is important. Your employees also have someone to turn to when they need to give or get information on the competition.

4. **Make it your priority to see that the system is carried out.**

   Make sure that competitor analysis is taken seriously in your company by including it in your own business plan. Then become an advocate, insisting that the competition be addressed in any planning document that comes across your desk.

Choosing your battles

The more thoroughly you understand your competitors – what they've done in the past, what they're doing now, and what they're likely to do in the future – the better you'll be able to plan for and choose the competitive battles that you want to be part of.

Naturally, you want to go after markets where you have a strategy and the capability to succeed. But you're never alone in any marketplace for long. By embracing the competition rather than ignoring it, you have the added advantage of knowing where the competition is weakest. Choose your battleground by combining your strengths with their weaknesses. That way, you win half the battle before the contest begins.

- Tracking and understanding your competition is an ongoing process.

- To keep up to date, create a system for gathering and organising information on your competitors.

- The better you know your competitors, the better you'll be able to choose battles that you can win.

Part III
Weighing Your Company's Prospects

"Still no luck with the bank loan, Mr. Blenkinsop?"

In this part . . .

Whenever you tackle something new, whether it's going back to school, buying a house, changing jobs – or starting a business – nagging questions come up. Is the new venture really the right decision? Are you up to the challenge? Will things work out in the end? They're good questions, because they force you to be honest about the capabilities and qualities that you bring to the table.

In this part, we help you look in the mirror and make an honest assessment about what you see. We set out to discover all the capabilities and resources that you have. We try to determine which of them are strengths and which are weaknesses by looking at what you need to succeed in your industry – and what opportunities and threats you face. We help you focus on what your company does best by looking at the areas where you provide the most value to customers, and then we help you figure out how you can maintain and extend the competitive advantages you already have in the market. Finally, we turn to your finances and help you create an objective portrait of your company based on your income, profits, assets, and cash position, and then we help you use them to create a forecast and a budget.

Chapter 8

Establishing Your Starting Position

. . . .

In This Chapter

▶ Discovering your capabilities and resources

▶ Reviewing critical success factors

▶ Identifying company strengths and weaknesses

▶ Recognising opportunities and threats

▶ Analysing your situation by using a SWOT grid

. . . .

*W*hen you look into a mirror, you expect to see an image of yourself. When you listen to your voice on an answering machine, you expect to hear yourself. When you look at photos or home videos, you expect to recognise yourself. But how many times have you said

> *That doesn't look like me.*

or

> *Is that what I really sound like?*

An honest self-portrait – whether it's seeing and hearing yourself clearly or making objective statements about your own strengths and weaknesses – is tough to put together. Strengths and weaknesses have to be measured relative to the situations at hand, and a strength in one circumstance may prove to be a weakness in another. Leadership and snap decision making, for example, may serve you extremely well in an emergency. But the same temperament may be a liability when you're part of a team that's involved in delicate give-and-take negotiations.

You're going to face similar problems in seeing clearly and objectively when you take on the task of measuring your company's internal strengths and weaknesses. You may be surprised by how many businesses fail miserably at the job of objective self-analysis – companies that cling to a distorted image of the resources that they command and the capabilities that they bring to the marketplace.

In this chapter, we help you get a handle on your company's strengths and weaknesses in relation to the opportunities and threats that you face. First, we look at ways that you can spot potential strengths and weaknesses by making a list of your capabilities and resources. Next, we show you how the critical success factors in your industry come into play to determine which of those capabilities and resources are strengths and which aren't. Then we help you pull all the pieces of the puzzle together – your company's strengths, weaknesses, opportunities, and threats – to create a complete picture. We also create a strategic balance sheet that helps you keep track of where you stand, what you should do, and when you should do it.

Situation Analysis

We examine your company's situation by using a tried-and-tested approach known as SWOT. Don't worry about guns or sharpshooters; *SWOT* is an acronym for *strengths, weaknesses, opportunities*, and *threats*.

Your company's strengths and weaknesses can't be measured in a vacuum, of course. Your situation depends not only on your own capabilities and resources, but also on the opportunities and threats that arise from things beyond your control. Check out Chapter 4 to review opportunities and threats. Depending on the situations that you face, opportunities and threats appear, disappear, and change all the time, and your company's strengths and weaknesses change with them.

A thorough SWOT analysis is something that you complete more than once. In fact, you probably should carry out a SWOT review on a regular basis, depending on how fast your business environment, the industry, and your own company change.

Identifying Strengths and Weaknesses

Your company's *strengths* are the capabilities, resources, and skills that you can draw upon to carry out strategies, implement plans, and achieve the goals that you've set for yourself. Your company's *weaknesses* are any lack of skills or a deficiency in your capabilities and resources relative to the competition that may stop you from acting on strategies and plans or accomplishing your goals.

To capture your own first impressions of your company, complete the Company Strengths and Weaknesses Questionnaire (see Figure 8-1). On the right side of the questionnaire, assess your capabilities and resources in each area. On the left side, rate the importance of these elements to your industry.

When a strength becomes a weakness

For 30 years, Marks and Spencer hired its managers and supervisors from a talent pool that consisted almost exclusively of young men and women under 26 years of age who had graduated from its own Management Training Programme. M & S saw this hiring policy as being a major corporate strength, creating a remarkable sense of unity and consistency in its outlook and its internal culture. The company didn't need seminars and workshops to develop a common sense of values and vision; M & S values were built in from the beginning.

But that apparent strength was challenged in the late 1980s, when M & S's dominance and the stability of the entire retail sector were thrown up for grabs. Big food companies – Tesco, Sainsbury's, and the others – encroached on M & S's traditional advantage in the quality pre-prepared market sector, and no one at M & S seemed to have the slightest idea what that was

going to mean. Many forward-thinking, out-of-the-mould managers had already been driven out of the strait-jacket management line-up. Everyone in the organisation came from the same background and thought in much the same way. Nobody understood the speed or magnitude of the competitive threat – or the changes that were about to engulf the company.

What started as an important company strength turned into a serious weakness as Marks and Spencer faced a battle for survival. The company began an aggressive campaign to hire managers with different backgrounds and diverse experience. It also moved to recruit its very top management from outside of the founding family members and time-serving employees in an all-out effort to prepare for a future in which fast-moving change and fierce competition became the name of the game.

Company Strengths and Weaknesses Questionnaire

Importance to Industry			Business Area	Your Capabilities and Resources			
Low	Moderate	High		Poor	Fair	Good	Excellent
❑	❑	❑	Management	❑	❑	❑	❑
❑	❑	❑	Organisation	❑	❑	❑	❑
❑	❑	❑	Customer base	❑	❑	❑	❑
❑	❑	❑	Research & development	❑	❑	❑	❑
❑	❑	❑	Operations	❑	❑	❑	❑
❑	❑	❑	Marketing & sales	❑	❑	❑	❑
❑	❑	❑	Distribution & delivery	❑	❑	❑	❑
❑	❑	❑	Financial condition	❑	❑	❑	❑

Figure 8-1: Company Strengths and Weaknesses Questionnaire.

Frames of reference

Once you complete the questionnaire shown in Figure 8-1, you should have an initial list of your company's strengths and weaknesses. In order to be objective, however, you need to go beyond first impressions and look at your business assets from more than one point of view. Different frames of reference offer the advantage of smoothing out biases that are bound to creep into a single viewpoint. They also offer the best chance of making your list as complete as it can be.

- ✔ **Internal view.** Draw on the management experience inside your company (use your own experience, or that of your friends and former co-workers if you're self-employed) to come up with a consensus on your business strengths and weaknesses. You may want to use the same people to get a sense of what's happened in the recent past as well. A little corporate history can show you how your company's strengths and weaknesses have changed over time – and how easily the organisation shifts gears.

- ✔ **External view.** Beware of becoming too self-absorbed in this analysis. It's important to step back and look around, using your competitors as yardsticks, if you can. All of your competitors do business in the same industry and marketplace that you do, and they're strong or weak in all the key areas that you're interested in. If your list is going to mean anything when the time comes to apply it to your own business situation, your strengths and weaknesses have to be measured against those of your competitors. (Flip to Chapter 7 for more information on the competition.)

- ✔ **Outside view.** Perhaps you identify company strengths that are assets only because your competitors haven't reacted yet, or maybe you ignore real weaknesses because everybody else has them, too. Every once in a while, you need an objective outside assessment of what's happening in your business. That's where consultants can actually be of some use. If you can't afford that kind of advice, make sure that you at least monitor the business press to get an outside view of what the experts are saying about your industry's key players. Business Link in England (and equivalents in Scotland and Wales) can generally help firms to set up an objective appraisal of the strengths and weaknesses of a business.

If you don't have a management team that can conduct a situation analysis, bring together one of the informal groups that you rely on for some of your other planning tasks. Ask the group members to spend a little time analysing strengths and weaknesses. Make sure that the group looks at your company's situation from various perspectives, using the different frames of reference in the preceding list.

Capabilities and resources

In putting together a list of your company's capabilities and resources, cast your net as widely as possible. Look at your capabilities and resources in a systematic way, reviewing all the business areas introduced in the Company Strengths and Weaknesses Questionnaire (refer to Figure 8-1 earlier in this chapter). In each area, try to identify as many capabilities and resources as possible by using different frames of reference. At the same time, assess how relevant each capability or resource is in helping you to carry out your plans and to achieve your business goals. You're going to use this master list as raw material when the time comes to identify your company's strengths and weaknesses.

Management: Setting direction from the top

Your company's management team brings together skills, talent, and commitment. You want team members to find their direction from your company's mission, vision, and values statements, as well as from the business goals and objectives that you plan to achieve. Top-notch managers and owners are particularly important in industries that face increasing competition or fast-changing technologies. It's hard to think of an industry that doesn't fit into one of these two categories.

Management is there to determine what your company's going to do. Senior managers are officially charged with setting the direction and strategy for your company, but all managers indirectly set a tone that encourages certain activities and discourages others. Office products leader 3M, for example, gives its managers the freedom to be entrepreneurs in their own right, allowing the company to recognise and invest in new business opportunities with the speed and flexibility of much smaller rivals. The Body Shop, on the other hand, is recognised for its environmentally aware management. The company attracts highly qualified men and women who want to work in a business environment that values both personal and corporate social responsibility.

Following are some key questions to ask about the management and/or ownership of your company:

- How long have managers been around at various levels in your company? (Alternatively, what variety of experiences do you have as an owner?)
- Does your company plan to hire from the outside or promote from within?
- What's the general tone set by you or your company's management?

- ✔ Do you have a management development programme in place? (Alternatively, how do you plan to develop your own skills, if you're a sole proprietor?)

- ✔ What backgrounds do you or your managers have?

- ✔ How is management performance measured in your company?

- ✔ How would you rate the general quality of your own skills or those of your management team?

Organisation: Bringing people together

The people who make up your company and its work force represent a key resource, both in terms of who they are and how they are organised. Although human resources are important to all companies, they're especially critical to companies in service industries, in which people are a big part of the product. (We take a closer look at your organisation in Chapter 15 when we talk about making your business plan work.)

Your organisation starts with who your employees are, and that depends first on how well you select and train them. Beyond that, the work environment and your company's incentive systems determine who goes on to become a dedicated, hard-working employee and who gets frustrated and finally gives up. The setup of your organisation (how it's structured and how it adapts) can be just as important as your employees are when it comes to creating a company team – even a small one – that performs at the highest levels, year in and year out.

Pharmaceutical companies, for example, hire hundreds of new sales people annually. Are these companies really growing that fast? Of course not. But the industry routinely loses up to 60 per cent of new employees by the end of the third year, after investing heavily in their training. Why? The industry discovered one problem was in their selection process: too many of their new sales people were unsuited to the stresses and strains of hitting challenging sales goals and making upwards of 20 field calls a day, with hundreds of miles of driving thrown in. After all, the typical industry sales new person was a young university graduate. So the industry revised its hiring practices – candidate advertising, interviewing, and psychometric testing – and has already started to see major improvements in both sales performance and longevity.

Following are some key questions about your organisation to consider:

- ✔ What words best describe the overall structure of your organisation?

- ✔ How many reporting levels do you have between a front-line employee and your CEO?

- ✔ How often does your company reorganise?

- ✔ What are your employees' general attitudes to their jobs and responsibilities?

- ✔ How long does the average employee stay with your company?

- ✔ How does your absenteeism level compare with industry benchmarks?

- ✔ Does your company have ways to measure and track employees' attitudes and morale?

- ✔ What does your company do to maintain morale and positive job performance?

Customer base: Pleasing the crowds

Your company's business depends, to a great extent, on the satisfaction and loyalty of your customers. In Chapters 5 and 6, you discover who those customers are and how you can find out as much as you can about them, because understanding your customers and satisfying their wants and needs are critical to the future of your company.

Nordstrom, for example, is an American department-store chain that appeals to upmarket shoppers. The company bases its reputation on the simple idea that the customer is always right. And the company means it. As the story goes, a disgruntled customer once stormed into the back loading dock of a Nordstrom store, demanding satisfaction and the immediate replacement of defective tyres that he'd recently purchased. The store managers were extremely polite. They quickly discovered that the man was indeed one of their best customers, and they arranged an immediate reimbursement for the full price of the tyres. In a better mood, the customer decided that he'd rather just have a new set installed. When he asked where he should take the car, he was informed that Nordstrom doesn't sell tyres. Obviously, this man became a satisfied customer – and a Nordstrom advocate for life.

Following are some key questions to consider when you study your own customer base:

- ✔ What does your company do to create loyal customers?

- ✔ How much effort do you put into tracking customers' attitudes, satisfaction, and loyalty?

- ✔ What do you offer customers that keeps them coming back?

- ✔ How easy and economical is it for your company to acquire new customers?

- ✔ How many years does a typical customer stay with you?

- ✔ How many markets does your company serve?

- ✔ Are you either number one or number two in the markets in which you compete?

Research and development: Inventing the future

Research and development (R&D) often plays an important role in the long-term success of a company, and R&D is particularly critical in industries in which new and better products are coming along. But research and product development must balance the other forces that are at work in your market-place. R&D is one business area in which even an A-1 team effort doesn't automatically pay off.

Consider the cosmetics industry. Estée Lauder or Revlon could easily spend millions of additional pounds on research and development. These companies could fund any number of studies to learn more about everything from the properties of skin to humans' sense of smell. They could construct state-of-the-art laboratories, hire teams of dedicated dermatologists and top-notch chemists, and in the process become unchallenged leaders in basic cosmetics research. But would the funds invested in these additional capabilities translate into enduring company strengths? Probably not. These companies don't want their products to be turned into drugs that have to be regulated by government departments. Most cosmetics products live or die on the strength of their images and on the resources invested in advertising and promoting them. Customers tend to buy the hype behind beauty aids – not the ingredients inside them.

On the other hand, the makers of integrated circuits and microprocessors – the brains of computers – have little choice but to commit themselves to aggressive R&D efforts. Intel and Motorola have world-class R&D organisations because their industry is driven by continuous product innovation. These companies continually push for greater processing speed and power in ever-smaller packages. Failure to maintain leadership in research could result in catastrophe for either company.

The following key questions help you examine the role of R&D in your company:

- ✔ To what extent is your industry driven by technology?
- ✔ Can you get enough results for your money to bother with R&D?
- ✔ Does your company have a consistent, long-term commitment to R&D?
- ✔ How many pounds do you spend on basic research as opposed to applied research?
- ✔ How long have the key people on your research staff been with you?
- ✔ Does your company protect what it owns with copyrights and patents?
- ✔ Have you set up partnerships with universities or outside research labs?

✔ Do you have technology agreements with other companies in your industry?

✔ Are you aware of the favourable UK tax treatment of R&D expenditure?

✔ Are you aware of possible UK government grant aid for R&D projects?

Operations: Making things work

The operations side of your business is obviously critical if you happen to be a manufacturing company. The products that you make (and the way that they work, how long they last, and what they cost) depend entirely on the capabilities and resources of your production facilities and work force – so much so that you can easily forget that operations are equally important to companies in the service sector. Customers demand value in all markets today, and they're simply unwilling to pay for inefficiencies in any business. Whether you make cars or carpets, produce cereal boxes or serial ports, run a bank or manage a hotel, operations are at the heart of your enterprise.

Operations in your own company probably are driven, to some extent, by costs on one side and product or service quality on the other. The tension between controlling costs and improving quality has led many companies to explore ways to reduce costs and increase quality at the same time. One way for you to do that is to involve outside suppliers in certain aspects of your operations, if those suppliers have resources that you can't match. Another way to achieve both goals is to streamline parts of your operations (through automation, for example).

Automation can also be a source of growth and may even create new business opportunities for your company. The airline industry is as big as it is today because of the computer revolution; computers enable airlines to track millions of passenger reservations and itineraries at the same time. Imagine the queues at airports if airlines were still issuing tickets by hand and completing passenger flight lists by using carbon paper.

When American Airlines developed its computer-based SABRE reservation system, however, it couldn't predict that *yield management* – the capability to monitor demand for flights and continuously adjust prices to fill seats – would become as important as on-time arrivals. The company has increased its profit margins because yield-management software ensures that each American flight generates as much revenue as possible. The software is so sophisticated and successful that Robert Crandall, American Airlines' chairman, spun off SABRE as a separate company. SABRE's expertise can now be used to benefit industries such as the hotel business, in which yield-management software can automatically adjust room rates and make sure that as many beds as possible are filled each night.

Following are some questions on the operations side of your business to mull over:

✔ Does your company have programmes for controlling cost and improving quality?

✔ Has your company taken full advantage of new technologies?

✔ Are your production costs in line with those of the rest of the industry?

✔ How quickly can you boost production or expand services to meet new demand?

✔ Does your company use outside suppliers?

✔ Is your operations workforce flexible, well trained, and prepared for change?

✔ Can you apply your operations expertise to other parts of the business?

Sales and marketing: Telling a good story

The best product or service in the world isn't going to take your company far if it's not successfully marketed and sold to all those potential customers out there. Your sales and marketing people (or you, if you're operating your own small business) are your eyes and ears, giving you feedback on what customers think about and look for. Your sales and marketing people are also your voice. They tell your company's story and put your products in context, offering solutions, satisfying needs, and fulfilling wants in the marketplace.

What could a marketing department possibly do, for example, to package and promote a boring old bulk chemical such as sodium bicarbonate? It turns out that such a department can do quite a bit, if it's connected with Arm & Hammer, which sells sodium bicarbonate (baking soda) toothpaste. The 'Wow' adverts, showing people smiling with gleaming white teeth, as if 'they had been cleaned by the dentist', ensured Arm and Hammer gained 4 per cent of the toothpaste market in Britain, just over a year after being launched. All this from a common, readily available chemical salt.

Following are a few key questions to ask about the marketing of your product line:

✔ How broad is your company's product or service line?

✔ Do consumers identify with your company's brand names?

✔ Do you have special processes or technologies that your competitors can't take advantage of?

> ✔ Are you investing in market research and receiving continuous customer feedback?
>
> ✔ Are you using all the marketing resources that are at your disposal?
>
> ✔ Is your company's sales force knowledgeable, energetic, and persuasive?

Distribution and delivery: Completing the cycle

Distribution and delivery means that your products and services are actually getting to their final destinations and into your customers' hands. No matter how good you think your products are, your customers have to be able to get their hands on them when and where they want them. How customers shop is often just as important as what they buy, so it's not surprising that when a different way to deliver products and services comes along (over the Internet, for example), the new system revolutionises a marketplace or even an entire economy. The Internet promises a future in which companies can reach out to their customers more directly, increasing company clout and at the same time lowering distribution costs.

Right now, your company probably distributes its products and services through *traditional channels* – time-tested ways in which you and your competitors reach customers – and your distribution and delivery costs may represent a significant part of your total expenses. The standard costs often include warehouse operations, transportation, and product returns. If you're in a retail business, you can end up paying for expensive shelf space as well. Supermarkets now routinely ask for money up front before they stock a new item, and you pay more for the best locations. After all, supermarkets control what customers see – and buy – as harried shoppers troop down the aisles, children and trollies in tow.

Many innovative products and companies succeeded in the past because of their novel approaches to the costs and other hurdles associated with traditional distribution networks. When Amazon decided to enter the book market, for example, Jeff Bezos, Amazon.com's founder faced established competition and a stodgy distribution system dominated by traditional retail outlets.

Rather than tackle all these problems head-on, the company set off in a new direction. Bezos realised that no single bookstore could carry a comprehensive inventory of the books in print. The distributors who carried thousands of titles acted as the warehouse for most stores, particularly smaller booksellers. When customers asked a store for a book it did not have in stock, they filled the customer's order through one of the handful of large distributors. These companies' inventory lists were digitised in the late 1980s. The online inventory lists would enable Bezos to offer books online through the company he planned to create.

The naming of Amazon.com was based on the importance of its relative size. Bezos reasoned that the Amazon River was ten times as large as the next largest river, which was the Mississippi, in terms of volume of water and Amazon.com had six times as many titles as the world's largest physical bookstore. Amazon has revolutionised traditional bookselling and buying, and has spawned many imitators.

Following are some questions about the distribution and delivery of your product or service:

- ✔ What are the costs associated with your company's inventory system?
- ✔ Can you reduce inventories by changing the way that orders are processed?
- ✔ How much time does it take for a customer order to get filled, and can the time be reduced?
- ✔ How many distribution channels does your company use?
- ✔ What are the relative costs in various channels, and which are most effective?
- ✔ How much control over your company do distributors have?
- ✔ Can you use any new channels to reach your customers more directly?

Financial condition: Keeping track of money

The long-term financial health of your company determines the health of your company, full stop. You simply can't survive in business for long without having your financial house in order. Come to think of it, the things that you have to track when it comes to company finances aren't all that different from the issues that you face in running your own household. If you're just starting in business, for example, how much money your company can get its hands on up-front (your *initial capital*) is a key to survival. (Does this sound like trying to buy and furnish your first house?) When your company's up and running, it's important to make sure that more money comes in than goes out (a *positive cash flow*), so that you can pay all your bills. (Remember those times when the mortgage and utility bills were due, and it wasn't payday yet?)

Figuring out how to keep your company financially fit is critical to planning your business. When you take the time to look over your important financial statements periodically, you give your company the benefit of a regular financial checkup. The checkup is usually routine, but every once in a while you uncover an early-warning symptom – profits that are too low, for example, or a promotional expense that's too large. That's when all your financial vigilance is worth it.

Following is a list of oh-so-painful questions to ask about your company's financial health. (If you don't know how to answer these questions, spend some time with Chapters 10 and 11.)

✔ Are your revenue and profits growing?

✔ Are you carefully monitoring your company's cash flow?

✔ Does your company have ready access to cash reserves?

✔ Does your company – and every business unit or area – have a budget for the coming year?

✔ Do you consistently track key financial ratios for the company?

✔ How does your company's financial picture compare with that of the competition?

Critical success factors

It's important to decide whether your capabilities and resources represent company strengths that you can leverage or weaknesses that you must correct as you plan for the future. To do that, you have to be clear about exactly what's important to your industry and the marketplace. The *critical success factors* (CSFs) are those capabilities and resources that absolutely have to be in place if you want your company to succeed over the long haul.

You may have already prepared a list of CSFs. (If you haven't, take a look at Chapter 4.) Along with a CSF list, you need a set of your company's capabilities and resources. You can use the two lists to construct a grid, which in turn allows you to compare your capabilities and resources with those that your industry thinks are important. In a perfect world, the lists would be identical, but that's seldom the case. The completed grid helps you identify your company's current strengths and weaknesses (see Figure 8-2).

To complete a grid similar to the one in Figure 8-2, remember the following:

✔ The capabilities and resources that you place up and down the left side of the grid are in your industry's 'must have' category. They represent critical success factors.

✔ The capabilities and resources that you place in the top-left corner of the grid are critical success factors in which your company is good or excellent. They represent your company's strengths.

✔ The capabilities and resources that you place in the bottom-left corner of the grid are critical success factors in which your company is only fair or even poor. They represent your company's weaknesses.

Figure 8-2:
Compare
your
capabilities
and
resources
with those
that are
thought to
be critical
success
factors
in your
industry.

Company Strengths and Weaknesses

Importance to Industry

Capabilities and Resources

Critical Success Factors

	Must Have	Nice to Have	Not Necessary
Excellent	Strengths		
Good			
Fair			
Poor	Weaknesses		

It's easy to find some value in the capabilities that your company already excels in, and it's just as easy to underestimate the importance of things that your company doesn't do as well. Try to be as objective as you can here. It's hard to admit that you're devoting valuable resources to things that don't really matter, and it's equally hard to admit that you may be neglecting key business areas.

✔ Different people have different ideas about what your company's strengths and weaknesses really are.

✔ By combining different viewpoints, both inside and outside your company, you get a more balanced picture.

✔ Be sure to assess your capabilities and resources in every area, from management to marketing to R&D to delivery.

✔ Strengths are strengths only if your capabilities and resources line up with the critical success factors in your industry.

Analysing Your Situation in 3-D

You must be prepared to take advantage of your company's strengths and minimise your weaknesses, which means that you have to know how to recognise opportunities when they arise and prepare for threats before they overtake you. Timing is everything here, and it represents a third major dimension that you have to think about.

Chapter 4 discusses where major opportunities and serious threats come from. These dragons can come from almost any source and from all directions. They often change the rules of the game and can even alter critical success factors that you assumed would always be part of your industry. Many opportunities and threats are the direct result of change (check out Chapter 12 if you don't believe us); others come directly from your competitors and the uncertainty that they introduce.

A glance at competitors

It's a good idea to create strengths-and-weaknesses grids for two or three of your most intense competitors. (Turn to Chapter 7 for a look at exactly who your competitors are and what information you have about them.) You won't know as much about your competitors as you know about yourself, of course, so the grids aren't going to be as complete as they may be about your own company. But what you *do* know is going to tell you a great deal.

Comparing the strengths and weaknesses of competitors with your own can help you see where competitive opportunities and threats to your business may come from. Opportunities often arise when your company has a strength that you can exploit in a critical area in which your competition is weak. And you can sometimes anticipate a threat when the situation is reversed – when a competitor takes advantage of a key strength by making a move in an area where you're not as strong. Because the competitive landscape is always changing, plan to monitor these grids on a regular basis.

Completing your SWOT analysis

A SWOT analysis (an analysis of your strengths, weaknesses, opportunities, and threats) allows you to construct a strategic balance sheet for your company. In the analysis, you bring together all the internal factors, including your company's strengths and weaknesses. You then weigh these factors against the external forces that you've identified, such as the opportunities and threats that your company faces due to competitive forces or trends in your business environment. How these factors balance out determines what your company should do and when you should do it. Follow these steps to complete the SWOT analysis grid:

1. **Divide all the strengths that you've identified into two groups, based on whether they're associated with potential opportunities in your industry or with latent threats.**

2. **Divide all the weaknesses the same way – one group associated with opportunities, the other with threats.**

3. **Construct a grid with four quadrants.**

4. **Place your company's strengths and weaknesses, paired with industry opportunities or threats, in one of the four boxes (see Figure 8-3).**

Figure 8-3:
The SWOT
grid bal-
ances your
company's
internal
strengths
and weak-
nesses
against
external
opportunites
and threats.

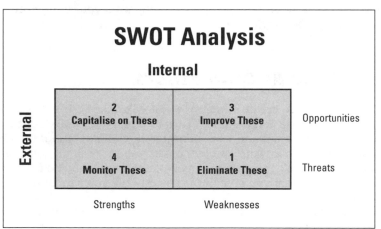

The SWOT analysis provides a bit of useful strategic guidance. Most of it is common sense. First, fix what's broken. Next, make the most of the business opportunities that you see out there. Only then do you have the luxury of tending to other business issues and areas. Be sure to address each of the following steps in your business plan:

1. **Eliminate any company weaknesses that you identify in areas in which you face serious threats from your competitors or unfavourable trends in a changing business environment.**

2. **Capitalise on any business opportunities that you discover where your company has real strengths.**

3. **Work on improving any weaknesses that you identify in areas that may contain potential business opportunities.**

4. **Monitor business areas in which you're strong today so that you won't be surprised by any latent threats that may appear.**

Change is the only constant in your business, your industry, and your marketplace. Constant change means that you can't complete your SWOT analysis only one time; you have to revise the grid regularly as your company grows and as the environment around you changes. Think of your SWOT analysis as being a continuous process – something that you do repeatedly as an important part of your business-planning cycle.

✔ To identify potential opportunities and threats, take a close look at the strengths and weaknesses of your competitors.

✔ A SWOT grid places your strengths and weaknesses in the context of opportunities and threats, and thereby tells you what to do.

✔ The SWOT strategy is to eliminate weaknesses in areas where threats loom and also to capitalise on strengths in areas where you see opportunities.

Chapter 9

Focusing On What You Do Best

· ·

· ·

*E*very time you leave the house to go shopping, you gear up to make a complex set of choices that together determine what you finally come home with at the end of the day. As you look down the shopping list over morning coffee, the decisions begin:

> ✔ Town centre shops or the out-of-town shopping precincts?
>
> ✔ Speciality shops or a department store?
>
> ✔ Designer brands or store labels?
>
> ✔ £25, £50, or £100 limit?

If you happen to be in the business of producing and selling products in shops, these are make-or-break decisions. How do shoppers make their choices? Why do they go into one shop and not the next? What determines where they stop to browse and what they take a second look at? How are customers different from one another? In what ways are they the same? No matter what industry you're in, the same kinds of questions are just as crucial.

As they go about making decisions on what to buy and where to shop, customers continually weigh various combinations of product or service benefits against price. When customers make their choices based on their own calculation of the best value they can find in the marketplace, they are using a *value equation*. (Check out Chapter 7 if you want to know more about that equation.) But what does it actually mean to have the best value out there? If you're one of the competitors, you need to know exactly where and how your products add value in the eyes of your customers.

In this chapter, we take another look at how you create customer value around your own products and services. The approach is called a *value-chain analysis* by people who try to make something simple sound difficult, and we use it to identify which parts of your business are responsible for adding the greatest value for customers. We show you how to use your value chain to help explain why you may have a competitive advantage in the marketplace. We also use the value chain to point out your company's *core competence*. We talk about how you can work to maintain your competitive advantage over the long term. Finally, we show you how to use an understanding of your value chain and core competence to make the most of your company's human and financial resources as you create your business plan.

Describing What You Do

You'd think that it would be easy to describe what your company does, summarising your key business activities in a few well-chosen sentences or in a clear diagram or two. It's not. From the inside of your business looking out, it's much harder than you may think to push away the everyday details to get at the core of what actually keeps you in business from one day to the next.

That's why consultants hang around a lot. Many of them would like nothing better than to help you describe what you do. Their little secret, of course, is that they're not really any smarter than you are. Consultants seem to have a clearer view of your business simply because they are on the outside looking in.

But chances are that you have a built-in understanding of your own business and what really makes your company successful – you just need to unlock what you already know.

Tom Farmer, the son of a Leith shipping clerk who earned £5 a week, launched Kwik-Fit, a company that grew into a £418 million public company with almost 1,000 outlets, before he sold out to Ford for £1 billion. In his own words, the enduring philosophy behind his business to which he ascribes its success is '100 per cent customer satisfaction. Just giving service – phoning back in half an hour if you say you will, standing by promises – puts you miles ahead of anyone else in the field.' Knowing that service is as important as the exhausts themselves is what has provided Kwik-Fit with a lasting competitive advantage.

This canny businessman had a real feeling for why he was successful at what he did. Given a little guidance, you can take the same gut-level understanding of your own business and develop a chain of activities that captures what your company really does to stay in business. In particular, we focus on creating customer value, and divide your business into the specific areas and activities that build value into the products and services that you offer.

Constructing a typical value chain

Your company constructs its *value chain* from the sequence of activities that it engages in to increase the value of your products and services in the eyes of your customers. (See Figure 9-1.) The chain connects you to the marketplace, making sure that you don't stray too far from the customers you serve.

The links in a value chain help you understand your company's activities.

Primary links in the value chain are the business functions that are at the heart of what your company does. Primary links are usually sequential. They're the essential stages that your company goes through in developing, producing, and getting products to market and they often involve the following:

- ✔ Research and development
- ✔ Operations
- ✔ Marketing and sales
- ✔ Distribution and delivery
- ✔ Service

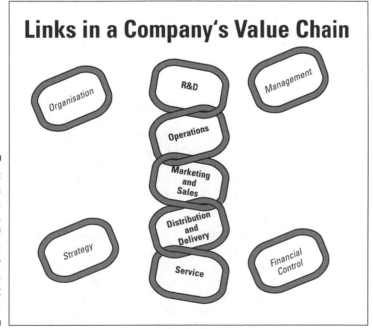

Figure 9-1:
A company's value chain has two types of links: primary activities and support activities.

Supporting links in the value chain contribute to the overall success of the business by strengthening your company's primary links. Supporting links are often spread throughout your organisation. They assist and tie together all the primary business functions, as well as support one another. The activities often involve the following:

- ✔ Management
- ✔ Organisation
- ✔ Strategy and planning
- ✔ Financial control

Try to concentrate on organising your basic business functions around customer value and the bright idea that everything you do in your company should somehow contribute to that effort. A value-chain analysis allows you to take your company apart and put it back together, making sure that each link in the chain contributes to the value that customers see when they buy your product or service.

Comparing different value chains

You can learn a great deal about a company by checking out its value chain: where and how it's creating customer value. In fact, the value chain is a relatively good way to compare and contrast competitors in your own industry. You may even want to use this information to revisit your strategic groups of competitors. (See Chapter 7 to find out what the phrase *a strategic group of competitors* means.)

To see how to compare value chains, take a closer look at the airline industry. That the experience of flying from London, Heathrow to Belfast, for example, is usually measured somewhere in the range of tolerable to terrible. Air travel always seems to generate metaphors that involve cattle trucks, the underground at rush hour, and Guinness records that have to do with people crammed into telephone booths or Volkswagens. But within these constraints, so to speak, airlines do in fact compete for your sky business in different ways.

easyJet, for example, is a major player in the so-called 'no-frills' segment. Compared with other airlines, easyJet can make several additional flights a day in each airplane, based on its capability to turn the plane around – unload, reload, and take off – in about 20 minutes. Most of the costs in the airline industry are tied up in things such as aircraft and buildings, so extra flights a day mean extra profits for an airline – or lower prices for customers. easyJet chooses to pass its savings along to its passengers. The company caters to people who have to pay for travel out of their own pockets and are looking for the best deal. easyJet always promises the lowest fares around and has attracted a loyal set of customers.

How does easyJet make its business work? A quick glance at its value chain highlights several important value-adding activities. Key links include

- **Operations.** easyJet prides itself on having efficient personnel, ace ground crews, and state-of-the-art equipment that allow the company to get planes in and out of airports as fast as humanly possible, meet tight flight schedules, and reduce overall costs.

- **Distribution.** The airline has built up a regional route system that tends to bypass the most crowded airports and overly competitive destinations. Periodic reviews of passenger traffic and competition suggest expansion opportunities that are in line with the carrier's low-cost strategy.

- **Management.** easyJet has put together a team of managers and professionals who have the skills, aptitude, and temperament to deal with considerable job stress and who work well together.

 By contrast, British Airways is a global, full-service carrier at the opposite end of the airline spectrum from easyJet. The company serves hundreds of destinations daily and offers frequently scheduled flights to most major commercial airports in the world.

Its extensive national network feeds into international routes that span the globe. BA has a freephone reservations number, close relationships with travel agents, a frequent-flyer programme offering worldwide awards, and credit cards tied to its mileage programme. Customers count on BA to provide in-flight meals and films, to transfer their bags, and to cater to them if anything goes wrong along the way. Who are these customers? Many of them are business passengers and other well-heeled travellers who are willing to pay the price to cover the costs of all these added services.

Although getting each plane turned around quickly on the ground certainly is important to British Airways, the company doesn't depend on it the same way that easyJet does. In fact, the services that BA's passengers demand make it almost impossible for its airline crews to keep up with easyJet on the ground. BA's value chain points out the areas in which the airline adds customer value. Key links include the following:

- **Research and development.** Whether it's developing more comfortable business-class seats, better in-flight entertainment, or Internet connections at 35,000 feet, British Airways works to please its most demanding customers. At the same time, its reservation system and yield-management software allow the airline to maximise revenue and match fares with other airlines in certain competitive markets.

- **Marketing and sales.** The company spends significant time and resources in promoting its image and worldwide brand. BA advertises in a wide range of global media, sponsors all sorts of special events, and maintains strong ties with travel agencies across the country and the world.

✔ **Service.** Customer service is a major link in BA's value chain. The company makes every effort to create a lasting relationship with its most loyal customers through its frequent-flyer programme. And it makes sure that these valued customers are pampered with special airport lounges, hassle-free check-in, and checked baggage that always arrives first in the baggage claim.

✔ **Financial control.** British Airways maintains the financial resources and flexibility to fund continued investments in the extensive ground facilities and huge fleet of aircraft that allow it to serve a global network of routes and destinations.

Both easyJet and British Airways are in the business of transporting passengers from one location to another by using aircraft on regularly scheduled flights, yet their value chains and the important links in creating customer value are quite different.

Forging your own value chain

To develop your company's own value chain – the sequence of activities that you go through in the process of adding customer value to your products and services – you need a list of your company's capabilities and resources. Take a look at Chapter 8 if you need help.

You can construct a framework for your value chain by creating a grid that divides your business into value-creating areas (see Figure 9-2). Then you place activities in the grid based on whether they are part of your primary business functions or are associated with supporting areas.

Follow these steps to create the grid that shapes your value chain:

1. **List all the key business areas that are directly involved in putting together your own company's products and services and getting them out to customers.**

   Include such things as R&D, operations, marketing, sales, distribution, delivery, and service.

2. **Arrange the list of key business areas in order, from the first good idea out of R&D to the finished product or service.**

3. **List the general business areas in your company that support the primary business functions.**

   Include such things as management, organisation and human resources, strategy and planning, and financial control.

4. **Construct a grid similar to the one in Figure 9-2, using your own lists of primary and supporting business areas.**

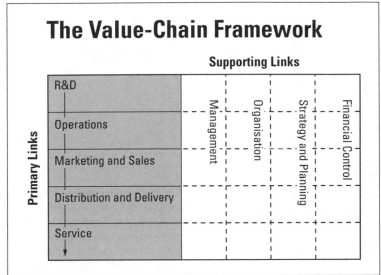

The Value-Chain Framework

Supporting Links

Primary Links		Management	Organisation	Strategy and Planning	Financial Control
R&D					
Operations					
Marketing and Sales					
Distribution and Delivery					
Service					

Figure 9-2:
The value-chain framework.

Your value chain may not look exactly like all those organisation charts that are floating around your company. The primary and supporting business functions that end up adding customer value may be framed differently, depending on whom you ask, so it's important to talk to customers as well as to co-workers. Ask your customers to describe your business as they see it. Your customers just may have a better vantage point.

To fill in the value-chain grid, you have to fill in all the specific value-adding activities – the capabilities and resources that your company uses to increase the value of your products and services in the eyes of your customers. Follow these steps:

1. **Go through the lists of capabilities and resources, and have a first go at placing them in the value-chain grid.**

2. **In the boxes on the left side of the value-chain grid, place value-adding activities that directly contribute to your primary business functions.**

   These activities make up the primary links in your value chain.

3. **Place value-adding activities that are associated with supporting functions in grid boxes across from the primary functions that they support.**

   These activities are the supporting links in the value chain.

4. **On the grid, include a description of the customer value that's added at each link, as well as how that value is added.**

A blueprint for change

An architectural and engineering firm in the northeast, that we'll call NAE, used to pride itself on being a full-service building consultant. Its professional staff ranged from structural engineers to interior designers and everyone in between. The company maintained a complete project-budgeting department and a full in-house blueprinting operation; in fact, the firm routinely turned down requests by small outside contractors to take over and supply blueprinting services. Business was booming, the company was growing, and its clients couldn't have been happier.

All that changed in 1989. A major downturn in the property market hit NAE quite hard, and the company was forced to think about ways to cut costs for the first time in its history. As part of the restructuring effort, NAE took another look at its internal blueprinting operations, and it learned that it should have taken the bids from outside suppliers more seriously. Independent contractors could provide the quality and reliability that NAE demanded and substantially lower the firm's blueprinting costs at the same time.

When NAE asked its most important customers what they thought about the proposed changes, the answers were surprising. No one chose the company because of the quality of its blueprints; clients saw real value in the breadth and expertise of the company's professional staff. By reviewing the value chain, NAE had an opportunity to refocus its resources and energy on the activities and links in the chain that provided the most value to its customers.

The value chain offers you a unique look at your company through your customers' eyes. Every link in the value chain is something that you do as a company. Every link is an activity that you spend money on. The value chain allows you to see exactly what value customers are getting out of each link. A value-chain analysis gives you a relatively clear picture of why you stay in business, as well as where you could be doing a better job.

✔ The value chain describes all the things that you do to add value to the products and services that you offer customers.

✔ Value is in the eyes of the customer.

✔ By comparing the value chains of other companies in your industry, you learn about the competitive landscape and how you fit in.

✔ A value chain shows exactly what value your customers are getting from each of your basic business functions.

Staying in Business

Companies don't just stay in business year after year by accident. Oh, maybe a manager somewhere gets lucky every once in a while, making a brilliant move without having a clue as to why it's so brilliant. But that kind of luck never lasts long, especially when the competition is intense. Companies succeed over the long haul because they understand what their customers place the most value on, and they translate that knowledge into products and services that consistently meet or exceed customers' expectations, often at the expense of unsuspecting competitors.

Using a value chain for your own company enables you to pinpoint the business areas and activities in which most of your customer value is created. Those key areas and activities tell you about your company's advantage in the marketplace and how it achieved that advantage. The value chain may highlight the importance of your cost advantage in the market, for example, and point out that your company achieved that advantage through careful, continuous improvements in manufacturing efficiency. Or maybe your value chain flags the calibre of your professional staff as being a key advantage in the marketplace, achieved through a commitment to recruit, develop, and support the most capable people out there.

A high-street video-rental outlet may highlight its convenient location and a club that offers a free tape for every ten rentals. A competitor that has a location on the outskirts of town may create value by offering a large selection that features hard-to-find videos. In the same way, large chain bookstores compete on the basis of savings, whereas local booksellers are valued for their knowledgeable staff, personal service, and friendly atmosphere.

Take a close look at what it means to have an advantage over the competition in your marketplace, where the advantage comes from, and how you can work to maintain it over the long haul.

Searching for competitive advantage

We all know people who like to take car trips – maybe up to the Lake District for a walking weekend or off in the family caravan whenever the weather's nice. If you ask them where they stop along the way, they always have a special burger van, a favourite pub or café, or a certain ice-cream place that they would never dream of missing. Why do these travellers develop such affection for specific stops on their route when hundreds of other places are available along the way? What makes particular establishments so unique?

If you push them, these travellers come up with all sorts of reasons. They may tell you that they've been stopping at the same places for years, that they love the food, that they like the atmosphere, that they know the owners, that they can count on the service . . . whatever. No doubt all these things are true. But take a careful look at the value chain for many of these businesses, and one important link that jumps right out at you is likely to be location. Distances and driving times most likely are the major reason why many of their customers find these businesses in the first place; the shopfronts literally happen to be in the right place at the right time. Location provides a significant competitive advantage in this on-the-move marketplace.

Competitive advantage means exactly what it says: a company has some sort of advantage over the competition. Where does it come from? Usually, out of the distinct and special value that the company can offer its customers – and from the premium that customers place on that value. Ask yourself this basic question:

> *Why do customers choose my company and its products when other competitors in the industry have more-or-less similar offerings?*

You can find the answer in the strongest links of your value chain. The links that produce the bulk of your customer value – whether it's location, service, image, or product features – are the links that create your competitive advantage in the marketplace.

In 1975, Microsoft was a partnership of two: Bill Gates and Paul Allen. They started out competing against a host of bright young entrepreneurs like themselves and eventually had to go head-to-head with IBM itself. Today, Microsoft has over 20,000 employees and £5.18 billion in revenue and offers a wide array of software products, ranging from word processing programs and spreadsheet applications to language tools and operating systems. Its Windows program alone has sold more than 100 million units. Where is Microsoft's competitive advantage?

- ✔ **Standards.** Microsoft's programs pretty much set the standards in the PC world. Microsoft offers the standard operating system and the standard suite of office applications. Although other companies sell better products here and there, Microsoft is seen as being the safe and sensible choice across the board.

- ✔ **Compatibility.** Microsoft programs promise to work with one another and with the operating system. You don't have to worry that your favourite application will become an outcast or somehow misbehave inside your computer.

✔ **Product range.** You name it, and Microsoft probably has a product that can do it. The company continues to aggressively develop new software to meet the needs of rapidly changing markets. Most recently, the company targeted Internet users with a host of new products.

✔ **Service and support.** With Microsoft, you know what you're getting. If something doesn't work, the company tries hard to fix it. In the meantime, it's comforting to know that you can always find other people who have the very same problem.

Hertz is by far the largest car-rental agency in the world. The company has rental locations in more than 150 countries and boasts a fleet of more than 500,000 vehicles. But Hertz faces competition at all levels, from the family-run rental companies at popular holiday spots to regional agencies such as Easy Car Hire, an offshoot of easyJet and other global companies, including Avis and National. Where is the Hertz Corporation's competitive advantage?

✔ **One-stop reservations.** When you call the Hertz free number, you gain immediate access to the company's worldwide fleet. You can quickly and conveniently book the kind of car that you want, when and where you want it. Changing your mind is just as easy.

✔ **International presence.** No matter where or why you need the car – for a safari in Africa, a tour of Italy, or a business trip to Birmingham – you can safely bet that Hertz can rent you what you need.

✔ **Peace of mind.** With Hertz, you don't have to worry that the car won't be there, that the rate will double, or that you'll end up paying for a rent-a-dent that's obviously a year old. Also, to help you find your way around, the company offers personalised maps and is introducing a new onboard navigation system.

✔ **Rewards for loyalty.** As a loyal Hertz customer, you're rewarded with membership in a club that provides extra service, attention, and the chance to apply the pounds that you spend toward free rental days.

Focusing on core competence

Your competitive advantage is created in the marketplace. That advantage has everything to do with your customers, with the relative value that they place on your products and services, and with the purchase decisions that they finally make. But what is it about your company that allows you to achieve this competitive advantage? What internal capabilities and resources do you have, and what business activities do you engage in that lead directly to your competitive advantage?

You probably already have the answer. Go back to your company's value chain, and focus on those links that are most responsible for your own competitive advantage. When you do, you come face to face with something that the gurus call your core competence. Simply defined, *core competence* is your company's special capability to create a competitive advantage for itself in the market-place. In almost all cases, this gift is specific to your company. Think of core competence as being corporate DNA. Unlike your personal genetic code, how-ever, your company's core competence is there for you to build on – or to lose, depending on how attentive you are to your markets and your business.

The section 'Searching for competitive advantage' earlier in this chapter exam-ined two well-known companies, each of which is a household name. Can you identify the core competence behind that competitive advantage for both Microsoft and Hertz?

Microsoft's core competence:

- **Visionary executives.** The executive team has a broad vision of the future, enabling the company to forge today's software standards and shape tomorrow's.

- **Top-notch development team.** The company is committed to supporting a dream-team corps of developers and programmers who are charged with creating and maintaining a state-of-the-art product line.

- **Management of complexity.** Microsoft manages a complex related set of software products that all have to behave and work together.

- **Capability to change direction.** The company has the capacity to redirect resources and energies when the fast-moving marketplace shifts course and the rules of the game suddenly change.

Hertz Corporation's core competence:

- **Information systems.** A sophisticated computer database allows the company to keep track of customer profiles and match them against an ever-changing supply of rental cars around the world.

- **Global logistics.** The company has the capability to track, distribute, arrange, and rearrange a huge fleet of vehicles in all shapes and sizes on a worldwide basis.

- **Scale of operations.** The company uses its sheer size and business volume to negotiate favourable terms when it comes to new-car pur-chases and even insurance premiums.

- **Relationships and tie-ins.** Hertz has the resources to work closely with travel agencies and the travel industry to create new business by expand-ing car-rental options and opportunities.

Sometimes, a company's core competence can point the way toward new market opportunities. Honda, for example, used a core competence in designing engines to expand its markets. The company created product lines in lawn mowers, snow throwers, snowmobiles, and all-terrain vehicles, to name just a few of its motor-based businesses. Honda benefits from a related competitive advantage in each of these distinct markets. Take another look at your own company's core competence to see whether you can come up with any new business directions, based on those things that you already do well.

Sustaining an advantage over time

Every company that manages to stay in business from one month to the next has some sort of competitive advantage and core competence to draw upon; otherwise, it simply wouldn't be there. But the million-dollar question has to do with how to renew and sustain that competitive advantage over years and even decades. Customers and their needs shift over time, competition gets more intense, and industries evolve, so your competitive advantage and the core competence that supports it aren't guaranteed to stay around. You rent them; you don't own them. You want to make sure that you keep a long-term lease on both.

Sustained competitive advantage – the business world's Holy Grail – is a company's capability to renew a competitive advantage over and over again in the face of a constantly changing business environment and marketplace. But if you want to sustain a competitive advantage over time, you need to have a long-term strategy in place. Chapter 7 introduces three common alternatives called generic strategies and gives you a handle on what your competitors may be up to. Chapter 13 takes a much closer look at your own strategic options.

Spend some time thinking about things that your company can do on an ongoing basis to see that your core competence is preserved or evolves to meet changed market needs. How can you sustain the competitive advantage that your company already has? Get a blank sheet of paper and jot down answers to these key questions:

- ✔ Where will changes in your business most likely come from?
- ✔ How are those changes likely to affect your company's competitive advantage?
- ✔ What can your company do to maintain core competence in the face of change?

Whatever happened to Daddy's Daimler?

Daimler used to be a synonym for *making it* in the UK. When a Daimler was parked in front of their house, it meant that they had finally arrived. In fact, it's hard to think of another product that could bestow quite as much status on its owner. The car was built for ultimate comfort, and it conveyed an image of wealth and luxury. Daimler owners were an intensely loyal bunch, typically ordering new models every few years, just to burnish that image.

Dailmer owners are still loyal today, but not to that brand. In the 1980s, a new generation of car buyers began to look for new status symbols. The young and wealthy began to chase foreign cars with names such as BMW, Mercedes, and Volvo (or Lexus, Infiniti, and Acura). Whatever happened to Daimler's enviable position in the luxury-car market? Competition, of course, and a failure on Daimler's part to respond quickly to changing tastes. The image of luxury and intense brand loyalty that the car once enjoyed simply weren't passed along to the next generation of buyers, and a once-powerful competitive advantage quietly slipped away.

Focus on each of the major forces that fuel change in your own industry:

- ✔ Your customers and their changing needs and requirements
- ✔ Your competitors and their changing capabilities, strategies, and goals
- ✔ Your company, its value chain, and its shifting strengths and weaknesses

As you create your business plan, make sure that you continue to track these forces so that they don't threaten the core competence you've worked so hard to achieve or so that your core competence evolves.

- ✔ Your core competence – what sets you apart – is based on the strongest links in your value chain.
- ✔ Competitive advantage in the marketplace is a direct result of your company's distinct core competence.
- ✔ Staying ahead of the competition means sustaining your competitive advantage, which requires a long-term strategy.

Earmarking Resources

The value chain paints a portrait of your company as your customers see it. Links in the chain reflect the value that customers place on aspects of your products and services. The strongest links capture your competitive advantage in the market and define your core competence as a business. Because the value chain is so good at weighing the importance of the things that your company does, it also comes in handy when you plan how your resources are going to be used.

Have you ever been to a horse race? If you have, you know that there's bound to be a group of regulars hanging around the stands or clustered at the fence. These people are serious about horse racing. They spend time poring over form sheets and newspapers, circling this, checking that. They pace back and forth, occasionally disappearing for a while to do something or other. What are they up to?

Well, they're placing bets, of course. But they're certainly not relying on Lady Luck alone to keep them flush. Instead, they're using all the information available – the condition of the track, the horse's health, the jockey's record, and the betting odds – to place their cash only on those wagers that are most likely to result in the best payoffs and the biggest winnings.

Betting on the horses is a serious business for these committed professionals. Maybe those punters can teach you something about how to divvy up working assets. Is it sensible to spread your company's limited resources equally among all the areas that make up your business? Probably not. Each time you set aside time and money for a particular business activity, you're placing a bet. What you're betting is that the resources you commit are going to contribute to your business, add value to what you do, and eventually come back around to generate revenue and profits.

Chapters 10 and 11 help you pore over the numbers (financial statements, ratios, and budgets) that keep track of where you spend money and then tell you whether you're winning. In short, your financial statements tell you a great deal about how you manage your cash, what bets you place, and how well you do at the track. But your financial statements alone don't tell you *what* to do. So how do you know where to place your bets in the first place?

You guessed it: you go back to your company's value chain. Consider this simple way to check your resource allocation based on your own value chain.

1. **Look at where your company currently spends money.**

   Make a quick-and-dirty estimate of how yearly expenses are divvied up among business activities – from R&D to delivery and service – and jot the numbers down on your value-chain grid. To keep things simple, use percentages. Make sure that the numbers add up to 100 per cent.

2. **Look at where customers think that you are providing them value.**

   Take the total value that customers think you provide, and divvy it up among your business activities. If customers pay £100 to buy your widget, for example, how much of that are they willing to pay for features, how much for service, and how much for convenience? Again, use percentages, and jot the numbers on the same value-chain grid. Make sure that the numbers add up to 100 per cent.

3. **As a reminder, highlight the boxes on the value-chain grid that represent your core competence and account for your competitive advantage in the marketplace.**

4. **Analyse the completed grid.**

   If the percentages line up and are concentrated in the highlighted boxes, you're in fairly good shape. But if you find a glaring mismatch in terms of where you're spending money, what your core competence is, and where your customers think that your products get their value, it's time to reassess where your company's resources are directed.

The value chain is invaluable when it comes time for you to earmark resources for your business activities. A clear understanding of your core competence and competitive advantage helps you make informed decisions when you have to allocate scarce resources.

✔ Value chains come in handy when it comes to planning the best way to allocate your company's resources.

✔ A value chain highlights mismatches between current spending and the areas that provide the most value to customers.

Chapter 10

Figuring Out Financials

*N*umbers. Some people love them; others are bored by them; still others begin to stammer, shake, and exhibit other physical signs of distress around them. But almost everyone agrees that, love 'em or hate 'em, numbers are the way that we keep track of things – football, cholesterol, the stock market, and our latest business venture. There's a lot more to numbers than simply the score at the end of game or the final Footsie closing, however. When they're put together in the right ways, numbers paint detailed pictures and tell stories about everything from the career of a football player to the state of the global economy.

You're probably familiar with the numerical snapshots that a bank requires when you want to borrow money for a new car, a bigger house, or the caravan in Devon that you've always wanted. Those snapshots always include a profit and loss account, as well as some sort of balance sheet. The profit and loss account tells the bank where you get your money and where you spend it. The balance sheet lists the value of all the things that you own and balances it against the money that you owe, including your car loans, mortgages, credit cards, even personal IOUs.

Financial statements tell the bank a great deal about you, and the bank learns even more by taking numbers from the statements and calculating a load of ratios. The bank totals your monthly loan payments and divides that number by your monthly income, for example, and then compares this ratio with the average for other borrowers. The result gives the bank a relatively good measure of your ability to repay the loan. Taken together, the statements and ratios create a financial portrait that the bank uses to get to know you better. And the better the bank knows you, the more reliable its decision is.

In this chapter, we introduce the basic financial statements and ratios that are widely used in business planning – which really are the same ones that paint a picture of your personal finances. First, we show you how a profit and loss account and a balance sheet are put together. Next, we explain cash-flow statements, which do pretty much what the name implies. Finally, we explore simple financial ratios that you can use to evaluate your business.

Understanding a Profit and Loss Account

A *profit and loss account* presents the proverbial bottom line. By adding all the revenue that you receive from selling goods or services and then subtracting the total cost of operating your company, the profit and loss account shows *net profit* – how much money the company has made or lost over a given period. Here's how to think of net profit:

Net profit = Revenue – Cost

The important thing to remember is the fact that the profit and loss account captures a simple idea. No matter what your accountants call it – a profit and loss account, earnings report, or statement of profit and loss – or how complicated accounting types make it look, it still uses the same basic principle of subtracting cost from revenue to come up with profit.

Your profit and loss account should cover a period that makes the most sense for your business planning: monthly, quarterly, or yearly. (The tax people, of course, are always interested in seeing your profit and loss account once a year.) You get a better financial picture of your company and where it's going if you look at profit and loss accounts over several periods and even over several years. In Chapter 11 you develop a pro-forma profit and loss account – a forecast of your profits based on projected revenue and costs.

Look at the various parts of a profit and loss account for Global Gizmos Company (see Figure 10-1). Notice that Global Gizmos includes a two-year comparison to show how revenue, costs, and profits have changed over time. Global Gizmos is a small company; if you want to make it a big company, add three zeros after all the numbers. In either case, the profit and loss account works exactly the same way.

Profit and Loss at a Glance

Global Gizmos Company

Figure 10-1:
The profit
and loss
account
starts with
gross
revenue
and then
subtracts
the costs
of various
business
activities
to arrive at
different
kinds of
profit.

PROFIT AND LOSS ACCOUNT AS OF DECEMBER 31	This Year	Last Year
1 ▷ Gross Revenue on Sales	£ 810,000	£ 750,000
2 ▷ Cost of goods sold	-560,000	-520,000
Gross Profit	250,000	230,000
3 ▷ Sales, general, and administration	-140,000	-140,000
Depreciation expense	-30,000	- 25,000
Operating Profit	80,000	65,000
4 ▷ Dividend and interest income	+ 3,000	+ 2,000
Interest expense	- 13,000	- 14,000
Profit Before Taxes	70,000	53,000
5 ▷ Taxes	- 20,000	- 18,000
NET PROFIT FOR YEAR	£ 50,000	£ 35,000

Figure 10-1:
The profit and loss account starts with gross revenue and then subtracts the costs of various business activities to arrive at different kinds of profit.

Revenue

Revenue refers to all the money that a company receives as a result of being in business. The most important source of revenue (usually, the sale of goods or services) always appears as the first item in the income statement – in the case of Global Gizmos, gross revenue on sales. In this context, *gross* doesn't mean anything unpleasant; it indicates that the revenue is a total, without costs subtracted. Revenue from sources other than sales usually shows up a bit later in the profit and loss account.

Gross revenue on sales

Gross revenue on sales is based on the number of units actually sold during a particular period multiplied by the prices actually paid. Global Gizmos sold 32,400 widgets at a price of £25 each, for a gross revenue of £810,000. Things can be a little more complicated than this example, of course; your company may have several products or kinds of service, or your prices may change over time. Maybe you have to make an allowance for items that are returned. All these considerations contribute to your own calculation of gross revenue on sales.

Dividend and interest income

Your company may have sources of revenue besides sales – the income from savings accounts and other securities, for example. Because you must have money to operate the company anyway, you probably want that money to make money while it's sitting around. You should keep this investment income separate from your revenue on sales, however, so that you always know how much money the company itself is generating. In your profit and loss account your dividends and interest income should appear separately from your other revenue.

Costs

Unfortunately, you have to spend money to make money. The cost of doing business usually is divided into general categories that reflect the separate activities that a company is involved in and the different kinds of expenses that it incurs. Major cost categories include cost of goods sold, sales and administrative expenses, depreciation, interest expense – and don't forget taxes. Each item deserves its own entry in the profit and loss account.

Cost of goods sold

The *cost of goods sold* (COGS) combines all the direct costs of putting together your product or service. Raw materials, supplies, and the labour involved in assembling a product are all part of the COGS; so are the electricity, water, and gas used in manufacturing, as well as the costs of maintaining production facilities. If you offer dog-walking for pet owners, for example, the costs associated with delivering that service – leads and pooper scoopers – go into the COGS.

You may have to make a judgement call here and there about what is or isn't part of the COGS. Just remember to be consistent over time.

Sales, general, and administration

Sales, general, and administration expenses (SG&A) combine all the costs associated with supporting your product or service. If the company is just you, a telephone, and a tiny rented office above the hardware shop, the costs won't amount to much. But for larger companies, these costs seem to go on and on. SG&A includes salaries and overhead for the sales staff as well as the

receptionist, secretary, and the boss. SG&A also includes advertising and promotion, travel, telephone calls, accounting fees, office supplies, dues and
subscriptions, and everyone's favourite, miscellaneous expenses.

SG&A costs are tracked separately because they're not tied directly to revenue and can easily get out of hand. Make sure that you keep an eye on this
particular entry.

Depreciation expense

Depreciation expense is a standard way to spread both the cost and the usefulness of expensive items out over time. Whether it's a building, a truck, or a
computer, almost any durable item that your company buys slowly declines in
value, because of simple wear and tear or because new technology makes the
item obsolete. Bean-counters have come up with various ways to calculate that
depreciation. All the methods allow you to allocate a portion of the purchase
price as a business expense each year, to reflect a decrease in value. (Land, by
the way, isn't included in depreciation expenses and can't be depreciated.)

Interest expense

Interest expense includes all the money that you pay out to the parties that
loaned you funds to operate the company. You don't want to overlook this
cost. You may have entered into agreements with banks or other investors,
for example, and are obligated to pay back interest on a fixed schedule. An
interest expense (often called a *fixed charge*) is isolated in the profit and loss
account because it absolutely, positively has to be paid year after year.

Taxes

Even Albert Einstein stopped short of trying to figure his own taxes. But taxes
are a fact of life and represent another cost of doing business. You can minimise your company's taxes by making sure that you keep careful track of all
your other expenses.

Profit

Profit is the Holy Grail. When you do things right, the total costs flowing out
of your business are less than all the revenue coming in. Your profit, of course,
represents the difference. But it's useful to talk about different kinds of profit
at various stages along the way. In particular, you can keep track of gross
profit, operating profit, and profit before taxes, as well as your overall net
profit. Comparing profit at different stages gives you a clearer picture of where
your company is most efficient and where you could do better.

Gross profit

Gross profit measures how much money your company still has after you subtract all the direct costs of putting together your product or service (COGS) from the total revenue generated by sales. This profit doesn't include the many indirect expenses that you have in running the company or any revenue sources other than sales.

Operating profit

Operating profit accounts for all those additional sales, general, and administration (SG&A) costs that you incur as part of operating your business; it also subtracts the depreciation expense of your costly purchases. Operating profit reflects the money that you make from your overall business operations.

Profit before taxes

Profit before taxes takes everything else into account, including any financial transactions that you make. Your income from other sources (such as investment dividends and interest) is included here, as well as your interest payments to creditors.

Net profit

Net profit, of course, is the bottom line after the company's tax bite is subtracted. Global Gizmos made money in its most recent period.

- ✔ A profit and loss account begins with your revenue and subtracts all your costs to come up with net profit, usually for a year.

- ✔ Revenue includes all the money that you take in from sales, as well as income that you receive from dividends and interest.

- ✔ Your costs include the cost of goods sold; sales, general, and administrative expenses; depreciation; interest expense; and taxes.

- ✔ By calculating profit at various stages – gross profit, operating profit, and profit before taxes – you can see precisely where the money comes from and where it goes.

Interpreting the Balance Sheet

Whereas a profit and loss account captures the financial results of your operations for a given period, a *balance sheet* is more like a snapshot of your financial condition at a particular moment. The profit and loss account lists your revenue, your costs, and the profit that you make. The balance sheet, on the other hand, addresses what your company owns, what it owes, and what it's worth at a given moment. Ideally, the balance sheet tells you just how much money you'd have left over if you sold absolutely everything and then paid every last one of your debts.

The things that your company owns are called *assets* by the same people who look forward to audits and dream about accounting standards. The amounts that you owe make up your *liabilities*. The difference between the two represents the *equity* in your business. Think of equity in terms of the following equation:

Equity = assets – liabilities

You have to admit that the equation is simple. Unfortunately, our accounting friends have dreamed up another, less straightforward way of looking at this equation:

Assets = liabilities + equity

Go work that out. Anyway, the US balance sheet is based on this second equation.

A US balance sheet is always divided into two parts. One part deals with all the company's assets; the other part lists liabilities and equity. Because of the second equation, the two parts are always in balance, adding up to exactly the same amount. Although the two totals always match, the entries along the way say a great deal about the overall financial health of the company.

Just as the profit and loss account usually covers a full year, the balance sheet is often compiled for the last day of the year. Figure 10-2 shows Global Gizmos' balance sheet. In this case, figures are provided for two years, so that the reader (you or the accountant) can make a comparison between those years.

Assets

Your company's *assets* include anything and everything you own that has any monetary value. When you think about your assets in terms of the balance sheet, all that you're concerned about is how much each asset is worth and how quickly it can be sold. So assets are separated into categories, depending on how *liquid* they are – how fast and easy it is to liquidate them, turning them into cold, hard cash. *Current assets* are those that you can dispose of within a year, if you have to, whereas *fixed assets* often take much longer to get rid of. *Intangibles* may never be converted to cash.

Balance Sheet at a Glance

Global Gizmos Company

BALANCE SHEET ON DECEMBER 31		
ASSETS	**This Year**	**Last Year**
Current Assets		
Cash	30,000	15,000
Investment portfolio	35,000	20,000
Debtors	135,000	150,000
Stock	115,000	120,000
Prepaid expenses	5,000	5,000
Total Current Assets	£ 320,000	£ 310,000
Fixed Assets		
Land	60,000	60,000
Buildings, equipment, machinery	355,000	315,000
Minus accumulated depreciation	-125,000	-95,000
Total Net Fixed Assets	£ 290,000	£ 280,000
Intangibles (goodwill, patents)	£ 5,000	£ 5,000
TOTAL ASSETS	**£ 615,000**	**£ 595,000**
LIABILITIES & OWNERS' EQUITY	**This Year**	**Last Year**
Current Liabilities		
Creditors	60,000	70,000
Accrued expenses payable	80,000	90,000
Total Current Liabilities	£ 140,000	£ 160,000
Long-term Liabilities	£ 90,000	£ 100,000
Owners' Equity		
Share capital	155,000	150,000
Reserves	230,000	185,000
Total Owners' Equity	£ 385,000	£ 335,000
TOTAL LIABILITIES & OWNERS' EQUITY	**£ 615,000**	**£ 595,000**

(markers 1–6 shown alongside the sections of the balance sheet)

Figure 10-2:
The US
balance
sheet.

Current assets

Current assets represent your company's readily available reserves. As such, they're the assets that you draw on to fund your day-to-day business operations, as well as the assets that you may have to turn to in a financial emergency. Current assets include the following:

- ✔ **Cash.** You can't get any more liquid than cash, which is just what you expect it to be: notes and coins in the till, the petty-cash fund, and money on deposit in the bank.

- ✔ **Investment portfolio.** Investments are also usually liquid assets. Your investment portfolio includes savings accounts, short-term government bonds, and other safe securities that you invest in to watch your cash earn a bit of money while you wait to use it.

- ✔ **Debtors.** *Debtors* represent the money that customers owe you for goods and services that you've already delivered. Maybe you give customers 30, 60, or 90 days to pay. You want to keep tabs on this particular asset. You may end up reducing it by some percentage if you run into deadbeat customers who just won't pay up.

- ✔ **Stock.** The cash value of your stocks can be a bit tricky to calculate, but it should reflect the costs of the raw materials and supplies that you have on hand, as well as the value of partially finished products and products that are ready to be shipped.

- ✔ **Prepaid expenses.** If you pay any of your business expenses ahead of time, you should treat them as current assets. These expenses may include paid-up insurance premiums or retainers for unused accounting or advertising services.

Fixed assets

Fixed assets are fixed in the sense that they can't be readily converted to cash. These assets are the items that usually cost a great deal of money up front and are meant to last for several years – things like buildings, trucks, machines, and computers.

In the balance sheet, the value of a fixed asset is based on its original cost minus its accumulated depreciation over time, so the figure doesn't necessarily reflect the true market value of the asset or how much it may actually cost to replace it. Fixed assets can include the following:

- ✔ **Land.** The land that your company owns is listed separately in the balance sheet, because it doesn't depreciate over time; its value on the books remains the same from year to year.

- **Buildings, equipment, machinery.** This asset represents the original cost of all the expensive items that you've invested in to operate your company. The entry should include anything you purchase that's expected to last more than a year.

- **Minus accumulated depreciation.** Depreciation measures the decline in the useful value of an expensive item over time, so the original cost of all your fixed assets (excluding any land) is reduced by an amount equal to the total depreciation accumulated over the years. Notice that Global Gizmos shows accumulated depreciation increasing by £30,000 in its most recent year. Because its fixed assets are now worth £30,000 less on paper, Global Gizmos also takes a £30,000 depreciation expense in its profit and loss account (refer to number three in Figure 10-1).

Intangibles

Even though you can't polish any of these assets, intangibles can be extremely important to your company. *Intangibles* include such things as your rights to a manufacturing patent, a long-term contract, or an exclusive service franchise. Intangibles also cover something called goodwill. Although it's not at all obvious from the name, *goodwill* represents the extra money that you may spend for an asset above and beyond its fair market value – maybe because it's worth more to your company than to anybody else.

By definition, intangibles are hard to describe and difficult to put a real value on. Some companies don't even try. Instead, they place a nominal value of £1 on all their intangibles to indicate that although these assets exist, there's no way to measure what they're actually worth.

Liabilities and owners' equity

Your company's *liabilities* cover all the debts and obligations that you enter into while you run your company. In the same way that assets are divided up, your liabilities are separated into categories, based on how soon they are due. *Current liabilities* are those that have to be paid off within a year; *long-term liabilities* may stay on the books much longer. When these liabilities are subtracted from total assets, you're left with *owners' equity*, which is a measure of how much the company is actually worth.

Current liabilities

Current liabilities are the debts that your company has agreed to pay in the short term (say, within a year), so you have to be able to cover them from your current assets. What's left over (the difference between your current assets and current liabilities) is so important that it has a name: *working capital,* which is the chunk of money that you actually have to work with. Here are some standard liabilities:

- **Creditors.** *Creditors* represent the amounts that you owe your regular business creditors as part of your ongoing operations. At any given time, you may have accounts payable to all sorts of outside suppliers and service people, including the merchants, professionals, and even utility companies that you deal with every day.

- **Accrued expenses payable.** On any given day, your company also owes salaries and wages to its employees, interest on bank loans, and maybe insurance premiums – not to mention the taxes that you haven't sent in. To the extent that any of the obligations are unpaid on the date of the balance sheet, these liabilities are totalled as *accrued expenses payable*.

Long-term liabilities

Long-term liabilities usually represent large chunks of money that you're scheduled to pay back over several years. These liabilities are often at the centre of your company's financing. You may have issued bonds or a 'Director's Loan' to investors, for example, or you may have gone directly to the bank and secured a loan against your company's assets. In any case, you're probably using the money to invest in long-term growth of the company – acquiring new equipment, building a new manufacturing facility, developing additional products, or expanding into new markets.

Owners' equity

A company's owners come in various shapes and sizes. Their investments and equity in the company are arranged and distributed in all sorts of ways and can become incredibly complicated, especially if the company is a traded public limited company (plc). But don't be confused. All this complexity boils down to two major sources of equity: money and resources that flow in from outside the company, and profits that the owners keep and pump back into the company. Owners' equity can be any of the following:

- **Share capital.** The money that's invested in your company can take various forms, from the direct infusion of cash by inside owners who manage the business to the buying and selling of shares that represent small chunks of the company owned by outside investors. Share capital represents the total of all this money, no matter where it comes from or how it's described.

- **Retained earnings.** Your company makes a profit each year (at least, we hope it does), and you choose what to do with that excess cash. You can distribute it to the owners (that arrangement is where dividends come from) or keep part of it to reinvest in the company. If you put profits back into the company, it can grow. And if the company grows, you can increase the company's net worth and owners' equity (at least, we hope you do). *Retained earnings*, also known as reserves, represent the profits that you plough back into the company year after year.

Keep the following in mind when interpreting the balance sheet:

- ✔ A balance sheet is a snapshot of your financial condition at a particular moment – usually, the end of the year.

- ✔ Your assets include everything that has monetary value, ranging from cash and investments to buildings and stocks.

- ✔ Liabilities include all the debts and financial obligations that you incur in running your company.

- ✔ Subtract liabilities from assets to calculate your equity in the business.

Growing Up

Unless you are working in the United States, where the balance sheet is always set out in the straightforward and logical way we have used so far, you will have to enter the 'grown up' world of UK accountancy. Here, instead of keeping assets and liabilities apart, we jumble them up all over the place. Actually once you get used to the UK method its logic is appealing and it certainly makes analysing accounting data rather easier.

So far we have kept to this system as it is much simpler to explain, but we're afraid we always had to make that leap, so here goes.

Figure 10-3 sets out the same data as in Figure 10-2, for one year only, but follows the layout of the UK balance sheet. The conventions, concepts, rules, regulations, resulting ratios, in fact the whole thing, is exactly the same, its just that things are in a different order.

In this layout we start with the *fixed assets*, rather than liquid assets such as cash, and work our way down. After the fixed asset sum has been calculated we arrive at the residual unwritten down 'value' of those assets, tangible (land, buildings etc.), and intangible: in this case £295,000. We then work our way down the current assets in the reverse order of their ability to be turned into cash. Don't ask why it's done this way, it just is. Actually, it doesn't really matter a jot which order things come in as long as they are slotted into the right section of the balance sheet. The total of the current assets comes to £320,000.

Next we get the *current liabilities*, which come to a total of £140,000, and take that away from the current asset total to come to a figure of £180,000. This is often referred to as the *working capital*, as it represents the money circulating through the business day to day.

Fixed assests	£s	£s	£s
Land	60,000		
Buildings, equipment, machinery	355,000		
Less accumulative depreciation	125,000		
Net book value		290,000	
Intangible (goodwill, patents)		5,000	
Total fixed assets			295,000
Current assets			
Pre-paid expenses	5,000		
Stock	115,000		
Debtors	135,000		
Investments	35,000		
Cash	30,000		
Total current assets		320,000	
Less current liabilities			
Creditors	60,000		
Accrued expenses payable	80,000		
Total current liabilities		140,000	
Net current assets			180,000
Total assets			475,000
Less creditors, amounts falling due in over one year			90,000
Net Total Assets			385,000
Financed by			
Share capital	155,000		
Reserves (retained earnings)	230,000		
Total owner's equity			385,000

Figure 10-3:
The UK
balance
sheet.

By adding the _net current assets_ (working capital) of £180,000 to the total fixed assets of £295,000 – bingo: we can see we have £475,000 tied up in net total assets. Deduct the money we owe long term, the creditors due over one year, a fancy way of describing bank and other debt other than overdraft, and we arrive at the net total assets. Net, by the way, is accountant-speak for deduction of one number from another, often adding a four-figure sum to the bill for doing so.

The net total assets figure of £385,000 bears an uncanny similarity to the total of the money put in by the owners of the business when they started out, £155,000, and the sum they have left in by way of profits undistributed over the years, £230,000. So the balance sheet balances, but at a very different total to that of the US balance sheet.

The UK balance figure is Shareholders Equity = (Assets – Liabilities)

The US balance figure is Assets = (Liabilities + Equities)

You will need to recognise both the UK and the US balance sheets, as chances are that some of the companies you compete with, buy from, won shares in, or perhaps plan to buy will be reporting using US balance sheets. Now you can see that the accounting processes, like the language, have much in common, but still have some pitfalls for the unwary.

Examining the Cash-flow Statement

If you know what your company is worth and how much it makes every year, can't you just relax and assume that your financial plan is in reasonably good order? After all, what else do you need to know?

As it turns out, you've got to keep close track of one other absolutely indispensable resource: cash. No matter how good things look on paper – no matter how bright the balance sheet and how rosy the income statement – you still need cash on hand to pay the bills. The fact that you've got assets and profits doesn't automatically mean that you have money in the bank. Cash can turn out to be much more important than income, profits, assets, and liabilities put together, especially in the early stages of your company.

The *cash-flow statement* monitors changes in your cash position over a set period. The top half of the statement tracks the flow of cash in and out of your company; the bottom half reports where the funds end up. Just like the balance sheet, the top and bottom halves of a cash-flow statement match. Given the importance of ready cash, you want to look at cash-flow statements on a regular basis – quarterly, monthly, or maybe even weekly.

Figure 10-4 shows a cash-flow statement for Global Gizmos Company. The cash-flow statement contains many of the same elements as a profit and loss account, but with a few critical adjustments.

Cash Flow at a Glance

Global Gizmos Company

CASH FLOW AS OF DECEMBER 31		
INFLOW AND OUTFLOW	**This Year**	**Last Year**
Funds Provided By:		
Gross receipts on sales	825,000	760,000
Dividend and interest income	3,000	2,000
Share capital	5,000	10,000
Total Funds In	**£ 833,000**	**£ 772,000**
Funds Used For:		
Cost of goods produced	555,000	515,000
Sales, general, and administration	160,000	150,000
Interest expense	13,000	14,000
Taxes	20,000	18,000
Buildings, equipment, machinery	40,000	50,000
Long-term debt reduction	10,000	5,000
Dividend distribution to owners	5,000	5,000
Total Funds Out	**£ 803,000**	**£ 757,000**
NET CHANGE IN CASH POSITION	**£ 30,000**	**£ 15,000**
CHANGES BY ACCOUNT	**This Year**	**Last Year**
Changes In Liquid Assets		
Cash	15,000	5,000
Investment portfolio	15,000	10,000
Total Changes	**£ 30,000**	**£ 15,000**
NET CHANGE IN CASH POSITION	**£ 30,000**	**£ 15,000**

1 ▷
2 ▷
3 ▷
4 ▷

Figure 10-4:
A cash-flow statement monitors changes in the company's cash position over time.

Cash in and cash out

The top half of the cash-flow statement deals with the inflow and outflow of cash, tracking where your company gets funds and what you use those funds for. Cash flow is a little more honest than a profit and loss account, because the cash-flow statement shows money coming in only when you actually deposit it and money going out only when you actually write a cheque.

Funds provided by

Where does all that money originate? Because the cash-flow statement reflects the actual receipt of cash, no matter where it comes from, the entries are a bit different from the revenue shown in a company's profit and loss account. These funds are usually made up of the following:

- **Gross receipts on sales.** This entry represents the total money that you take in on sales during the period. Gross receipts are based on your gross revenue, of course, but they also take into account when you actually receive payment. Global Gizmos, for example, received all of its £810,000 in gross revenue this year, plus £15,000 in debtors that the company was owed from last year, for a total of £825,000.

- **Dividend and interest income.** Your income from savings accounts and other securities is also reported in your profit and loss account. The amounts should be the same, as long as you actually receive the money during the period covered by the cash-flow statement.

- **Share capital.** The money invested in your company shows up as part of the owners' equity in your balance sheet. Invested capital doesn't represent revenue from your business operations, of course, so it never appears in the profit and loss account, but it can be a source of cash for the company. As Figure 10-4 shows, Global Gizmos received an additional £5,000 in invested capital this year.

Funds used for

Where does all the money go? The cash-flow statement keeps track of the costs and expenses that you incur for anything and everything. Some of the expenses appear in the profit and loss account; others don't, because they don't directly relate to your costs of doing business. These funds usually consist of the following:

- **Cost of goods produced.** This entry represents the total cost of producing your product or service during the period. The cost of goods produced often differs from the cost of goods sold shown in your profit and loss account, because the cost of goods sold also includes sales out of stock (items that your company has already produced and paid for) and doesn't include the cost of products that you add to stock. Global Gizmos, for example, reduced its overall inventory by £5,000 this period, so the company's cost of goods produced was £5,000 less than its cost of goods sold from the profit and loss account.

- **Sales, general, and administration (SG&A).** These expenses are the same SG&A expenses that appear in a profit and loss account, except that paying off bills that you owe or postponing payments may change the amount. Global Gizmos paid down £10,000 in both its accounts payable and expenses payable this year, increasing its SG&A cash outflow by £20,000, for a total of £160,000.

✔ **Interest expense.** Interest expense shows up in the profit and loss account as well. The number reflects the amount that you actually pay out during the period.

✔ **Taxes.** Taxes also appear in the profit and loss account. But in the cash-flow statement, taxes are the ones that you actually pay out during the period.

✔ **Buildings, equipment, machinery.** When your company buys an expensive item, it doesn't appear in your profit and loss account as an expense, because you're really just trading cash for another asset. Instead, you take a depreciation expense each year to reflect the spread of that cost over the asset's useful life. When you buy the building, lorry, or whatever, however, you've got to pay for it. The cash-flow statement reflects those costs. Global Gizmos, for example, shelled out £40,000 this year for new equipment.

✔ **Long-term debt reduction.** It costs you money to reduce any long-term debt that your company may have, and that expense doesn't appear in the profit and loss account. Global Gizmos reduced its long-term debt by £5,000 last year and £10,000 this year.

✔ **Dividend distribution to owners.** The portion of your company's profits that you decide to give back to the owners comes directly out of your cash box. Again, this entry isn't a business expense in the profit and loss account, but it costs you nonetheless. Global Gizmos distributed £5,000 to its owners this year.

What's left over

The flow of cash in and out of your business is like water flowing in and out of a reservoir. If more water comes in than goes out, the water level goes up, and vice versa. When your company's cash reserves rise, however, the money flows into one or more of your liquid-asset accounts. The bottom half of your cash-flow statement keeps track of what's happening to those accounts.

Changes in liquid assets

With cash flowing in and out of the company, your liquid assets are going to change during the period covered by the cash-flow statement. The items listed in this portion of the cash-flow statement are the same ones that appear in the balance sheet. This year, for example, Global Gizmos improved its cash reserves and investment portfolio by £15,000 each.

How to make a profit and go broke at the same time

Meet poor Fred Finance, a classic example of the manager and company owner who falls into a common financial trap. Fred used to work for Global Gizmos. But one night, after working late on widget sales, he decided that it was high time to start a small business of his own. Fred developed a business plan to make and sell a little doodah that he invented in high school. He figured that he could make it for 75 pence and sell it for £1. To test his concept, Fred took all his savings and had 2,000 doodahs made up. He sold 1,000 right off the bat.

Armed with a product, a market, and a plan, he opened his doors for business on January 1. His total assets were £1,000 in cash, 1,000 doodahs in stock, and £1,000 in debtors from those first customers.

Fred's business plan was relatively straightforward. He gave his doodah customers 30 days to pay, he always maintained a 30-day supply of doodahs stock, and he paid his own bills promptly. And business was great. He sold another 1,000 doodahs in January. After that, sales steadily climbed by 500 a month, and all his customers paid in 30 days. Within six months, his profits hit £2,500.

But none of that really matters now, because Fred Finance is broke.

How did that happen? Take a look at his books:

Profit and loss account

	January	February	March	April	May
Revenue on sales	£1,000	£1,500	£2,000	£2,500	£3,000
Cost of goods sold	750	1,125	1,500	1,875	2,250
Monthly profit	250	375	500	625	750
Yearly profit to date	£250	£625	£ 1,125	£1,750	£2,500

Cash-flow Statement

	January	February	March	April	May
Funds in	£1,000	£1,000	£1,500	£2,000	£2,500
Funds out	750	1,500	1,875	2,250	2,625
Change in cash position	250	−500	−375	−250	−125
Total cash on hand	£1,250	£750	£375	£125	£0

Poor Fred just didn't understand that a growing company can eat up capital even while it's making a profit. Each month that he was in business, Fred took the preceding month's revenue (his debtors) and paid out the next month's costs (his stock). The difference between the two kept growing as his business expanded. It's called 'over-trading'. Fred's business plan simply didn't include the financial cushion to support his growth.

Whatever you do, don't become a Fred Finance. Don't assume that as long as you make a profit every month, you'll always have money in the bank. It ain't necessarily so.

Net change in cash position

Raising the level of your liquid-asset accounts has the happy effect of strengthening your cash position. Global Gizmos increased its liquid assets and cash position by £30,000 this year. Not coincidentally, this £30,000 is also the difference between the £833,000 that Global Gizmos took in during the year (Total Funds In) and the £803,000 that it spent (Total Funds Out).

- ✔ A cash-flow statement tracks the movement of cash in and out of your company.

- ✔ Cash in represents money that you deposit; cash out, the cheques that you write.

- ✔ Cash flow can be more important than income, assets, and profits combined, especially for a new business.

Evaluating Financial Ratios

Armed with a profit and loss account, a balance sheet, and a cash-flow statement, you have a relatively complete financial picture of your company in front of you. But when you look everything over, what does that financial picture actually tell you? Is it good news or bad news? What things should you plan to do differently as you go forward?

Your financial picture may tell you that you pay your bills on time, keep a cash cushion, and make some money. But could your company do a better job down the road? It would be nice if you could look at the picture year after year and compare it against a competitor, several competitors, or even your entire industry. But companies come in all shapes and sizes, and it's hard to compare numbers from any two companies and make sense of them.

As a result, companies use *financial ratios*. When you divide one number by another, thereby creating a ratio, you eliminate many of the problems of comparing things on different scales.

Take your personal finances as an example. You're looking for help on invest-ments. One friend boasts that they made £5,000 on the stock market last month; another made only £1,000. Who do you ask for advice? It depends. If the first friend has £500,000 invested and the second friend has only £20,000, who's the savvy investor?

A ratio gives you the answer. The first friend saw a return of only 1 per cent (5,000 ÷ 500,000), whereas the second friend realised a better return of 5 per cent (1,000 ÷ 20,000).

Comparing two companies of different sizes works just the same way. If you want to compare your company's financial ratios with those of major competi-tors or with an industry average, you need to get your hands on some outside data. You can always start by asking your banker, accountant, or investment adviser, because financial institutions keep close track of standard ratios across industries. But you should also check out financial-data services such as Standard and Poor's, Value-Line, and Moody's. Also, Dun & Bradstreet offers a publication called *Industry Norms and Key Business Ratios*.

With all this data in hand, you can see how your company measures up, because you can bet that your investors, creditors, and competitors are going to, even if you don't.

Financial ratios fall into three categories. The first two categories take your company's vital signs to see whether you're going to make it (remain solvent). One set of ratios measures the company's capability to meet its obligations in the short term; the other looks at the long term. The final set of ratios indicates just how strong and vigorous your company really is, measuring its relative profitability from several points of view.

Short-term obligations

The overriding importance of being able to pay your bills every month is the major reason why current assets and current liabilities are separated in the company's balance sheet. The difference between the two – your working capital – represents a safety net that protects you from almost certain finan-cial catastrophe.

How much working capital do you need to ensure survival? Having the liquid assets available when you absolutely need them to meet short-term obligations is called *liquidity*. You can use several financial ratios to test your company's liquidity. You can monitor the following ratios year by year and measure them against your competitors' ratios and the industry averages.

Current ratio = current assets ÷ current liabilities

You determine your company's current ratio by looking at the balance sheet and dividing total current assets by total current liabilities. Global Gizmos Company, for example, has a current ratio of £320,000 ÷ £140,000, or 2.3 (refer to Figure 10-2). You can also express this ratio as 2.3 to 1 or 2.3:1.

Like most financial ratios, the current ratio isn't an especially precise measurement, so there's no point in calculating it to more than one or two decimal places.

What's the magic number to aim for? If your company falls below a current ratio of 1.0, you're in serious financial danger. In most cases, you want the number to stay above 2.0, meaning that you have more than twice the current assets that you need to cover current liabilities. But again, the answer depends on your industry. Companies that move stocks quickly can often operate with somewhat lower current ratios, because the stocks themselves are a little more liquid. You don't want your current ratio to get too high, either. Then you could be sitting on excess cash that should really be put to work and invested back in the company.

Quick ratio = (cash + investments + debtors) ÷ current liabilities

The quick ratio sometimes is called the *acid test,* because it's more stringent than the current ratio. The quick ratio doesn't allow you to count stock and prepaid expenses as part of your current assets, because it's sometimes hard to turn them back into cash quickly, especially in an emergency. This situation is particularly true in industries in which products go out of fashion rapidly or are quickly outdated by new technology.

Global Gizmos has a quick ratio of £200,000 ÷ £140,000, or 1.4, this year (refer to Figure 10-2). You want to keep your own company's quick ratio above 1.0 by a comfortable margin that is in line with your industry.

Stock turnover = cost of goods sold ÷ stock

Stock turnover tells you something about how liquid your stocks really are. This ratio divides the cost of goods sold, as shown in your yearly profit and loss account, by the average value of your stock. If you don't know the average, you can estimate it by using the stock figure as listed in the balance sheet at the end of the year.

Global Gizmos has a stock turnover of £560,000 ÷ £115,000, or 4.9. (Refer to Figures 10-1 and 10-2 for the company's profit and loss account and balance sheet, respectively.) This ratio means that Global Gizmos turns over its stocks almost five times each year. Expressed in days, Global Gizmos carries a 75-day (365 ÷ 4.9) supply of stock.

Is a 75-day inventory good or bad? It depends on the industry and even on the time of year. A car dealer who has a 75-day supply of cars at the height of the season may be in a strong stock position, but the same stock position at the end of the season could be a real weakness. As automation, computers, and information systems make business operations more efficient across all industries, stock turnover is on the rise, and the average number of days that stock of any kind hangs around continues to shrink.

Debtor turnover = sales on credit ÷ debtors

Debtor turnover tells you something about liquidity by dividing the sales that you make on credit by the average debtors. If an average isn't available, you can use the debtors from a balance sheet.

If Global Gizmos makes 80 per cent of its sales on credit, its debtor turnover is (£810,000 × .8) ÷ £135,000, or 4.8. (Refer to Figures 10-1 and 10-2 for Global Gizmos' profit and loss account and balance sheet.) In other words, the company turns over its debtors 4.8 times per year, or once every 76 days, on average. That's not so good if Global Gizmos' payment terms are 30 or 60 days. Unlike fine wine, debtors don't improve with age.

Long-term responsibilities

Your company's liquidity keeps you solvent from day to day and month to month, but what about your ability to pay back long-term debt year after year? Two financial ratios indicate what kind of shape you're in over the long haul. The first ratio gauges how easy it is for your company to continue making interest payments on the debt; the second tries to determine whether the principal amount of your debt is in any danger.

If you've read this chapter from the beginning, you may be getting really bored with financial ratios by now, but your lenders – bankers and bondholders, if you have them – find these long-term ratios to be incredibly fascinating, for obvious reasons.

Times interest earned = earnings before interest and taxes ÷ interest expense

Don't get confused – earnings before any interest expense and taxes are paid (EBIT) really is just the profit that you have available to make those interest payments in the first place. Global Gizmos, for example, has an EBIT of £57,000 and an interest expense of £13,000 this year for a times-interest-earned ratio of 4.4. (Refer to Figure 10-1 for the company's income statement.) In other words, Global Gizmos can meet its interest expense 4.4 times over.

You may also hear the same number called an *interest coverage*. Lenders get mighty nervous if this ratio ever gets anywhere close to 1.0, because at that point, every last penny of profits goes for interest payments on the long-term debt.

Debt-to-equity ratio = long-term liabilities ÷ owners' equity

The debt-to-equity ratio says a great deal about the general financial structure of your company. After all, you can raise money to support your company in only two ways: borrow it and promise to pay it back with interest, or sell pieces of the company and promise to share all the rewards of ownership. The first method is debt; the second, equity.

Global Gizmos has a debt-to-equity ratio of £90,000 ÷ £385,000, or .23. (Refer to Figure 10-2 for Global Gizmos' balance sheet.) This ratio means that the company has more than four times as much equity financing as it does long-term debt.

Lenders love to see lots of equity supporting a company's debt, because they know that the money they loan out is safer. If something goes wrong with the company, they can go after the owners' money. Equity investors, on the other hand, actually want to take on some risk. They like to see relatively high debt-to-equity ratios, because that situation increases their leverage and (as the following section points out) can substantially boost their profits. So the debt-to-equity ratio that's just right for your company depends not only on your industry and how stable it is, but also on who you ask.

Relative profitability

If profit is the bottom line for your business, profitability is the finishing line. Profitability tells you how well you measure up when it comes to creating financial value out of your company. Profitability ratios allow you to keep track of your own performance year by year. They also allow you to compare that performance against that of other competitors, other industries, and even other ways of investing resources.

You could easily invest the money that flows into your company in other businesses, for example, or in bank accounts, property, or government bonds. Each of these investments involves a certain level of risk. By comparing profitability ratios, you begin to see whether your own company measures up, generating the kinds of financial rewards that justify the risks involved.

Profitability ratios come in three flavours. The first type of ratio examines profit relative to your company sales. The second type examines profit relative to total assets. The final type examines profit relative to owners' equity. Each of the ratios reflects how attractive your company is to an investor.

Net profit margin = net profit ÷ gross revenue on sales

The net profit margin is your net profit divided by your gross revenue. The ratio really says more about your costs in relation to the prices that you charge, however. If your net profit margin is low compared with that of other companies in your industry, your prices are generally lower or your costs are too high. Lower margins are quite acceptable if they lead to greater sales, larger market share, and bigger profits down the road, but you want to monitor the ratio carefully. On the other hand, no one's going to quibble with net profit margins that are on the high side, although they're an awfully good way to attract new competitors.

Global Gizmos Company has a net profit margin of £50,000 ÷ £810,000, or 6.2 per cent, this year. (To examine Global Gizmos' profit and loss account, refer to Figure 10-1.) That result is a substantial increase from the 4.6 per cent for the year before. The company didn't grow just in terms of revenue, but also became more profitable.

When you calculate your own net profit margin, you should also think about calculating margins based on your operating profit and gross profit. Together, these ratios give you a better idea of where your company's profitability really comes from.

Return on investment = net profit ÷ total assets

Net profit divided by total assets gives you the overall return that you're able to make on your company's assets – referred to as *return on assets* (ROA). Because these assets are equal to all your debt and equity combined, the ratio also measures an average return on the total investment in your company. What does the ratio mean? It's similar to the yield on Grandma's savings bonds or the return on that hot new mutual fund that you've discovered. *Return on investment* (ROI) is widely used as a test of company profitability, because you can compare it to other types of investments that an investor can put money into.

Watch out for one thing, though: The value of the total assets used in the calculation of ROI usually is taken from a company's balance sheet and can be misleading. If the assets have been around for a while, the numbers on the page may not reflect real replacement costs, and if the assets are undervalued, the ROI is bound to be a bit exaggerated.

Global Gizmos has an ROI of £50,000 ÷ £ 475,000, or 10.5 per cent, this year. (Refer to Figures 10-1 and 10-2 for the company's profit and loss account and balance sheet.) That figure is up from 7.1 per cent the year before, and the increase certainly is good news.

Whether your own company's ROI is where it should be depends to a large extent on your industry, as well as on what the economy is doing at the moment.

Return on equity = net profit ÷ owners' equity

Net profit divided by the owners' equity in your company gives you the return on just the equity portion of the investment (ROE). Keep in mind that you've already taken care of all your bankers and bondholders first by paying their return – the interest expense on your debt – out of your profits. Whatever is left over goes to the owners and represents their return on equity.

Your creditors always get paid first, and they get paid a fixed amount; everything else goes to the owners. That's where *leverage* comes in. The more you finance your company by using debt, the more leveraged you are, and the more leveraged you are, the more you're using other people's money to make money. Leverage works beautifully as long as you're good at putting that money to work – creating returns that are higher than your interest costs. Otherwise, those other people may end up owning your company.

Global Gizmos, for example, has an ROE of £50,000 ÷ £385,000, or 13.0 per cent. (The profit and loss account and balance sheet shown in Figures 10-1 and 10-2, earlier in this chapter, shed some light on where these figures come from.) Without any leverage, that ROE would be the same as the company's ROI, or only 10.5 per cent. More leverage probably would raise the ROE even higher, upping the risk at the same time. In short, leverage makes the good years better for the owners and the bad years much worse.

✔ Financial ratios allow you to compare your performance with that of other companies, especially your competitors.

✔ One set of ratios examines your company's vital signs to see if your company is going to remain solvent.

✔ Another set of ratios examines your company's financial health by measuring profit in terms of sales, assets, and equity.

Chapter 11

Forecasting and Budgeting

. . . .

In This Chapter

▶ Constructing your financial forecast

▶ Putting together a pro-forma profit and loss account

▶ Estimating a balance sheet

▶ Projecting your cash flow

▶ Exploring financial alternatives

▶ Preparing your company's budget

. . . .

*H*ow many times have you sat around the table with your family (or maybe just your dog) and talked about the importance of putting the household on a budget? Everybody knows what a budget is, of course: It's a way of figuring out how much you're going to spend on essentials (the things that you need) and incidentals (all the frills). By its very nature, a budget is something that looks ahead, combining a forecast and a set of guidelines for spending money.

As you probably know from experience, it's a lot easier to put together a budget if you have some basic financial information to work with. It's nice to know how much money's going to come in, for example, and when you expect it to arrive. It's also important to keep track of the expenses that absolutely have to be taken care of, such as the mortgage and the car payment. Only then can you begin to get a handle on what you have left over, which is called your *working capital*.

For your company, this kind of basic financial information resides in its financial statements. (For more information on financial statements, refer to Chapter 10.) These financial statements – profit and loss accounts, balance sheets, cash flow – are fairly straightforward, because they're based on how your company performed last year or the year before. Unfortunately, financial information is not quite as easy to put together and use when you have to plan for next year, three years from now, or even five years from now.

Why go to all the trouble of putting financial information together in the first place? The answer is simple: Although the numbers and financials aren't your business plan by themselves, they help you to fulfil your business plan. Without them, you're in real danger of allowing your financial condition – money (or the lack of it) – to take control of, or even replace, your business plan.

In this chapter, we help you construct a financial forecast for your company, including a pro-forma profit and loss account, an estimated balance sheet, and a projected cash-flow statement. Because nothing in the future is certain, we also introduce scenario planning and what-if analysis as ways to consider several financial alternatives. Finally, we talk about how you can use the financial information to create a budget, explaining what goes into a budget and how to go about making one.

Constructing a Financial Forecast

Every philosopher-wannabe has spoken profound words about the future and about whether we should try to predict it. But we can't avoid the future. It's there, it's uncertain, and we're going to spend the rest of our lives in it.

All of us make decisions every day based on our own personal view of what's ahead. Although things often end up surprising us, our assumptions about the future at least give us a basic framework to plan our lives around. Our expectations, no matter how far off the mark they are, encourage us to set objectives, to move forward, and to achieve our goals somewhere down the road.

You can think about the future of your company in much the same way. Assumptions about your own industry and marketplace – that you'll have no new competitors, that a new technology will catch on, or that customers will remain loyal, for example – provide a framework to plan around. Your expectations of what lies ahead influence your business objectives and the long-term goals that you set for the company.

You want to be clear about what your business assumptions are and where they come from, because your assumptions are as important as the numbers themselves when it comes to making a prediction. If you are convinced that no new competitors will enter the market, say why. If you see a period of rapid technological change ahead, explain your reasons. Don't try to hide your business assumptions in a footnote somewhere; place them in a prominent position. That way, you make your financial forecast as honest, adaptable, and useful as it can be. If all your assumptions are out in the open, nobody can possibly miss them.

✔ Everybody who looks at your forecast knows exactly what's behind it.

✔ You know exactly where to go when your assumptions need to be changed.

As you may have guessed, coming up with predictions that you really believe in isn't always easy. You may trust some of the numbers (next year's sales figures) more than you do others (the size of a brand-new market). Some of your financial predictions are based on your best estimate. You may arrive at others by using sophisticated number-crunching techniques. When you get the hang of it, though, you begin to see what a broad and powerful planning tool a financial forecast can be. You'll find yourself turning to it to help answer all sorts of important questions, such as the following:

✔ What cash demands does your company face in the coming year?

✔ Can your company cover its debt obligations over the next three years?

✔ Does your company plan to make a profit next year?

✔ Is your company meeting its overall financial objectives?

✔ Do investors find your company to be an attractive business proposition?

With so many important questions at stake, a financial forecast is worth all the time and effort that you can spend on it. Because if you're not careful, a forecast can turn out to be way off base. Did you ever hear the old computer programmer's expression 'Rubbish in, rubbish out'? The same is true of financial forecasts. Your financial forecast is only as good as the numbers that go into it. If the numbers are off the mark, it's usually for one of the following reasons:

✔ Expectations were unrealistic.

✔ Assumptions weren't objective.

✔ Predictions weren't checked and rechecked.

The following sections examine the financial statements that make up a financial forecast. After we explain how to put these statements together, we point out which of the numbers are most important and which are the most sensitive to changes in your assumptions and expectations about the future.

Pro-forma profit and loss account

Pro forma refers to something that you describe or estimate in advance. (It can also mean something that is merely a formality and can be ignored – but don't get your hopes up; we're talking about a serious part of a business plan.) When you construct your financial forecast, you should try to include *pro-forma profit*

and loss accounts – documents that show where you plan to get your money and how you'll spend it – for at least three years and for as long as five years in the future, depending on the nature of your business. You should subdivide the first two years into quarterly profit projections. After two years, when your profit projections are much less certain, annual projections are fine. (For a look at a profit and loss account, flip to Chapter 10.)

Your company's pro-forma profit and loss accounts predict what sort of profit you expect to make in the future by asking you to project your total business revenue and then to subtract all your anticipated costs. The following should help you get ready:

- ✔ If you're already in business and have a financial history to work with, get all your past financial statements out right away. You can use them to help you figure out what's likely to happen next.

- ✔ If you have a new company on your hands and don't have a history to fall back on, you have to find other ways to get the information that you need. Talk to people in similar businesses, sit down with your banker and your accountant, visit a trade association, and read industry magazines and newspapers.

The pro-forma profit and loss account has two parts – projected revenue and anticipated costs.

Projected revenue

Your company's projected revenue is based primarily on your sales forecast – exactly how much of your product or service you plan to sell. You have to think about two things: how much you expect to sell, naturally, and how much you're going to charge. Unfortunately, you can't completely separate the two things, because any change in price usually affects the level of your sales.

Your sales forecast is likely to be the single most important business prediction that you'll ever make. If you get it wrong, the error can lead to mountains of unsold stock or a sea of unhappy, dissatisfied customers – a financial disaster in the making. A souvenir-T-shirt company that *over*estimates how many Cup Final T-shirts customers will buy, for example, is going to be left with an awful lot of worthless merchandise. By the same token, the corner toy shop that *under*estimates how many kids will want the latest Bratz will have to answer to many frustrated parents and unhappy children – and will suffer lost sales.

How do you get the sales forecast right? Start by looking at its formula:

Sales forecast = market size × growth rate × market-share target

✔ Market size estimates the current number of potential customers.

✔ Growth rate estimates how fast the market will grow.

✔ Market-share target estimates the percentage of the market that you plan to capture.

Because your sales forecast has such a tremendous impact on the rest of your financial forecast – not to mention on the company itself – you should try to support the estimates that you make with as much hard data as you can get your hands on. Depending on your situation, you can also rely on the following guides:

Company experience. If you already have experience and a track record in the market, you can use your own sales history to make a sales prediction. But remember that your sales are a combination of the size of the market and your own share of the market. You may still need other sources of data (listed in the following paragraphs) to help you estimate how the market and your share of it are likely to change in the future.

Using data from outside your company also ensures that you're taking full advantage of all the growth opportunities that are available. All too often, companies use last year's sales as a shortcut to estimating next year's sales, without taking the time to look at how their markets are changing. Because a sales forecast can be self-fulfilling, those companies may never know what they missed!

Industry data. Industry data on market size and estimates of future growth come from all quarters, including trade associations, investment companies, and market-research firms (covered more extensively in Chapter 4). You can also get practical and timely information from industry suppliers and distributors.

Outside trends. In certain markets, sales levels are closely tied to trends in other markets, social trends, or economic trends (a phenomenon described in Chapter 12). Car sales, for example, tend to move with the general economy. So when car dealers track what's happening with the Gross Domestic Product (GDP), they get an estimate of where car sales are headed.

Even if a product is brand-new, you can sometimes find a substitute market to track as a reference. When frozen yogurt first appeared on the scene, for example, frozen-yogurt makers turned to the sales history of ice cream to help support their own sales forecasts.

Speaking of ice cream, don't forget to factor sales cycles into your forecast; in most of the UK, ice cream sales freeze over in January and February. Other markets may have other cycles.

Next, multiply your sales forecast by the average price that you expect to charge. The result is your projected revenue and it looks like this:

Projected revenue = sales forecast × average price

Where does the average price come from? Your average price is based on what you think your customers are willing to pay and what your competitors are charging. Use the information that you pack away on your industry and the marketplace. (Refer to Part II for how to analyse your industry and customers.) The price should also take into account your own costs and your company's overall financial situation.

Now put all the numbers together and see how they work. We'll use a company called Global Gizmos as an example. Sally Smart, widgets product manager, is putting together a three-year revenue projection. Using industry and market data along with the company's own sales history, Sally estimates that the entire market for widgets will grow about 10 per cent a year and that Global Gizmos' market share will increase by roughly 2 per cent a year, with projected price increases of approximately £1 to £2. She puts the numbers together in a table so that she can easily refer to the underlying estimates and the assumptions that support them (see Table 11-1).

Table 11-1   Widget Revenue Projection for Global Gizmos Company

Revenue projection	Year 1	Year 2	Year 3
Projected market size (units)	210,000	231,000	254,100
Projected market share (%)	20	22	24
Sales forecast (units)	42,000	50,820	60,980
Average price	£26	£27	£29
Projected revenue	**£1,092,000**	**£1,372,140**	**£1,768,420**

Anticipated costs

When you complete your revenue projection, you're still not quite finished. You still have to look at anticipated costs – the price tag of doing business over the next several years. To make life a little easier, you can break anticipated costs down into the major categories that appear in a pro-forma profit and loss account: projected cost of goods sold, projected sales, general and administration expenses, projected interest expenses, and projected taxes and depreciation. The following list defines these categories.

Projected cost of goods sold (COGS). COGS, which combines all the direct costs associated with putting together your product or delivering your service, is likely to be your single largest expense. If you have a track record in the industry, you have a useful starting point for estimating your company's future COGS.

Even though the following formula may look ugly, it's actually a simple way to calculate your projected COGS. Based on the assumption that the ratio of your costs to your revenue will stay the same:

> Projected COGS = (current COGS ÷ current revenue on sales) × projected revenue

If you haven't been in business long or if you're just starting a company, you won't have access to this kind of information. But you can still estimate your projected COGS by substituting industry averages or by using data that you find on other companies that have similar products or services.

Although this ratio approach has the advantage of being simple, you can get into trouble if you don't confirm the COGS that you come up with. At the very least, you should sum up the estimates of the major costs looming ahead (materials, labour, utilities, facilities, and so on) to make sure that the projected COGS makes sense. This method is tougher, but it gives you a chance to make separate assumptions and projections for each of the underlying costs. You may be pleasantly surprised; you may discover that as your company gets bigger and you're in business longer, your projected revenue goes up faster than your costs do. The effect is called the experience curve (explained thoroughly in Chapter 13), and it means that your COGS-to-revenue ratio will actually get smaller in the coming years.

Sales, general, and administration (SG&A). SG&A represents your company's overheads: sales expenses, advertising, travel, accounting, telephones, and all the other costs associated with supporting your business. If your company is brand-new, try to get a feel for what your support costs may be by asking people in similar businesses, cornering your accountant, or checking with a trade association for average support costs in your industry. Also come up with ballpark numbers of your own, including estimates for all the major overhead expenses that you can think of.

If you've been in business for a while, you can estimate a range for your SG&A expenses using two calculations. The first method projects a constant spending level, even if your company's sales are growing. In effect, you assume that your support activities will all get more efficient and will accommodate your additional growth without getting bigger themselves. The other method projects a constant SG&A-to-revenue ratio. In this case, you assume that support costs will grow as fast as your revenue and that you won't see any increase in efficiency. An accurate SG&A forecast probably lies somewhere in between. Given what you know about your company's operations, come up with your own estimate, and include the assumptions that you make.

Interest expense. Your interest expense is largely the result of decisions that you make about your company's long-term financing. Those decisions, in turn, are influenced by your ability to pay your interest costs out of profits. Think about what sort of financing you will need and what interest rates you may be able to lock in, then estimate your interest expense as best you can.

Taxes and depreciation. Taxes certainly affect your bottom line, and you want to include your projections and assumptions in your anticipated costs. It's usually pretty simple to estimate their general impact in the future by looking at their impact on your company now. If you're starting a new business, do a bit of research on tax rates.

Depreciation, on the other hand, is an accountant's way of accounting for the value that your asset purchases lose over the time in which you will be using them. As such, it's an expense that doesn't really come out of your pocket every year. You can estimate the numbers, but don't get too carried away. In the future, your depreciation expense will include a portion of those expensive items that you have to buy to keep the business healthy and growing (computers, cars, forklifts, and so on).

When you plug the numbers into your pro-forma profit and loss account and calculate your net profit, be prepared for a shock. You may discover that the profit you were expecting in the first year or two has turned into a projected loss. But don't panic. New business ventures often lose money for some time, until their products catch on and some of the startup costs begin to get paid off. Whatever you do, don't try to turn a projected loss into a profit by fiddling with the numbers. The point isn't to make money on paper; the point is to use the pro-forma profit and loss account as a tool that can tell you what sort of resources and reserves you need to survive until losses turn into predicted profits.

Even if your projection shows a healthy profit, ensure you also complete a Cash Flow Projection (see below) to make sure you can afford to trade at the projected level. Making a profit does not always mean that you will have *cash* on hand to buy raw materials, pay staff and pay taxes.

Estimated balance sheet

Another part of your financial forecast is the *estimated balance sheet,* which, like a regular balance sheet, is a snapshot of what your company looks like at a particular moment – what it owns, what it owes, and what it's worth. Over the years, these snapshots (estimated balance sheets) fill a photo album of sorts, recording how your company changes over time. Your estimated balance sheets describe what you want your company to become and how you plan to get it there. The estimated balance sheets that you put together as part of your financial forecast should start with the present and extend out three to five years in a series of year-end projections. (For much more information on balance sheets, check out Chapter 10.)

While the pro-forma profit and loss accounts in your financial forecast project future revenue, costs, and profits, your estimated balance sheets lay out exactly how your company will grow so that it can meet those projections. First, you want to look at what sorts of things (*assets*) you'll need to support the planned size and scale of your business. Then you have to make some decisions about how you're going to pay for those assets. You have to consider how you'll finance your company – how much debt you plan to take on (*liabilities*) and how much of the company's own money (*equity*) you plan to use.

Assets

Your company's projected assets at the end of each year include everything from the money that you expect to have in the petty-cash drawer to the buildings and machines that you plan to own. Some of these assets will be current assets, meaning that you can easily turn them into cash; others will be fixed assets. Don't be confused by the word *current;* we're still talking about the future.

Current assets. The cash on hand and your investment portfolio, as well as debtors and stocks, add up to your current assets. How much should you plan for? That depends on the list of current liabilities (debts) you expect to have, for one thing, because you'll have to pay short-term debts out of your current assets. What's left over is your working capital. The amount of working capital that you will need depends on your future cash-flow situation.

Your estimates of future debtors (money that customers will owe you) depend on the payment terms that you offer and on the sales that you expect to make on credit.

Projected stocks (the amount of stuff in your warehouse) depend on how fast your company can put together products or services and get them to customers. The longer it takes to build products, the bigger the stock cushion you may need.

Fixed assets. Land, buildings, equipment, machinery, and all the other things that aren't easy to dispose of make up your company's fixed assets. Your estimated balance sheets should account for the expensive items that you expect to purchase or get rid of. Your capital purchases (such as additional buildings, more equipment, and newer machines) can play a major role in company growth, increasing both your revenue and the scale of your business operations.

Extruding better returns

A small, up-and-coming West Country company (we'll call it Klever Kitchens) has made a big name for itself in the kitchen-accessories business. Klever Kitchens produces all sorts of new-fangled gadgets and utensils for the gourmet chef – everything from pasta hooks to melon scoops. Because many of the company's products are made of plastic, the owners face a decision about the purchase of a second plastic-extruding machine. They know that the investment is sound, because the new £20,000 machine will allow the company to grow, and they expect it to generate an additional £4,000 a year in profit, resulting in an estimated payback period of about five years (£20,000 divided by £4,000). The question is whether to pay for the extruder by borrowing the funds or by using some of the company's equity reserves.

The owners understand that using debt is a way of gearing the company. The bank has already agreed to loan Klever Kitchens 75 per cent of the £20,000 investment at a fixed 8 per cent interest rate. But what do the numbers say?

Return on equity (ROE) really measures how much money Klever Kitchens makes on the money that it invests (ROE = (added profit – interest expense) ÷ equity). By taking on debt, the owners expect to earn an additional £2,800 on their investment of £5,000 in the new extruder, for an ROE of 56 per cent. That figure is almost three times the return that they would receive by putting up the funds themselves.

Acting like a financial gearbox, gearing allows Klever Kitchens to use other people's money to generate profits for itself. The risks are also a bit higher, of course, because the owners have to make added interest payments or face losing the extruder and maybe the entire company. In this case, Klever Kitchens should borrow the funds, deciding that the rewards are well worth the risks.

Additional plastic extruder	No gearing	75% geared
Liability	£0	£15,000
Equity	£20,000	£5,000
Net profit	£4,000	£4,000
Interest expense	£0	£1,200
Profit minus interest expense	£4,000	£2,800
Return on equity (ROE)	20%	56%

Keep an eye on how each machine or piece of equipment will help your bottom line. If you plan to buy something big, make a quick calculation of its *payback period* (how long it will take to pay back the initial cost of the equipment out of the extra profit that you'll make). Is the payback period going to be months, years, or decades? As you plan for the future, you also want to keep track of your overall expected *return on assets* (ROA), which is your net profits divided by your total assets. This figure monitors how well you expect all your assets to perform in the future. Compare your estimated ROA with industry averages and even with other types of investments.

Liabilities and owners' equity

Estimated balance sheets have to balance, of course, and your projected assets at the end of each future year have to be offset by all the liabilities that you intend to take on, plus your projected equity in the company. Think about how *leveraged* you intend to be (how much of your total assets you expect to pay for out of money that you borrow). Your use of leverage in the future says a great deal about your company. It shows how confident you are about future profits; it also says, loud and clear, how willing you are to take risks for future gain. For more about how leverage works, check out the sidebar 'Extruding better returns', or flip to Chapter 10.

Current liabilities. This category consists of all the money that you expect to owe on a short-term basis. That's why these debts are called *current liabilities,* although we're still talking about the future. Current liabilities include the amounts that you expect to owe other companies as part of your planned business operations, as well as payments that you expect to send to the tax people. You have to plan your future current assets so that they not only cover these estimated liabilities, but also leave you some extra capital to work with.

Long-term liabilities. The long-term debt that you plan to take on represents the piece of your company that you intend to finance. Don't be surprised, however, if potential creditors put a strict limit on how much they will loan you, especially if you're just starting out. It's hard to buy a house without a down payment, and it's almost impossible to start a company without one. The down payment is your equity contribution. In general, bankers and other lenders alike want to see enough equity put into your business to make them feel that you're all in the same boat, risk-wise. Equity reassures them that you and other equity investors have a real financial stake in the company, as well as tangible reasons to make it succeed.

How much are lenders willing to loan you, and how much of a down payment do you need to come up with to satisfy them? The answer depends on several things. If you're already in business, the answer depends on how much debt your company already has, how long your company's been around, how you've done up to now, and what the prospects are in your industry. If your company is new, financing depends on your track record in other businesses or on how well you do your homework and put together a convincing business plan.

Before you take on a new loan, find out what kind of debt-to-equity ratios similar companies have. (For help, turn to Chapter 10.) Make sure that yours will fall somewhere in the same range. As an additional test, run some numbers to make sure that you can afford the debt and the interest payments that come along with it.

Owners' equity. The pieces of your company that you, your friends, relatives, acquaintances, and often total strangers lay claim to are all lumped together as *owners' equity*. Although the details of ownership can become ridiculously complex, the result of the process is fairly straightforward. All owners own part of your company, and everybody sinks or swims, depending on how well the company does.

In general, you can estimate how well the company is likely to do for its owners by projecting the return that you expect to make on the owners' investment (refer to Chapter 10 for the details). Then you can compare that return with what investors in other companies, or even other industries, are earning.

In the initial stages of your company, equity capital is likely to come from the owners themselves, either as cash straight out of the wallet or from the sale of shares to other investors. The equity at this stage is crucial, because if you want to borrow money later, you're going to have to show your bankers that you have enough invested in your business to make your company a sound financial risk. When the company is up and running, of course, you can take some of your profits and (rather than buy the little sports car that you've always wanted) give them back to the company, creating additional equity.

Unfortunately, profit has another side, and the down side is definitely in the red. Although you probably don't want to think about it, your company may lose money some years (especially during the early years). Losses don't generate equity; on the contrary, they eat equity up. So you have to plan to have enough equity available to cover any anticipated losses that you project in your pro-forma profit and loss accounts (refer to the section 'Pro-forma profit and loss account' earlier in this chapter).

Projected cash flow

The flow of cash through a business is much like the flow of oil through an engine; it supports and sustains everything that you do and keeps the various parts of your company functioning smoothly. We all know what happens when a car's oil runs dry: the car belches blue smoke and dies. Running out of cash can be just as catastrophic for your company. If you survive the experience, it may take months or even years for your company to recover.

Cash-flow statements keep track of the cash that comes in and the cash that goes out of your company, as well as where the money ends up. These statements are crucial. Projected cash-flow statements ensure that you never find the cash drawer empty at the end of the month when you have a load of bills left to pay.

Cash-flow statements should project three to five years into the future, and for the first two years, they should include monthly cash-flow estimates. Monthly estimates are particularly important if your company is subject to seasonal cycles or to big swings in sales or expenses. (If you're not sure what a cash-flow statement looks like and how it's different from a profit and loss account, flip to Chapter 10.)

You get a bonus from all this work: The effort that you put into creating cash-flow statements for the company gives you a head start when the time comes to create a budget for your business (see 'Making a Budget' later in this chapter).

✔ Your financial forecast should include a pro-forma profit and loss account, an estimated balance sheet, and a projected cash-flow statement.

✔ The business assumptions behind your forecast are as important as the numbers themselves.

✔ Your company's pro-forma profit and loss account predicts the profit that you expect to make in future years.

✔ Your estimated balance sheet lays out how you expect your company to grow in the future.

✔ Your company's projected cash-flow statement tracks your expected cash position in coming years.

Exploring Alternatives

Wouldn't it be nice if you could lay out a financial forecast – create your pro-forma profit and loss accounts, estimated balance sheets, and projected cash-flow statements – and then just be done with it? Unfortunately the uncertain future that makes your financial forecast necessary in the first place is unpredictable enough to require constant attention. To keep up, you have to do the following things:

✔ Monitor your financial situation and revise the parts of your forecast that change when circumstances – and your own financial objectives – shift.

✔ Update the entire financial forecast regularly, keeping track of when past predictions were on target or off, and extending your projections another month, quarter, or year.

✔ Consider financial assumptions that are more optimistic and more pessimistic than your own best predictions, paying special attention to the estimates that you're the least certain about.

Why take the time to look at different financial assumptions? For one thing, they show you just how far off your forecast can be if things happen to turn out a bit differently than you expect. Also, the differences that you come up with are an important reminder that your forecasts are only that. You have to be prepared for alternatives.

The DuPont formula

If you really want to get a feel for what's going to happen when you change any of the estimates that make up your company's financial forecast, you have to understand a little bit about how the numbers relate to one other. The DuPont company came up with a formula that turned out to be so useful that other companies have been using a similar one ever since.

The idea behind the *DuPont formula* is simple. The recipe describes all the ingredients that play a role in determining your return on equity (ROE) – a number that captures the overall profitability of your company. ROE is your company's overall net profit divided by the owners' equity. But knowing that your ROE is 13 per cent, for example, is a lot like getting B+ on a test. You think that you did relatively well, but why did you get that particular mark? Why didn't you get an A? You want to know what's behind the mark so that you can do better next time.

By learning what's behind your company's ROE, you have a way to measure the impact of your financial predictions on your profitability. The DuPont chart shown in Figure 11-1 turns the formula into a pyramid, with the ROE at the top. Each level of the pyramid breaks the ratio into more basic financial ingredients.

Figure 11-1:
The DuPont chart turns the DuPont formula into a pyramid, with return on equity (ROE) at the top.

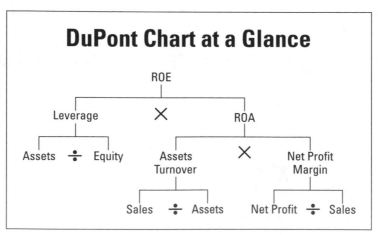

First level

ROE = ROA × leverage

You can increase your company's return on equity by increasing the overall return on your company assets or by increasing your leverage (the ratio of your total company assets to equity).

Second level

Leverage = assets ÷ equity

As your debt increases relative to equity, so does your company's leverage.

ROA = asset turnover × net profit margin

You can increase your return on company assets by turning those assets into more sales or by increasing the amount of money that you make on each sale.

Third level

Asset turnover = sales ÷ assets

Asset turnover is the amount of money that you take in on sales relative to your company's assets. The bigger your asset turnover, the more efficient you are at turning assets into sales.

Net profit margin = net profit ÷ sales

Net profit margin is the profit that you make after subtracting expenses divided by the amount of money you take in on sales. The larger your profit margin, the lower your overall costs relative to the prices that you charge.

What-if analysis

After you see how the DuPont formula is put together, you can start exploring different assumptions and what happens when you change the financial forecast. With the DuPont formula, you can look at how those changes are likely to affect your projected profitability, measured by your return on equity. The DuPont formula makes answering questions like the following much easier:

- ✔ What if you cut prices by 3 per cent?
- ✔ What if you increase sales volume by 10 per cent?
- ✔ What if cost of goods sold goes up by 8 per cent?
- ✔ What if you reduce your leverage by 25 per cent?

If you get your computer and a spreadsheet programme involved in the analysis (see your local computer guru for help, if necessary), you can ask ten what-if questions and get the answers before you have time to think of the next ten.

The better you understand where your revenue and profits come from, the better prepared you are to meet financial challenges. For more help on preparing for change, check out Chapter 12.

- ✔ Looking at different financial assumptions allows you to cover your bets in an uncertain future.

- ✔ The DuPont formula describes exactly what goes into your return on equity, which is a measure of your overall profitability.

- ✔ Using the DuPont formula, you can ask what-if questions to gauge the effects of changing your financial assumptions.

Making a Budget

The pieces of your financial forecast – the pro-forma profit and loss accounts, estimated balance sheets, and projected cash-flow statements – are meant to create a moving picture of your financial situation tomorrow, next month, next year, and three or even five years out. Your financial picture is likely to be much clearer in the near term, of course, and much cloudier the farther out you try to look. Fortunately, you can use the best of your forecasts to make near-term decisions about where, when, and how much money to spend on your company in the future.

Making a budget for your company is one of the most important steps that you'll take as you prepare your business plan. Your budget, in effect, consists of a series of bets that you're willing to place, based on what you expect to happen in your industry and in the marketplace in general. Your budget spells out exactly where your company's resources will come from and where they're going to go, and helps ensure that you make the right financial decisions.

A budget is more than a collection of numbers, though. Your budget is also a business tool that helps you communicate, organise, monitor, and control what's going on in your business. Your company's budget does the following things:

- ✔ Requires managers to communicate with one another so that they can agree on specific financial objectives, including revenue levels and spending targets

- ✔ Establishes roles and responsibilities for managers, based on how much money they're in charge of bringing in and how much they're allowed to spend

- ✔ Creates a standard way of measuring and monitoring management performance by keeping track of how well the revenue targets and spending limits are met

✔ Promotes the efficient and effective use of your financial resources by making sure that all your resources point toward a common set of business goals

What's in the budget

The rough outlines of your company's budget look a lot like your projected cash-flow statement. In fact, the cash-flow statement is the perfect place to start. Projected cash flow is a forecast of where you think the company's money will come from and where it's going to go in the future. Your budget fills in all the details, turning your financial forecast into a specific plan for taking in money and doling it out.

The *master budget* that you create is meant to account for everything that your company plans to do over the next year or two. Although you spend your company's money in all sorts of ways, all those ways can be divided into short-term and long-term spending. In the short term, you use money to keep the business up and running every day, covering the costs and expenses of putting together and selling products and services. Over the longer term, you use money to invest in things that will make your company bigger, better, or more profitable.

If your company is small and you have only a few employees, a single master budget should be all that you need to keep your day-to-day finances on track as well as to make decisions in the future. When your company gets a little bigger, however, you may want to think about your company's finances in terms of more than one budget, each of which covers a different aspect of your business. You may want to create the following budgets:

✔ **Operating.** This budget deals with all the costs that are directly associated with putting your product or service together, such as materials, supplies, labour, utilities, services, and facilities.

✔ **Administrative.** This budget deals with the expenses that are involved in supporting your products and services, sales and advertising, administrative salaries, phone and fax lines, and travel expenses.

✔ **Financial.** This budget deals with the overhead expenses involved in managing your assets, including keeping your books, doing your taxes, controlling your product stock, and keeping track of your debtors (the money that customers owe you).

✔ **Capital.** This budget deals with funds that are earmarked for the purchase of expensive items, such as new equipment, computers, a company car, and additional office space.

✔ **Development.** This budget deals with money that is set aside for developing new products, opening branches in other cities, or marketing to brand-new groups of customers.

When you need several budgets, like those in the preceding list, you use a master budget to pull all the separate budgets together and make sure that they meet your company's larger goals and financial objectives.

Global Gizmos Company put together a budget for the next two years based on a financial forecast and its projected cash flow (see Figure 11-2). The company's master budget looks a great deal like one of its cash-flow statements (flip to Chapter 10 for a comparison). But the budget goes into more detail in dividing the broad financial objectives into actual revenue and expense targets for specific company activities. The cost of goods produced, for example, is broken down into the cost of raw materials and supplies, labour, and utilities and facilities.

How budgets are made

Somehow, it's never the right time to sit down and make a budget, there's always something much more important to do. This situation seems to hold true for household and company budgets alike. Why doesn't anybody like to do them? Often, there doesn't seem to be enough financial information around to make a budget that's of any real use. If you complete a financial forecast first, however, your company's budget is much easier to complete.

So when do you get started? If you're just starting your company, there's no time like the present. If you're already up and running, when you create a budget depends on the company's size. For really big companies, the yearly budget process may begin six to nine months in advance. No wonder that the job can feel a bit like never-ending drudgery! Most companies, however, can count on spending some serious time with their budgets three or four months before the next year gets under way.

Established companies can use their track records and financial histories as starting points for next year's budget. But be careful. When you're a veteran, it's all too easy to get a bad case of budgetary laziness, using last year's numbers as a shortcut to next year's numbers. Unfortunately, you can veer off financial course before you know it. A good compass for this situation is something called *zero-based budgeting*. When you insist on zero-based budgeting, you ask everybody – including yourself – to go back and start from the bottom in preparing a budget. Rather than use last year's budget numbers, you make full use of your financial forecast, building up a new set of numbers from scratch. The process takes a little longer but is almost always worthwhile.

Master Budget

Global Gizmos Company

REVENUE AND EXPENSES		
	Next Year	Year After
Budgeted Revenue:		
Gross receipts on sales	£895,000	£970,000
Dividend and interest income	4,000	5,000
Total Revenue Available	**£ 899,000**	**£ 975,000**
Budgeted Expenses:		
Cost of goods produced	£ 600,000	£ 650,000
Raw materials and supplies	250,000	275,000
Labor costs	300,000	325,000
Utilities and facilities	50,000	50,000
Sales, general, and administration	£ 165,000	£ 170,000
Sales and distribution	90,000	95,000
Advertising and promotion	30,000	30,000
Product service	15,000	20,000
Accounting and office support	30,000	30,000
Interest expense	12,500	12,000
Taxes	22,000	24,000
Buildings, equipment, machinery	40,000	£100,000
Equipment and computers	35,000	25,000
Expanded warehouse	5,000	75,000
Development projects	10,000	15,000
New product development	8,000	5,000
New market development	2,000	10,000
Long-term debt reduction	2,500	2,000
Dividend distribution to owners	6,000	7,000
Total Expenses Out	**£ 858,000**	**£ 980,000**
NET CHANGE IN CASH POSITION	**£ 41,000**	**£ -5,000**

Figure 11-2:
The master budget looks a lot like the company's projected cash-flow statement.

The process of making a budget often gets a bad name in the business world. Rather than see budgeting as being a helpful business tool, business owners often rank budgeting among the greatest evils on earth, and managers often talk about it in unprintable ways. So what gives? When the budgeting process falls apart in a company, at least one of the following things probably happened:

MANAGER'S TIP

✔ The budget was handed down from above and used to control the company's managers, taking away their ability to influence the business decisions that they were ultimately responsible for carrying out.

✔ The budget was based on short-term thinking, ignoring the company's longer-term plans and strategic goals.

✔ The budgeted revenue and expense targets had nothing to do with the company's larger financial objectives or its real financial situation.

To make sure that your own company's budget doesn't suffer these fatal flaws, take a close look at two ways to put together a budget.

Top-down budgeting approach

The top-down approach to making your budget is the simplest way to work through your company's financial plans. The process pretty much begins and ends with the people who are in charge. If your company is small, you may want to invite some outside people to join you – people whom you trust, such as your banker, accountant, or maybe a close business associate. The process goes something like this:

1. **Put the finishing touches on your company's financial forecast, including pro-forma profit and loss accounts, expected balance sheets, and projected cash-flow statements.**

   If certain pieces are missing or incomplete, try to get the information that you need, or make a note that the document you need is unavailable.

2. **Meet with the company's decision-makers (or your trusted group, if you're self-employed) to review the financial forecast.**

   Take time to discuss general expectations about the future. Talk about the business assumptions that go into the forecast and the key predictions and estimates that come out of it.

3. **Meet again to explore possible financial alternatives.**

   Look at different sets of business assumptions and weigh their potential effects on the forecast. Continue to meet until the group either agrees or agrees to disagree about the future.

4. **Come up with revenue and expense targets for each of your company's major business activities or functional areas (whichever is more appropriate to your company).**

5. **Meet one last time after the budget is in place to review the numbers and get it approved.**

   Put together a written summary to go along with the numbers so that everyone in the company knows what the budget is, where it comes from, and what it means.

Although top-down budgeting does a fairly good job when you know all the people in your company by their first names, the approach has some definite disadvantages when your company gets bigger. By including only the managers at the top, you run the risk of leaving out large chunks of the organisation and losing track of your real business situation when it comes time to plug in the numbers.

Bottom-up budgeting approach

The bottom-up approach to creating your budget really is just an expanded version of the top-down process, taking into account the demands of a bigger company and of more people who have something to say. You still want to begin putting together your budget by getting a group of senior managers together. That group should still spend time coming to a general understanding of, and agreement on, your company's financial forecast, along with the business assumptions and expectations for the future that go with it. But rather than forcing a budget from the top, this approach allows you to build the budget up from the bottom.

Don't ask the group of senior managers to go on and dictate the company's budget. At this point in the budget process, the bottom-up approach means that it's time to get managers and supervisors at all levels of the company involved. The process goes like this:

1. **Meet with senior managers and ask them to review the company's broad financial objectives for each of the major business areas.**

   Try to come up with guidelines that set the tone and direction for budget discussions and negotiations throughout the company.

2. **Ask managers to meet with their managers and supervisors at all levels in the organisation.**

   Meetings can start with a recap of the budget guidelines, but discussions should focus on setting revenue and expense targets. After all, these managers are the ones who actually have to achieve the numbers and stay within the spending limits.

3. **Summarise the results of the budget negotiations.**

   If necessary, get the senior group members together again to discuss revisions in the financial objectives, based on the insights, perceptions, and wisdom of the company's entire management team.

4. **Go through the process again, if you have to, so that everyone at every level of the organisation is on board (or at least understands the reasoning behind the budget and its numbers).**

5. **Approve the budget at the top.**

   Make sure that everybody in the company understands what the budget means, applying the budget not only to financial objectives but also to larger business goals.

- Your budget spells out exactly where your company's resources will come from and where they will go.

- Your budget should be based on your projected cash-flow statements.

- Top-down budgeting is done by the top people – owners or senior managers – and works best in small companies.

- Bottom-up budgeting involves all management levels, which can mean more realistic revenue targets and spending limits.

Part IV
Looking to the Future

"OK – Here's the business plan. Nigel takes charge of marketing, Tristram sales, Keith accounts and Psycho makes sure clients pay on time."

In this part . . .

Wouldn't life be easier if you could predict the future? You'd never second-guess any of your decisions again. We have some good news: although you can't predict the future with 100 per cent accuracy, you can *prepare* yourself for the future. And planning for the future – whether in life or in business – is a great way to cut down on all the second-guessing that comes later.

In this part, we help your company look to the future. We prepare you for change by looking closely at where changes are likely to come from. We talk about how you can anticipate changes ahead of time, assessing what effect these changes will have on your business, and how likely they are to really happen.

Of course, you don't necessarily have to accept the future that you predict, so we help you shape your own future by thinking strategically. We introduce tried-and-true business strategies that have worked in the past, and show you how to create your own company strategy for the future. Finally, we explore different ways your business can grow. We look at ways to extend your product line, expand into new markets, and branch out into brand new businesses.

Chapter 12

Preparing for Change

· ·

In This Chapter

▶ Defining the dimensions of change

▶ Tracking economic, government, technology, and cultural trends

▶ Anticipating changes

▶ Using trend forecasting and scenario planning

▶ Assessing the effects of change

▶ Making use of probabilities and impacts

· ·

*L*ife is defined by change. When we get up in the morning, we expect to live through a day that's different in all sorts of ways from the day before. As far as we know, only Bill Murray in the film *Groundhog Day* ever had to live the same day over and over again, and it almost drove him crazy.

All of us expect change. At one time or another, no doubt, each of us has said, 'I really need a change.' But you don't often hear people say that they *want* a change or *like* change. Change makes things uncertain, uncertainty makes planning difficult, and people like to plan. (After all, you are reading this book.)

Companies don't want or like change, either, and they have come up with hundreds of excuses for trying to keep things just the way they are. Following are some of the top excuses:

✔ It's never been tried before.

✔ We tried it before.

✔ It's too radical.

✔ It's working fine as it is.

✔ We don't have the time.

✔ We're not ready for it.

✔ We can't take a chance.

✔ Our company's different.

✔ We should, but . . .

✔ It's impossible.

Although companies try to avoid change, they can never escape it, because change is what makes a market work in the first place. Change is the necessary evil that allows companies to form and grow, products and services to get better, competitors to come from everywhere, and customers to go on shopping. In a competitive marketplace, if you stop changing, you die. Harsh, but true.

Good companies understand this fact but often have a hard time acting on it when they become successful – maybe because they have more at stake. The original Footsie 100, first calculated in 1984, represents the biggest British companies. Today, only a few of the original companies are still on the list, and many are in completely different businesses.

Across all industries, the list of companies whose stars have dimmed continues to grow:

✔ Silver Reed (outstanding manual typewriters)

✔ Sinclair Computers (built the personal-calculator market)

✔ Land Rover and Aston Martin (now subsidiaries of BMW and Ford, respectively)

✔ GEC (the colossus of UK electronic engineering metamorphosed into Marconi and all but disappeared for ever)

In this chapter, we try to prepare you for change. We start by defining the elements of change, including economic, technological, governmental, and cultural trends. We go on to look at ways in which you can anticipate change by forecasting those trends and creating alternative scenarios. We also show you how to assess the possible effects of change.

Defining the Dimensions of Change

Events and forces that are beyond your control continuously change the business conditions around you. You can't fiddle with the laws of physics or human nature, but you must keep track of changes as they're taking place. The experts would say that you're doing *environmental scans* – not the kind that the UK Government does with the Health and Safety Executive, but the kind that look at anything that might affect your business situation.

Although thousands of factors can influence your business environment, you can simplify matters by looking at only the ones shown in Figure 12-1. (For the details, check out the following sections.) When radical changes threaten to reshape your business, it's safe to bet that you should look more closely at broad economic, technological, governmental, or cultural trends.

Economic trends

A bank account, a mortgage, a car loan, and credit cards seem to be relatively straightforward financial arrangements, which we all take advantage of every day. When combined, these financial arrangements create the glue that holds our economy together. It's not surprising that the economy, on a large scale, is complex and complicated, but the biggest mystery in economics is why no one seems to understand the basic forces at work.

Calculating to fail

It's not just the big slow-moving companies that get swept away by change. Did you ever hear of Sinclair's pocket calcululcators? In 1971, Clive Sinclair, then the boss of a tiny Cambridge hi-fi company, returned from a visit to Texas Instruments in America armed with a new integrated circuit chip. He used this revolutionary piece of circuitry to invent the world's first pocket calculator. Up until that point, calculators had been clumsy, deskbound things, which relied on mains power. His single chip calculator, which was born after six months' research, was pocket-sized as opposed to hand-held. Using the same PMOS chip as the American hand-held calculator, which required large batteries owing to the heavy demand the PMOS chip made on its power supply, Sinclair found a

way of cutting the power consumption by about 20 times. This meant that a truly hand-held calculator was possible. Sinclair Radionics made it and started the calculator boom with 'The Executive', earning £2.5 million in export revenue alone. At the time, Sinclair had a staff of about 60. By 1977, Sinclair had become world famous as a calculator manufacturer, and the 'Cambridge' programmable outsold all programmable and scientific calculators.

What happened? You guessed it: The world changed. Competitors saw a lucrative market and responded to the changing tastes of calculator users. HP and Texas Instruments quickly captured and dominated the market, whilst Sinclair was distracted with his Black Watch, C5 electric car, and portable computer.

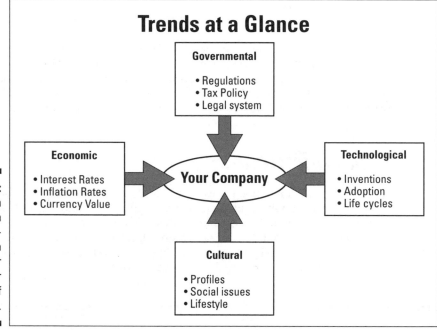

Figure 12-1:
You can
break an
environ-
mental scan
into four
major
groups of
trends.

Economics involves numbers, which are called *indicators*. Indicators include inflation rates, growth rates, interest rates, blah, blah, blah – the list goes on and on. Fortunately, you need to focus on only four key economic indicators, which reflect major trends in the economy:

✔ Gross Domestic Product, or GDP (the total value of the nation's annual production of goods and services)

✔ Interest rates (the cost of borrowing money)

✔ Inflation rates (the rate at which prices go up)

✔ Currency value (the value of a nation's money in the international arena)

Dealing with economic uncertainty can be difficult, but economic trends are important enough that you have to keep track of them, even if your information is incomplete. What numbers should you keep your eye on? The answer depends on your business. We outline a number of trends and help you figure out the important ones you need to be aware of.

GDP. The GDP (short for Gross Domestic Product) is the total value of a country's annual production of goods and services, and it is the broadest measure of the economy. You probably want to keep track of the change in

GDP from year to year, because that change reflects what's happening with the economy. Moderate, consistent growth in the GDP generally produces a healthy economy, with expanding opportunities for many businesses. A drop in the GDP, on the other hand, often leads to lower demand for products and services, increased competition, and lower profits for everyone.

You can't always generalise about the GDP, though. Businesses can go bankrupt even when the economy is booming, and even in the worst of times, the entertainment industry rakes in cash. Don't rely completely on the GDP; also look at how your industry and your company is performing within the larger economy.

Interest rates. Interest rates are simply the cost of renting money – how much you have to pay a bank, for example, to use its cash for a certain period. Short-term rates apply when you borrow money for periods ranging from a month to two years. Long-term rates apply to loans that extend all the way out to 25-year home mortgages. As you can imagine, the cost of money affects every facet of the economy, from consumer spending to business expansion.

In the UK, short-term interest rates are pretty much set by the Bank of England, the bank that holds the nation's bank account. With the rise of the almighty credit card, short-term rates influence shopping habits, which means that if you're thinking about starting a retail business, you have to pay special attention to short-term interest rates.

Long-term interest rates rise and fall in the corporate and government bond markets. Long-term rates have a major impact on how easy it is for consumers to afford houses, cars, and anything else that's big and expensive, because these items are usually financed with long-term loans. Long-term rates, therefore, affect consumer demand for expensive items. Long-term rates also affect business decisions such as building big new factories and buying expensive new equipment.

Inflation rates. Inflation, which is a continuous rise in wages and prices, is a nasty habit that economies often suffer from. Consumers are the first to know when inflation rears its ugly head, because prices go up and money just doesn't buy as much as it used to.

When inflation is high, companies find that things are more expensive for them as well. They have to pay more for everything from materials to employees' wages and benefits. Investors turn their attention to things that have intrinsic value, such as gold, property, and art – anything that will protect them against money that's worth less and less. Consumers may borrow more money, partly to pay the higher prices and partly because they can pay back today's cash with money that's not going to be worth as much. Lenders know what's happening, so interest rates go up. All these factors tend to be a real drag on the economy over time, and inflation can lead to a recession if it's left untreated.

Not all companies suffer equally from inflation, however. If you're in the business of mining precious metal, pumping oil, or selling property, for example, you can often do quite well during a period of inflation. You have to balance the broad economic trend against its effect on your own company.

Currency value. In the past, the value of the pound against the US dollar, the Euro, or the Japanese yen was something that only the biggest multinational companies ever had to worry about, because economies didn't rely much on the economies of other countries. That's no longer the case. In today's global economy, the rise or fall of the pound can have an enormous impact on your entire industry. Your suppliers, competitors, and customers may be anywhere in the world, no matter what industry you're in or how small your company is.

Currencies change their relative values daily for all sorts of reasons. As a result, short-term fluctuations in the value of the pound, say, are unpredictable. The effects of longer-term currency trends, on the other hand, are a little easier to predict.

When the value of the pound is relatively low, for example, British goods turn into bargains, so consumers around the world have a little extra incentive to buy British. To compete, foreign competitors have to lower their own prices (and watch profits go down) or see their share of the market get smaller. These companies also have a third option: come to Britain, build plants, and produce products to take advantage of the weak pound.

The reverse is also true. A strong pound leads to bargain prices on foreign products, a shift toward imports, and sometimes the relocation of UK companies abroad to take advantage of cheaper foreign currencies.

Technological trends

You can argue that technology is good, technology is bad, or technology is ugly. But no matter which side you're on, everyone agrees that technology means change. In the past 150 years, we've gone from horse and carts to space shuttles and from the mail coach to the Internet.

But every new technology that comes along isn't guaranteed to change the world overnight. You could produce a weekly TV show on the world's funniest inventions. For the most part, the technologies that finally make it have been around for quite some time. No matter how fast a new technology takes over from the old, it usually follows a *diffusion curve* – which traces how a new technology catches on in an industry (see Figure 12-2).

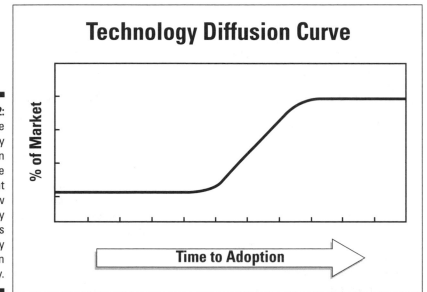

Figure 12-2:
The
technology
diffusion
curve
shows that
when a new
technology
finally takes
off, it usually
catches on
rapidly.

The diffusion curve demonstrates that it always takes a certain amount of time for any new technology to take off. When (and if) it does catch on, the technology usually sweeps through an industry quickly, because companies don't want to be left behind. The technology reaches a plateau when most of the companies that planned to adopt the new technology have done so.

Failing to adopt a new technology that's sweeping your industry can be disastrous. The advent of audio CD technology, for example, put most manufacturers of vinyl records, turntables, and diamond-tipped needles out of business in a couple of years. But not all technologies live up to their early press. Just look at nuclear power and its promise of cheap, clean, unlimited energy. Plenty of the utilities that jumped on that bandwagon now find themselves saddled with hugely expensive nuclear plants – and little to show for it.

For the majority of new technologies that come along, reality lies somewhere between eureka and potential disaster. Think about the electronics industry – transistors succeeded but did not kill off their older cousins, vacuum tubes. The older technology managed to hang in there, because for certain applications, tubes are still preferred. After funeral services were held for radios (supposed to be replaced by television), glasses (considered to be outdated with the advent of contact lenses), and razor blades (not much use in the world of electric razors), these industries all turned around and actually grew. Radio stations are some of the hottest properties around, designer eyewear is definitely in, and sales of safety razors never stopped expanding.

What do these examples all say about trends in technology? Although each industry is different, a few generalisations come to mind:

- ✔ Older technologies often have time to adjust to innovations.
- ✔ Older technologies can get better even after they're mature.
- ✔ New technologies usually begin by focusing on specialised markets.
- ✔ New technologies can create new customers, expanding the marketplace.
- ✔ Old and new technologies often live together for many years.

It's hard to predict when a new technology is going to come along, and you can't even say for certain what's going to happen when it arrives. Computer printers are a perfect example of changing technologies. Not too many years ago, four major technologies were represented in that marketplace, each in a different stage of its *technology life cycle* – a four-stage process that every new technology goes through. Laser printers were just being released, inkjet printers were in their growth stage, daisywheel printers were in a mature market, and printer-ball printers (typewriter-style) were in slow decline.

To prepare yourself for possible changes in technology and their potential effects on your industry, review the major technologies that are currently in use. For each technology, do the following things:

- ✔ Find out which research laboratories specialise in the technology and what technical journals and publications cover and report on it. Make sure that you check out academic, private, and government institutions.
- ✔ Attend major conventions and scientific meetings on the technology, and subscribe to any relevant journals and publications.
- ✔ Monitor press releases on the technology, and keep track of patents that are filed in the field.
- ✔ Compare your company's capability to adapt to and apply the technology relative to that of your key competitors.
- ✔ On a regular basis, reexamine the likelihood of a fundamental technological breakthrough, and check the status of small, step-by-step process improvements in the technology.

Although technologies within your own industry may be unpredictable, you can at least track them over time and take them into account as you create your business plan. The technology advances in unfamiliar areas, however, have the potential to bite you before you know what's happened. When Xerox introduced its first copier in 1959, it pretty much stopped mimeograph machine makers cold. When Sinclair came out with his hand-held calculator in 1971, with Hewlett Packard hot on his heels, slide-rule manufacturers took a fast slide into oblivion. So you want to make a point of keeping your eye on technology trends beyond your immediate industry. That way, you'll be better prepared for changes in your business that might come at you from out of the blue.

UK and EU governmental trends

We're not going to grab any headlines by reminding you that government has a profound effect on your company, no matter what industry you're in. From the rules and regulations that it issues to the tax policies and legal system that it supports, the government is a major player in your marketplace. Because of its sheer size and impact, there's a continuing national debate on how large, how wide, and how deeply involved government should be in the day-to-day running of our economy.

No matter which side of the more-or-less-government debate you're on, you don't have much choice but to keep track of where the discussion is heading. Government actions at any level – local, national, and EU – can rapidly and dramatically alter your business environment.

What kinds of issues should you be watching for? Topics that arouse public opinion and finally lead to some sort of government reaction seem to have an eight-year cycle. During the first five years, nothing much happens. Oh, the issue may come up in an article here or an opinion poll there. But it's usually not until around the sixth year that the national press picks up on it in a serious way and mounting public pressure finally results in some sort of government legislation. The earlier you spot a smouldering issue that may affect you, the more time you'll have to prepare a response. The following companies have done just that.

✔ In May 2003, Rolls Royce had to change its corporate structure to prepare for planned accounting changes that the government aimed to introduce five years later. FRS 17, as the rule is known, could curtail the company's ability to keep paying dividends at 2003 levels.

✔ In the spring of 2003, after 40 years of continuous service, the 'meals on wheels' service aimed at housebound pensioners and those too ill to cook for themselves looked set to change out of all recognition. The government mooted plans to give service users credits to be spent buying takeaway meals from local Chinese, Indian, and pizza outlets. The aim was to provide more choice for users, but the result would be vastly increased trade for local takeaways.

> ✔ In 2003 sweeping plans to eradicate sex discrimination in areas ranging from medical insurance to pension payments were being drawn up by the European Union. The proposals looked set to bring big changes to the way insurance premiums are calculated, which traditionally had discriminated by, for example, giving men higher annuities as their life expectancy is shorter. Whilst insurers drew up robust responses, they also drew up plans to live with the new legislation, should it become law.

What parts of 'government' should you pay most attention to? Government can be thought of as having four major levels – the EU (European Union), national government, local government, and the judiciary – and each can affect your company.

The European Union. The European Union was formally established on 1 November 1993. It is the most recent in a series of European cooperative organisations that originated with the European Coal and Steel Community (ECSC) of 1951, which became the European Community (EC) in 1967.

The EU countries cooperate in three areas, often referred to as pillars. At the heart of this system is the EC pillar with its supranational functions and its governing institutions. The EC pillar is flanked by two other pillars, Common Foreign and Security Policy (CFSP) and Justice and Home Affairs (JHA).

Now, all the unpopular legislation coming out of the EU, or from 'Brussels', as it's known, influences every aspect of corporate life from the hours you can expect people to work, to the wording of your job advertisement. Its rules impact on how you can produce and distribute products and even on how you can protect ideas and inventions.

How might the EU's agenda influence the future of your industry?

National government. Westminster, the shorthand for government in the UK, still holds sway over most legislation and still has some influence over how Brussels' rules and regulations should be enacted, if at all. In the Thatcher years, the aim was to lower taxes, slim back public services, and get out of industries' way. The Blair government is on a diametrically opposite tack. Taxes have risen in the UK, whilst in many other European countries they have contracted. The government is the largest consumer of advertising and consultancy services, amongst many others. 'Inclusion' is a Blair government watchword and policies abound to help single mothers get back to work, to encourage entrepreneurs to start up, and to aid various disadvantaged groups, for example. The government has dramatically increased spending on health and education services, with an enormous spin off of extra business to companies in those sectors. Today, legislatures in Wales and Scotland have assumed some of the central government's powers.

How do you think the government's agenda might impact on your industry?

Local government. When London's mayor, Ken Livingston, introduced his congestion charge soaking every central London visitor with a £5-a-day bill, it wasn't long before easyCar entrepreneur Stelios Haji-Ionnau's car rental business took a bath. The car hire market in central London dipped substantially. Mr Haji-Ionnau cited 'Red Ken's' tax as the primary reason for laying of half his London staff, reducing opening hours from 16 to 8 a day, and trimming back his fleet of 3,500 cars.

Local governments can be either councils or authorities at the county, borough, or district level. Local councils are controlled by laws and policies established by the central government, particularly concerning budgets and spending. Councils at the local level in Britain are responsible for police and fire services, roads, traffic, housing, building regulations, libraries, environmental issues, and schools paid for by direct grants from central authorities.

Judiciary. Britain has a long judicial history. The British legal system relies on common law, which is based on custom and on decisions in previous legal cases, called precedents. Common law originated in the 12th century, growing out of the rules and traditions that ordinary people had worked out over time. Through the centuries common law evolved as it incorporated legal decisions made in specific cases, and it remains the basis of British law except when superseded by legislation. The responsibility of reviewing legislation to determine its constitutionality falls to Parliament.

The Law Lords, the final court of appeal, decided that the Equitable Life insurance company, for example, did not treat all its members as equal, having given one group special rights in terms of guaranteed pension annuities. This decision in effect caused the business to cease taking in new business and all but close its doors.

Although we focus here on the UK government, the governments of other countries can create just as many complications.

You may need a little help in picking out the government activities and trends that are most likely to affect your own business environment. Almost every industry has a trade association, along with an industry newsletter or two. There are also local Chambers of Commerce. These organisations devote much of their time and resources to keeping tabs on – and influencing – what's going on at all levels of government. Check in with your trade association or Chambers of Commerce from time to time.

Cultural trends

Take two frogs and a pan. Place the pan on the stove and bring a small amount of water to boil. Drop one of the frogs into the pan. The frog will most likely jump out of the pan, onto the floor, and out the door. Let it go.

The juice on Jewson's

For decades, Jewson's operated a chain of old-fashioned building-supply shops in Cambridgeshire. Their first provisions shop opened in 1836, but they quickly changed tack and concentrated on meeting the needs of the fast-growing army of self-employed contractors or small-time builders, who sprang up on the back of the wealth created by the industrial revolution. Then, in the late 1970s, the company recognised an emerging trend that the company was ill-prepared for: the growing ranks of do-it-yourselfer. These people weren't at all like Jewson's traditional customers. They didn't know what they were doing, they expected a great deal of helpful advice, and they wanted lots of options.

Jewson's prepared for change. Today, you can find its 440 stores throughout the whole country. The stores don't look anything like they once did; most of them have been built or extensively refurbished over the past decade or so. Inside, you can find doors, windows, cupboards, counters, fixtures, wood, tools, plumbing materials, bathroom fittings . . . you name it. If you need help, you can take advantage of kitchen planners, interior designers, and even gardening and landscape experts, all for free.

Today, more than 60 per cent of Jewson's customers are retail buyers rather than contractors. Many of the customers are women and they come back because of the service that they receive. Customer service is a top priority, and every employee receives extensive and continuous training. Their 10,000 staff members have all been chosen for their knowledge and experience witin all trades. Their customers can approach them with any query, rely on their advice and know that they are getting the best service available.

Place the pan back on the stove, this time filled with cold water and the second frog. As the water slowly heats, the frog sits there agreeably, never noticing that the temperature's rising. (Don't try this experiment at home unless you're planning to have frogs' legs for dinner.) The moral? When you ignore the slow changes that are taking place around you, you boil.

Cultural changes don't happen overnight (after all, the greying of the Baby Boomers has taken many years). But the glacial speed of these trends reflects the glacial forces that lie behind them. The real danger lies in ignoring these trends simply because you can always worry about them later. Well, later always gets here sooner than you realise. Consider the cultural shifts described in the following sections.

Demographic changes. *Demographics* refers to the general profile of a specific population – anything from your company's customers to the citizens of a nation. Demographic data include things that you might find in a national census form, such as age, gender, and family size.

Changes in the profile of a nation are bound to have profound effects on its economy and business. Western Europe, Japan, and the United States, for example, are all trying to come to terms with the slow aging of their populations. Their governments have to figure out how to take care of all these older people, and companies are scurrying around trying to figure out how to sell them things.

Social changes. A society is made up of the combined values, customs, and traditions that its people hold in common. Social behaviour changes over time, of course, but people tend to give up their traditions slowly and grudgingly. American children still have the the summer off from school, for example, even though the children are no longer usually needed to help in the fields.

But what happens to customs and traditions as the population changes – as people move from place to place, as families start to look different, and as new citizens bring their own customs and traditions? Any change in broad social behaviour, no matter how slowly it occurs, can have a dramatic effect on your company and on industries across the economy.

Lifestyle changes. Changes in the way people live their lives affect how they work, what they buy, how they play, and where they live. About ten or 15 years ago, for example, the health-and-fitness craze caught on in the UK. Today, the industry includes the makers of sports shoes, sportswear, exercise equipment, tennis rackets, mountain bikes, kayaks, yogurt, diet drinks, bottled water, and many other products.

Other major lifestyle changes that affect all sorts of industries include:

- Growing gender equality in every area
- At-home companies and telecommuting
- At-home shopping, education, and entertainment
- Multiple-career professionals
- Alternative family units
- Workers who continue to work past retirement age
- Workers who opt for early retirement

When you define the dimensions of change, you have to look at trends in a number of areas:

- In a competitive marketplace, if you ignore change, you lose.
- The four major dimensions of change are economic, technological, governmental, and cultural trends.

✔ To track economic changes, keep an eye on the Gross Domestic Product, interest rates, inflation rates, and currency value.

✔ Technological changes are driven by the diffusion of innovation (how fast new technologies catch on).

✔ When the government changes its mind on regulation, taxes, or spending, shock waves can transform entire industries.

✔ Cultural trends are like glaciers – slow-moving but powerful enough to flatten you if you don't pay attention.

Anticipating Change

Obviously, it's hard just to keep track of what's going on all around you, never mind trying to anticipate what's going to happen in the future. The point is not to predict the future, however; we'll leave that to the palm readers and the people who gaze into crystal balls. The point is to have a better understanding of what *may* happen so that you can be better prepared than your competition.

To do that, you need to sort out which of the many trends – economic, technological, governmental, and cultural – are going to turn into the megatrends that will make tomorrow's entrepreneurs rich. What trends will influence your industry, your strategies, and the competition?

Start by turning to the professionals and seeing what they have to say. Scan the publications that make it their business to follow these trends. After a while, you can judge which of them are most useful. Along with *The Economist* and *The Financial Times,* try *The Wall Street Journal, Business Week, Forbes,* and *New Scientist* among others.

You should also check out organisations that specialise in the future, including The Centre for Policy Studies (CPS), The Fabian Society, and the Policy Studies Institute in the UK and The Aspen Institute, Global Business Network, Foresight Institute, Institute of the Future, and Millennium Institute in the US.

Trend forecasting

You can use several tricks of the trade to peer into the future and see whether a particular trend is likely to continue. Given the nature of the challenge, however, you may not want to rely on any one of these tricks too heavily. Each approach provides its own unique look forward.

Extrapolation

Sometimes, you can use mathematical sleight of hand to project a historical trend into the future. This process, called *extrapolation,* works particularly well for trends that aren't changing rapidly and can be measured in numbers. The idea's fairly simple: You take your favourite trend (the inflation rate, for example) and assume that it's going to change in exactly the same way as it has in the past. Certain economic measurements, customer profiles, and even a few technology trends are likely candidates for extrapolation.

The easiest way to extrapolate a trend is to find someone who's already done it for you, which means tracking down a magazine article or an academic paper. But don't despair if you have to do the job yourself. Computers make the job much easier, and the current crop of spreadsheet programs have buttons that you can click to generate an extrapolation. You need historical data to get started, of course.

Any sudden changes in a trend really mess up your extrapolation. Unfortunately, many trends are getting less and less predictable these days, which makes forecasting more difficult – and the abrupt changes are exactly the ones your business needs to know about ahead of time. Judgement forecasting and Delphi studies may help you predict some of these changes.

Judgement forecasting

Judgement forecasting relies on the information, experience, and gut feelings of the people in and around your company to predict specific trends. Use a short questionnaire or a brainstorming session to get your managers, employees, and even suppliers and customers to give you their judgements about where trends are likely to head.

Judgement forecasting isn't mathematical; you can use it to make predictions about things that can't be described in terms of numbers. You should do some sort of judgement forecasting periodically, just so that you can stay one step ahead of the most recent events and changes in your business environment.

Delphi study

A *Delphi study* is a set of questionnaires that you put together to send to a group of experts when you have a particular question about the future. Then you summarise the answers and send the questionnaires out again to get another set of responses. A Delphi study is really a way to bring in the big guns without having to get them together in the same room.

Suppose that you want to forecast trends in the use of solar energy to heat, cool, and provide electricity for entire housing developments. You know that the issue is best addressed by experts in the solar-energy field. Ideally, you'd like to bring a group of these experts together for a face-to-face discussion of the issues, but that meeting would cost big bucks and would be hard to organise. Instead, you can use a Delphi study. Follow these steps:

1. **Send a questionnaire to each of your experts, asking for his or her judgement on an issue.**

   For this example, the issue is solar energy and the feasibility of solar-driven housing developments in the future.

2. **Read the completed questionnaires when the experts return them to you.**

3. **Summarise the experts' forecasts, including majority judgements, minority opinions, and any dissenting views.**

4. **Send the summary back to each of the experts, along with a second copy of the questionnaire.**

   You ask the experts to review the first-round summary and then fill out and return the questionnaires again. Some experts may alter their original judgements and respond to new issues and concerns that are raised.

5. **Continue the process of responding and getting feedback until you're satisfied that a consensus has been reached.**

Scenario planning

Sometimes trends are too unpredictable or too numerous to track, so you can't project a single view of the future that seems to make any sense. *Scenario planning* allows you to imagine several complete versions of the future and consider how each version might affect your company's fortunes.

Start with a trend (the inflation rate, for example), and think about how you might create two or three alternative scenarios, based on different levels of inflation in the future. (For more information on inflation, refer to the section 'Economic trends' earlier in this chapter.) Try to include a fairly complete description of what your business environment might look like in each case.

Don't be too surprised if you feel the need to introduce another important trend into your scenario. Maybe your company's future is also tied to government regulations that are to be announced sometime in the next five years; you can put together another set of scenarios that involve those regulations. But if you have three possibilities for regulation, with three possible levels of inflation, you now have nine scenarios to juggle. Obviously, this situation can get out of hand rather quickly.

Experienced scenario jugglers are quick to point out the wisdom of working with no more than three or four scenarios at a time. Rather than add trend after trend into a growing set of scenarios, limit yourself to three complete scenarios based on different views of your industry in the future:

✔ A scenario based on an optimistic view

✔ A scenario based on a pessimistic view

✔ A scenario based on the most likely view

You may decide that low inflation, minimum regulation, and a technology breakthrough create an optimistic scenario, while high inflation, heavy regulation, and no technology breakthroughs are the pessimistic view. The most likely view probably falls somewhere in between.

You may decide to create a business plan for the future by looking backward and doing what you've always done in the past. That method is easy, comfortable – and dangerous. Scenario planning isn't meant to predict the future; its real value lies in offering you new options and a wider range of possibilities to think about. Different business scenarios stimulate your imagination and bring to life compelling glimpses of your company's future.

✔ Effective plans don't have to predict the future, but they do have to anticipate change.

✔ One way to forecast trends is to go by the numbers, using mathematical tricks such as extrapolation.

✔ You can look to the smart people around you to brainstorm and make judgements about what the future holds.

✔ When you have too many uncertainties, try several scenarios: optimistic, pessimistic, and most likely.

Assessing the Effects of Change

All sorts of changes take place around you all the time. Some of the changes have a big effect on your company; you scarcely notice others. Some of the changes are obvious and predictable; others come out of nowhere. The critical questions for your company are:

✔ Which changes will actually take place?

✔ What do the changes mean for your industry?

✔ What do the changes do to your company?

Rolling the dice

What are the odds that something – a specific event, a particular activity, a given scenario – will actually occur in the future? Fortunately, you don't have to dust off the crystal ball just yet. *Probability theory* is a respectable branch of mathematics that's been around for a long time. Probabilities are important, because they give you a rough idea about the likelihood that a prediction will come true.

You probably understand more about probability theory than you think. If you toss a coin, for example, you probably have a gut feeling that half the time, you'll get heads. The odds of getting heads, then, are 1 in 2. What other probabilities can you come up with? Here are some coin-tossing odds:

- ✔ Probability of tossing heads: 1 in 2

- ✔ Probability of tossing two heads in a row: 1 in 4

- ✔ After tossing three heads in a row, probability of tossing another heads: 1 in 2

These probabilities are all based on something called *random statistics*. Every time you toss a coin, the outcome is going to be random; it doesn't depend on anything else that happened before or around it. That's why it doesn't matter whether you've already tossed three heads in a row; your next toss is still random, and tossing heads is still a 50–50 possibility.

But many activities and events aren't at all random. The weather, for example, is certainly unpredictable and subject to change (that's why we talk about it so much). But weather is not random; it's influenced by all sorts of factors and forces. What's the probability that the thermometer will hit the 30 C mark tomorrow? The answer depends on your location and the season. The probability is higher in summer than in winter, and higher still during a heatwave.

Many of the business trends that we look at in this chapter behave much like the weather; they're unpredictable and subject to change, but not random. The probability that inflation, for example, is going to reach a certain level over the next six months depends on past inflation rates as well as on underlying factors that include economic demand, factory output levels, and wage pressures. That's why the experts tell us that they can forecast inflation, and their track records are about as good as those of weather reporters. Still, everybody's interested in forecasts, because they're better than guesses.

Win or lose

The impact that a trend or an event will have on your business tells you just how hopeful or worried you should be if predictions actually do come true. A trend may be the best thing to happen to one industry and a complete disaster for another. An event may create a major opportunity for your company or have no noticeable effect at all.

Review your own business trends and scenarios, and place significant events or possible outcomes in one of the four probability/impact categories shown in Figure 12-3. Each category requires a different level of planning and preparation on your part:

- ✔ High probability, high impact events demand careful preparation.
- ✔ High probability, low impact events call for routine planning.
- ✔ Low probability, high impact events require contingency planning.
- ✔ Low probability, low impact events suggest routine monitoring.

Figure 12-3:
The
Probability
and Impact
Grid divides
events into
categories
based on
how likely
they are
to occur
and what
effect they
may have.

Probability and Impact Grid

Probability

	Low	High	
Impact	Contingency Planning	Careful Preparation	High
	Routine Monitoring	Routine Planning	Low

If you need help figuring out which trends and scenarios belong in which categories, you can always open your wallet to the experts. But first, see what you can do on your own. Get together a group of your colleagues and maybe one or two of your best customers for a brainstorming session on the future of your company. You may be surprised by the insights that can come out of this kind of get-together when you start the ball rolling. Here's what you do:

1. **Give the group a fixed amount of time to review the trends and scenarios that you come up with and to throw in any new ones of their own.**

2. **Have someone make a list as the group generates ideas.**

3. **Put the complete list of trends and scenarios in front of the group.**

4. **Rank trends and scenarios, based on their potential to affect your company's future.**

5. **Rank these trends and scenarios again, this time in terms of the probability that they will actually occur.**

6. **Divide the trends and scenarios into the four probability/impact categories (refer to Figure 12-3).**

The Probability and Impact Grid tells you where to concentrate your efforts. Putting the trends and scenarios that you come up with in probability/impact categories gives you a place to begin. You can prepare for change, allocate time and resources, and plan for possible events based on a practical combination of probabilities and potential effects on your company.

✔ It's not enough just to predict change; you also have to figure out what it means for your company.

✔ Probabilities tell you the likelihood that your best guess will come true.

✔ By weighing the impact of your best guess, you know whether to be excited, worried, or unconcerned.

✔ Looking at probability and impact together gives you a better idea of how to plan.

Chapter 13

Thinking Strategically

• •

In This Chapter

▶ Discovering why strategy can make a difference

▶ Exploring the low-cost leadership strategy

▶ Applying differentiation strategies

▶ Focusing on a focus strategy

▶ Examining other strategic alternatives

▶ Coming up with your own strategy

• •

*I*n this chapter, we help you formulate a strategy for your company that's in keeping with its basic mission. First, we explore why strategy is so important to the business-planning process. We examine what it means to have a strategy and when that strategy works best, and introduce several basic strategies that you can apply across many industries. These off-the-shelf strategies include efforts

✔ To be the low-cost provider

✔ To differentiate your products

✔ To focus on specific market and product areas

We talk about several other general strategic alternatives as well, answering questions such as 'What does it mean to become more vertically integrated as a company?' and 'How should you act when you're the market leader or a market follower?' We also give you some pointers about creating a strategic blueprint for your own company.

Making Strategy Make a Difference

Some companies think that *strategy* and *planning* are four-letter words. Those companies would never think of using either term in the context of their own organisations. It isn't that these companies don't move forward; it's just that they don't talk much about it ahead of time. So why do the two terms have such bad reputations in certain quarters? More than likely, it's because they've been misunderstood or applied incorrectly. *Strategy* and *planning* have become such buzzwords in today's business world that their real meanings are easily lost in all the muddle surrounding them.

The colourful and outspoken Wall Street trader Alan 'Ace' Greenberg, head of the Bear Stearns brokerage house, is no fan of strategic planning. He has even gone so far as to suggest that because strategic plans have such poor track records, he should establish a Backward Planning Committee to guarantee his company's success. What a card. Still, although Greenberg won't give business planners the time of day, it's clear that he has a strong personal vision, strategy, and plan to make Bear Stearns successful over the long haul.

At the opposite end of the playing field from Ace Greenberg is a fictional character named Joe Clueless, who doesn't give a hoot about the future. Joe doesn't have a personal vision or a strategy. He doesn't have his own plan, because he's an opportunist. Maybe he's in the right place at the right time, right now. But no one can consistently survive on short-term breaks alone. As the old saying goes:

> *Luck sometimes visits a fool, but it never sits down with him for long.*

The process of strategic planning creates a framework and a discipline to guide those of us who find ourselves somewhere in between Ace, who has built-in business radar, and Joe, who can't be bothered. We know that strategic planning works, because we've seen it with our own eyes. We've also seen where a lack of strategic planning can lead. A 2000 survey of close to 500 small companies backs us up; it found that companies that have strategic plans have 50 per cent more revenue and profit growth than companies that fail to plan. It's that simple.

What strategy means

The word *strategy* comes to us from the ancient Greeks and translates literally as *the art of generalship*. When you compete, you probably feel that you're suiting up for battle, jousting with your competitors for the hearts and minds of customers.

Modern definitions of the word are even less precise, so we're proposing our own standard definition of *strategy* in the business arena. A strategy does the following things:

- Describes how to reach the goals and objectives that you set for the company
- Takes into account the personal and social values that surround your company

✔ Guides the way that you allocate and deploy your human and financial resources

✔ Creates an advantage in the marketplace that you can sustain, despite intense and determined competition

Putting together a strategic business plan requires you to gather data, analyse the information, and then do something with it – something more than just reformatting it, printing it, and packaging it in a tidy report titled 'The Five-year Plan'. In most cases, that kind of report begins and ends with numbers – revenue projections, cash flows, expense allocations, and the like, which are things that don't help you figure out what to do next. Reports like this are sure to fall victim to the dreaded SPOTS (Strategic Plans on Top Shelves) syndrome: they gather dust and little else. These reports don't represent strategy or planning; they represent a waste of time.

What can you do to make sure that this doesn't happen to your business plan? For one thing, a healthy dose of plain old common sense works wonders as you pull all the pieces together to create your strategy. Experience in your industry and some nous are advantages, too. Unfortunately, we can't give you any of these gifts. But we can offer you some solid advice about laying out your strategy, including some hints that make you look like a planning pro.

Keep the following questions in mind as you begin to formulate your strategic plan:

✔ What markets and segments does your company plan to compete in?

✔ Which products and services will your company develop and support?

✔ Where is your company's competitive advantage in these markets and products?

✔ How will your company sustain that competitive advantage over time?

The answers that you come up with go a long way toward keeping your strategy focused and on target, so you want to return to them from time to time at each phase of the planning process.

When strategy works

Strategy works when you have a process to ensure that planning is consistently tied to the ongoing operations of your business. If strategic plans fail, it's usually because they don't seem to be relevant to the issues and problems at hand. Strategy and planning get linked with committee meetings, bureaucracy, overheads, and all those other barriers that are thrown up to ensure that results aren't achieved. As a result, strategy and planning are seen by some companies as a part of the problem, not a solution.

Strategy works best when strategic planning is integrated into every aspect of your business, every day of the week and every week of the year. An ongoing strategic-planning process means that you do the following things:

- ✔ Always question what makes your company successful.
- ✔ Continually observe customers and markets, tracking their wants and needs.
- ✔ Relentlessly examine the competition and what it's up to.
- ✔ Steadily work at maintaining your competitive advantage.
- ✔ Continually search for ways to leverage your core competence (check out Chapter 9 for the definition of core competence).

Some managers may do all these things automatically and intuitively. But if you want to make sure that strategy and planning are carried out in all parts of your company, you have to create a framework to ensure that it happens. When you make strategic planning a basic responsibility, you get the added benefit of including all levels of employees in the planning process. Employees often have different and equally valuable viewpoints about shaping strategy, and a strategic-planning framework ensures that their voices are heard.

To start the ball rolling in your own company, pull together a group of employees who represent different functions and various levels in your organisation. Meet on a regular basis to talk about strategy and planning. Concentrate on how to set up a framework to promote strategic thinking, and focus on problems associated with the strategic-planning process itself. Then group members can take what they learn back to their own areas and begin to integrate strategic planning into the way that they do business.

- ✔ Strategy is the art and science of creating a business plan that meets your company's goals and objectives.
- ✔ Strategy works best when strategic planning is integrated into every aspect of your business.
- ✔ Don't fall victim to the SPOTS (Strategic Plans on Top Shelves) syndrome.
- ✔ On average, small companies that have strategic plans have 50 per cent higher revenue and profit growth than companies that fail to plan.

Applying Off-the-Shelf Strategies

Maybe you think your company's situation is absolutely unique and the issues you face are one-of-a-kind. Does this mean that your strategy and business plan have to be unique as well? Not entirely. If you look through a microscope, every snowflake is different. But snowflakes have a great deal in common when you stand back and watch them pile up outside. Companies are like snowflakes. Although all the details give companies their individual profiles, companies and industries in general display remarkable similarities when you step back and concentrate on their basic shapes.

Master business strategist and Harvard University professor Michael Porter was one of the first to recognise, and take an inventory of, standard business profiles. Based on what he saw, he came up with three generic approaches to strategy and business planning. These *generic strategies* are important because they offer off-the-shelf answers to a basic question: What does it take to be successful in a business over the long haul? And the answers work across all markets and industries.

Generic strategies boil down to the following standard approaches (highlighted in Figure 13-1):

- ✔ **Cut costs to the bone.** Become the low-cost leader in your industry. Do everything that you can to reduce your own costs while delivering a product or service that measures up well against the competition.

- ✔ **Offer something unique.** Figure out how to provide customers with something that's both unique and of real value, and deliver your product or service at a price that customers are willing to pay.

- ✔ **Focus on one customer group.** Decide to focus on the precise needs and requirements of a narrow market, using either low cost or a unique product to woo your target customers away from the general competition.

It's not surprising that cutting costs and offering something unique represent two generic strategies that work almost universally. After all, business, industry, and competition are all driven by customers who base their purchase decisions on the value equation – an equation that weighs the benefits of any product or service against its price tag. (Refer to Chapter 7 for more information on the value equation.) Generic strategies merely concentrate your efforts on influencing one side of the value equation or the other.

Low-cost leadership

Becoming the low-cost leader in your industry requires the commitment and coordination of every aspect of your company, from product development to marketing, from manufacturing to distribution, from raw materials to wages and benefits. Every day and in every way, you track down and exterminate unnecessary costs. Find a new technology that simplifies manufacturing? Install it. Find a region or country that has a more productive labour force? Move there. Find suppliers to provide cheaper raw materials? Sign 'em up.

Figure 13-1:
Generic
strategies
involve
deciding
whether to
become the
low-cost
leader or
provide
unique
customer
benefits.

A cost-leadership strategy is often worth the effort because it gives you a powerful competitive position. When you're the low-cost leader, you call the shots and challenge every one of your competitors to find other ways to compete. Although the strategy is universal, it works best in markets and industries in which price tends to drive customer behaviour – the bulk- or commodity-products business, for example, or low-end, price-sensitive market segments.

The following sections describe the ways in which you can carry out a cost-leadership strategy.

No-frills product

The most obvious and straightforward way to keep costs down is to invoke the well-known KISS (Keep It Simple, Stupid!) principle. When you cut out all the extras and eliminate the options, your product is bound to be cheaper to put together. A no-frills product can be particularly successful if you're able to match it with a market that doesn't see any benefit in (or is even annoyed by) other products' bells and whistles – the couch potatoes whose video recorders sport a flashing 12:00, for example, or famous-writers-to-be who are baffled by their word processors.

In addition to removing all the extras, you can sometimes take advantage of a simple product redesign to gain an even greater cost advantage. Home developers have replaced plywood with pressed board, for example, to lower the costs of construction. Camera makers have replaced metal components with plastic. And, of course, there's always the Pizza Express solution; the company reduced costs at one point simply by making its pizzas a wee bit smaller.

Stripped-down products and services eventually appear in almost every industry. The most obvious examples today are:

- No-frills airlines such as easyJet and Ryanair
- Warehouse stores such as Aldi, Costco, and Lidl, which offer a wide selection, low prices, and no help
- Bare-bones brokerage houses such as Hargraves Lansdown and TD Waterhouseand Quick & Reilly, which charge low commissions on trades without any hand-holding or personal investment advice

Experience curve

Cost leadership is often won or lost based on the power of the *experience curve,* which traces the declining unit costs of putting together and selling a product or service over time (see Figure 13-2).

The curve measures the real cost per unit of various general business expenses: plant construction, machinery, labour, office space, administration, advertising, distribution, sales – everything but the raw materials that make up the product in the first place. All these costs combined tend to go down over time when they're averaged out over all the products that you make or services that you provide.

Figure 13-2:
The experience curve traces the declining unit costs of putting together and selling a product as total accumulated production increases.

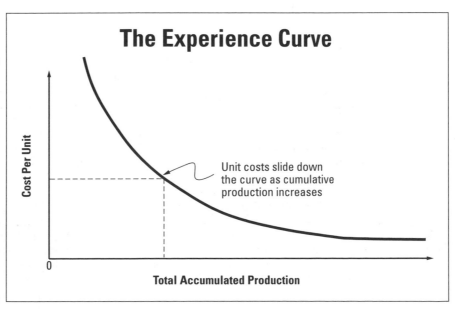

The underlying causes of the experience curve include the following:

✔ **Scale.** *Scale* refers to the fact that you have fixed business costs, which are fixed in the sense that they're not affected by how much of your product you make and sell. (Fixed costs usually include such things as your rent, the equipment that you buy, and some of your utility bills.) The more products you produce, the more you gain an immediate scale advantage, because the fixed costs associated with each unit go down automatically.

Think about widgets for a moment. Suppose that you rent a building at £1,000 a month to house widget production. So as not to lose money, you have to add that rental expense into the cost of the widgets that you make. Perhaps the first month, you turn out only ten widgets. No matter what else they cost, you have to add £100 rent (£1,000 divided by ten units) to the price of each widget. But if you can boost production to 100 units the next month, you have to add only £10 in rent (£1,000 divided by 100 units) to the price of each widget, and you reduce your rental costs per unit by a whopping 90 per cent. Scale is good for business and your bottom line.

✔ **Scope.** *Scope* works a little like the scale effect, but scope refers to the underlying cost benefit that you get by serving larger markets or by offering multiple products that share overhead expenses associated with such things as advertising, product service, and distribution. (Chapter 14 provides more information on juggling your product expenses.) These expenses aren't exactly fixed, but you do gain an automatic scope advantage if the ad that you decide to run reaches a larger market or if your delivery trucks deliver two or three products to each of your sales outlets instead of one.

✔ **Learning.** Remember the first time you tried to tie your shoelaces? Big job. A lot of work. Now you can do it in your sleep. What happened? The more you tied your shoes, the better you got at it. The same is true whether you're on a factory floor, at a computer workstation, or in a conference room. You (and your employees) get better at something the more you do it. As you learn, the overall cost of doing business goes down.

A general rule suggests that all these underlying causes result in what's known as an 80 per cent experience curve. Every time you double the total number of products produced, unit costs go down by about 20 per cent – to 80 per cent of what they were before.

The cost benefit that you actually get out of your own company's experience is bound to vary and depends partly on your industry. A few industries don't benefit from experience effects at all. In industries in which the basic costs of raw materials are high, for example, there's not much room for gaining a big advantage through experience. Many service industries may not get much of an advantage from experience, either. It doesn't matter how good hairstylists become at what they do; it still takes them about an hour to wash and style each customer's hair, so the company's costs don't change.

Low-cost culture

You can sustain low-cost leadership only if every part of your company is committed to keeping costs under control, reducing or eliminating expenses and unnecessary spending. This kind of commitment doesn't occur without leadership and the example set by the owners themselves.

Perhaps more than any other strategy and business plan that you can pursue, the push to be the low-cost leader in your industry succeeds or fails based on how well you actually carry it out. Knowing where and when to bring in cost-saving technology may be one important aspect of your drive, for example. But at the heart of your plan, it's absolutely critical that you figure out how to structure the company, reward your employees, and create the spirit of a 'lean, mean fighting machine'. In the end, your employees determine just how efficient your company really is. This may mean that you don't drive a company car or that you never, ever make personal long-distance calls from work. You can bet that your employees will follow your lead.

Low-cost leadership means exactly what it says. It's just not good enough to be first, second or third runner-up; it's not even all right to be first among equals. If you can't assume the cost-leadership position, you run the risk of playing a part in your own worst nightmare: a high-stakes, cut-throat industry in which price-war shoot-'em-outs threaten to destroy all the players. After all, if no one's a clear leader, everyone's a challenger, and when low-cost challengers decide to battle for market-share advantage, they use price as their favourite weapon. If you happen to find yourself in such a Wild West industry, take action. Look for new and different ways to compete – alternative strategies that are more likely to reward you in the end.

Standing out in a crowd

Not every company can be the low-cost leader in an industry, and many companies don't even want to be. Instead, they prefer to compete in the marketplace by creating products and services that are unique, offering customers things that they just have to have – things that they're willing to pay a little extra for. The strategy is known as *differentiation*.

Differentiation has a great deal going for it, because companies can be different in many ways, which means that there are many ways to be successful. Although the low-cost strategy that we talked about in the preceding sections can easily produce a win-lose situation for many companies, differentiation often creates room for more players, each of which competes successfully in its own special ways. That's not to say that competition isn't fierce, even when companies offer distinctly different products or services.

Companies that can make themselves distinct from their competitors often enjoy enviable profits, and they frequently use those extra pounds to reinforce their unique positions in the marketplace. A premium winery, for example, earns its reputation based on the quality of grapes and expertise of the winemaker, but it goes on to polish that reputation through expensive packaging and promotional campaigns. All these added investments make it more difficult for competitors to join in, but they also raise the cost of doing business. Although a maker of house wine has trouble competing in premium markets, a premium winery really can't afford to compete on price alone. No company can ignore cost, of course, even if it offers something that no one else does. Wine-lovers may be willing to spend £15 for a special bottle of chardonnay but may baulk at a £30 price tag.

Chances are that you can make your company unique in a number of ways. You can set your product or service apart based on what it can do, how well it works, or the way that it is packaged and distributed. Then you can go on to develop any of these aspects into a successful differentiation strategy, creating a loyal set of customers along the way.

Because a differentiation strategy hinges completely on your relationship with customers, however, stop and ask yourself several questions before you move ahead:

✔ Who are your customers?

✔ How would you best describe them?

✔ What are their basic wants and needs?

✔ How do they make choices?

✔ What motivates them to buy things?

Check out Chapters 5 and 6 for insight on customers. The following sections describe ways that you can set yourself apart from the competition.

Product features

You can often find the basic outlines of a successful differentiation strategy in what your product can and can't do for customers. After all, a product's features are frequently among the first things that a potential buyer considers. How do your products stack up? Are you particularly strong in product design and development? (Chapter 9 may help you decide whether you are.) If so, you probably want to consider how to leverage your strength in developing new features to make your company's product stand out.

Unfortunately, product features represent a big target for your competitors to aim at, and trying to be different based on major product attributes alone is sometimes hard to sustain over the long haul. Technology-driven companies such as Sony, 3M, and Intel have managed to stay one step ahead of the competition for many years by always offering the latest and greatest products. But it's not easy (or inexpensive) to be chased all the time.

Rather than always take the lead in product development, you can make your company stand out by enhancing a product in more subtle ways, offering customers unique and tailored options that are appreciated all the more because they're often unexpected. Examples include a camera that senses when you've forgotten to put the film in, an insurance policy that makes it easy to keep track of what you own and then automatically updates your coverage, and software that actually helps you remove every bit of itself from your hard drive when you want to get rid of it.

Product quality

When you offer a product or service that's known for its quality, you take a big step toward standing out in the marketplace. In some sense, quality captures what differentiation is all about. Quality of one sort or another is what everybody seems to be looking for, and it's often in the eyes of the beholder. Although customers can't always tell you exactly what quality is, they know it when they see it, and when they see it, they like it – and may even pay a little extra for it.

Customers are likely to perceive quality in your product a bit differently than they do quality in a service that you may offer. The differences between product and service quality are big enough, in fact, that we treat the two separately in Table 13-1.

Table 13-1	Product and Service Quality Examples
Product quality	*Example*
Performance	Do pots and pans get clean in the dishwasher?
Consistency	Is the restaurant's pasta special always tasty?
Durability	How long will the hiking boots last?
Reliability	Will the answering machine save all the messages?
Appearance	Does the watch have that special look and feel?
Brand name	Which stereo system is known for its quality?

(continued)

Table 13-1 *(continued)*

Service quality	Example
Capability	Does the brain surgeon know what she's doing?
Dependability	Will the newspaper be delivered in the morning?
Responsiveness	Can the 999 emergency team arrive in time?
Integrity	How much should the lawyer be trusted?
Attentiveness	Does the bank clerk smile and say hello?
Tangibles	Which airline has the cleanest onboard toilets?

The different quality dimensions depend on the industry that you're in and on the customers you're serving. Even in a particular industry, companies create successful differentiation strategies for distinct dimensions. The car industry is a prime example. When you think of Porsche, for example, you think of performance; Volvo means safety; and Toyota and Honda are reliable choices. These differences allow competitors to prosper in the same industry, each in its own way.

Things are a bit different in service industries. For one thing, you can't help but face the importance of customers' impressions when you're dealing with services. By definition, a service is something that can't be held; you can't really touch it, feel it, or kick its tyres. So customers are in a bit of a quandary when it comes to making well-informed decisions. Figuring out what is and isn't a quality service is harder. How do you really know whether your doctor's a genius or a quack, for example? Is the pilot of today's flight an ace or just so-so? Is your dentist a saint or a sadist?

It's all in how it's packaged

✔ Calvin Klein underwear costs more than the Jockey brand, but Calvin Klein boxers and briefs are big sellers because they capture the imagination of men who want to look like Calvin Klein models in nothing but their undies.

✔ Avon products look a great deal like cosmetics that you can buy almost anywhere, but the Avon Lady still gets the attention of women across the country who want to be pampered on their own sofas with their favourite skin-care products.

✔ Local gift shops may not offer the lowest prices, but by serving up homemade cakes and jams when you come in the door, they provide a unique shopping experience that keeps many customers coming back.

A special kind of Cat

Caterpillar, Inc. is the giant company that builds those giant yellow machines that build motorways, bridges, dams, and airports around the globe. Caterpillar makes some of the best heavy-construction machines in the world, but its customers are impressed by much more than just equipment specs. What really sets this company apart is its unmatched capability to deliver service and spare parts on short notice. Caterpillar makes this commitment to each of its customers: no matter where you are in the world, no matter what replacement part you need, they'll see that you have it to hand within 24 hours.

It's a big and expensive promise. Caterpillar has spent a fortune creating a global service network with distribution depots that can fulfil its pledge, which of course means higher prices for Cat equipment. But customers don't mind paying those extra pounds, because they know how much they stand to lose if they have to shut down huge construction projects for want of a spark plug or fan belt. So Caterpillar sells peace of mind along with its machinery.

That's why perceptions come into play. When customers don't have all the data, they go with what they see. No matter what other dimensions are important, the tangibles – equipment, facilities, and personnel – play a significant part in customers' perceptions of service quality. As an airline executive said:

Filthy toilets and dirty trays are bound to lead to engine failure.

Because customers have no way of evaluating the quality of an airline's engine-maintenance programme, they look at the things that they *can* judge, and they form their opinions accordingly.

Product packaging

Customers often look beyond the basics in making the final decision on what to buy. In fact, your customers may be influenced as much by the packaging as by the standard set of features that your product or service has to offer. Accordingly, you can develop an effective differentiation strategy based on product packaging – how it's advertised, when it's serviced, and where it's sold.

Given creative advertising, attentive service, and sophisticated distribution, almost anything can be made unique in one way or another. If you don't believe us, check out the produce section in a classy supermarket. Fruit and vegetables are routinely identified by country, state, or even farm of origin. Signs tell customers whether the produce was grown with or without chemicals and even specify the harvest date. Each combination represents a differentiated product to be advertised, displayed, and priced based on the unique benefits that it offers.

A focus on focus

The two generic strategies that we've talked about so far concentrate on one side of the customer value equation or the other. A cost-leadership strategy points out the price tag, whereas differentiation emphasises the unique benefits that a product or service has to offer. The final generic strategy plays off the first two strategies. A *focus strategy* still aims at either price or uniqueness, but it concentrates on a smaller piece of the action.

A focus strategy works because you concentrate on a specific customer group. As a result, you do a better job of meeting those customers' particular needs than do any of your competition, many of whom are trying to serve larger markets. The following sections discuss several ways to concentrate your efforts.

Niche markets

Small, well-defined market segments provide an opportunity not only to meet customers' needs, but also to exceed their expectations. If these market segments happen to be at the high end, you're likely to be well rewarded for your attentions as the money keeps rolling in. Small, upmarket hotels, for example, pamper their well-heeled customers with valets, butlers, and even a chauffeured service to restaurants and the airport. A new breed of takeaway food services treats customers to mix-and-match offerings from the best restaurants in town, well-dressed delivery people, and even sit-down catering complete with china, crystal, and kitchen staff.

Customers are willing to pay a premium for this kind of service, and that means big profits. Niche markets don't have to be upmarket, of course; factory outlet stores are thriving by serving cost-conscious customers who have high-end tastes.

Targeted products

Companies that are driven by volume sales in large markets often ignore so-called speciality products and services – all those non-standard items and services that have limited appeal and not much market potential. If these companies do get into a speciality business, they're usually fairly inefficient at it; size and overhead costs simply work against them. Speciality products and services spell potential opportunity for a focused strategy to be successful.

Speciality hardware manufacturers, for example, have found a ready market for their new lines of old hardware. As it turns out, antique screws, hinges, doorknobs, and hundreds of other hard-to-find items are absolute necessities for turning rundown terraced houses back into elegant period dwellings.

Limited territory

Sometimes, a focus on geography results in cost advantages, better-served markets, or both. Where local tastes are strong, for example, or service and distribution costs are particularly high, a regional business can flourish. Independent restaurants and grocery shops, TV stations, and newspapers all attract a community of customers who want local news, buy regional products, and like to patronise neighbourhood shops. Commuter airlines focus on regional service, offering frequent flights and the best schedules to out-of-the-way destinations, and they keep costs down by flying smaller planes, limiting facilities, and running bare-bones operations.

A focus strategy works especially well if you're the new kid on the block, trying to establish a foothold in an industry in which the big guys have already staked out their claims. Rather than go after those fat, juicy markets (and get beaten up right away), you can sometimes avoid head-on competition by focusing on smaller markets, which may be less attractive to existing players. Once you're established in a niche market, you may decide that it's time to challenge the market leaders on their own turf. Morrisons, the supermarket chain, for example, started out as a small local chain offering bargain prices and a limited range. The company became a major regional player, and with its acquisition of Safeways, is now the third most successful supermarket nationally.

For small established companies in a market, a focus strategy may be the only ticket to survival when the big guys decide to come to town. If your company has few assets and limited options, concentration on a specific customer segment at least gives you a fighting chance to leverage the capabilities and resources that you do have.

Customer loyalty can prove to be a potent weapon, even against much larger companies. Tesco, for example, finds moving their superstores into small rural towns to be increasingly difficult, because the neighbours rally around local businesses and merchants that have made them satisfied customers over the years, despite the fact that Tesco probably has a wider selection of products at lower prices.

Unfortunately, a focus strategy is one of the most difficult to defend over time. Dangers lurk both inside and outside the company. If the market segment that you're in suddenly takes off, you can pretty much count on intense competition down the road from much bigger players with much deeper pockets.

If your market niche stays small, you face a powerful urge to spread your wings and expand into new and different markets, knowing full well that you may lose many of your original strengths and advantages. Your best bet is to stay focused. Small companies have the best chance of sticking around over the long haul if they stick to a strategy and business plan that concentrate their resources and capabilities, focusing their energies on serving a specific market segment better than anyone else out there.

- Planning pundits highlight three generic strategies that can jump start your planning efforts: cutting costs, offering unique products or services, and focusing on one customer group.

- To be a low-cost leader, track down and exterminate unnecessary costs.

- To set your company apart, offer something new and different – faster, stronger, tastier, longer-lasting, or more reliable.

- To adopt a focus strategy, zero in on a specific group of customers, and serve them better than anyone else does.

Checking Out Strategic Alternatives

A successful strategy and plan depend on your business circumstances – what's happening in the industry and marketplace, and what your competitors are up to. In particular, consider a couple of common business situations that you may find yourself in.

Up, down, or sideways

The range of activities that define your industry – called *vertical integration* – measures how many phases of the business you and your competitors are involved in. Vertically integrated companies are involved in many parts of an industry, from supplying raw materials to selling products and services to customers. Companies that are not vertically integrated tend to focus on one or two major aspects of the business. Some breweries, for example, concentrate on one central activity: the brewing of beer. Other breweries also get involved in growing the barley and hops; in making the beer bottles, labels, and cans; in trucking the beer around; and even in running the pubs that sell the beer to all those loyal customers.

Exactly where does your company stand in terms of vertical integration in your own industry? The question's important, because it affects your decision about whether to become more or less vertically integrated over time. Several terms have been coined by business gurus to describe the strategic moves that you may decide to make:

- **Backward integration.** *Backward integration* means extending your business activities in a direction that gets you closer to the raw materials, resources, and expertise that go into creating and producing your company's products.

✔ **Forward integration.** *Forward integration* means extending your business activities in a direction that gets you closer to the marketplace by involving the company in packaging, marketing, distribution, and customer sales.

✔ **Outsourcing.** *Outsourcing* means concentrating on your core business activities by farming out other parts of your company's operations to outside contractors and vendors that specialise in those particular areas.

✔ **Divesting.** *Divesting* means reducing your company's activities to focus on specific aspects of your business by spinning off or selling other pieces of the company.

Tables 13-2 and 13-3 describe some of the pros and cons of vertical integration.

Table 13-2	Pros of Vertical Integration
Pro	*Reason*
Efficiencies	If you're in charge, it's sometimes easier to coordinate activities at the various business stages along the way, combining related functions or getting rid of overlapping areas to streamline your overall operations.
Resources	If you have a hand in the upstream (early-stage) activities of a business, you can guarantee that your company has access to the raw materials and resources that it needs to stay in business.
Customers	If your company is involved in downstream (late-stage) activities, you not only get to know a great deal about customers, but also create lasting relationships and secure your own long-term access to the market.

Table 13-3	Cons of Vertical Integration
Con	*Reason*
Overhead	If your company tries to control all stages of its industry, it can run into all sorts of extra expenses because of mismatched operations, idle resources, and added coordination costs.
Mediocrity	If your company is involved in a wide range of activities, it's much tougher to be the best at any of them, and the company risks becoming average in everything that it does.
Size and slowness	If your company is vertically integrated, its size often makes it difficult to quickly respond to change, and commitments to various parts of the industry leave it little room to be flexible.

There's both good news and bad news in terms of deciding just how much vertical integration is best. Over the years, there have been swings in the popularity of vertically integrated companies: A rush toward control of all aspects of an industry is followed by the race to break up companies and concentrate on specific business activities. Then the cycle repeats itself.

Today's wisdom seems to come down on the side of breaking companies apart. Worldwide competition in all industries over the past decade has made it more cost-effective to go out and buy what you need rather than to try to build up resources and expertise inside the company. That practice has resulted in a wave of downsizing and restructuring as companies struggle to remain competitive at what they do best.

And the future? One thing seems to hold true across the swings and cycles: The most successful and profitable businesses most often do business at one of the two extremes of integration. Companies that are heavily integrated reap all the real benefits of vertical integration; those that concentrate on a single activity eliminate all the costs and inefficiencies. Whatever you do, try not to get stuck in the middle, with few of the benefits and too many of the costs.

Leading and following

No matter what industry you're in, you can divide your competition into two major groups: the market leaders and all the market followers nipping at their heels. *Market leaders* are those top-tier companies that set the agenda for the industry and make things happen; they're the ones in the driver's seat. The *market followers,* well, they follow along. But in this second group, you find the companies that work hard, think big, and keep the market leaders on their toes.

Depending on the market situation, companies in both groups behave very differently. Whether you're already a part of an industry or are thinking of joining it as a new business owner, it's important that you understand what motivates both the market leaders and the rest of the pack. The following sections explore some market strategies.

Market-leader strategies

Market leadership comes in various forms, from the absolute dominance of one company to shared control of the industry by several leading players. If you're a market leader, here are some possible strategic approaches for you:

> ✔ **Full speed ahead.** In this situation, your company is the clear market leader. Even so, you always try to break further away from the pack. You're always the first to make a move, whether in implementing new

technology and introducing innovative products or in promoting new uses and setting aggressively low prices. You not only intend to stay on top, but also want to expand your lead.

✔ **Hold the line.** Your company's certainly in the top tier in the market, but it doesn't have a commanding position of strength in the industry, so your goals centre on hanging on to what you've already got. Those goals may involve locking distributors into long-term contracts, making it more difficult for customers to switch to competing brands or going after new market segments and product areas to block competitors from doing the same thing.

✔ **Steady as she goes.** In this case, your company is one of several powerful companies in the market. As one among equals, your company takes on part of the responsibility of policing the industry to see that nothing upsets the boat. If an upstart challenger tries to cut prices, for example, you're there to quickly match those lower prices. You're always scanning the horizon for new competitors, and you work hard to discourage distributors, vendors, and retailers from adding new companies and brands to their lists.

Market-follower strategies

Market followers are often forced to take their cues and develop strategies based on the strength and behaviour of the market leaders. An aggressive challenger, for example, may not do well in an industry that has a powerful, assertive company on top. Fortunately, you can choose among several strategic alternatives if you find yourself in a market-follower position:

✔ **Make some waves.** In this case, your company has every intention of growing bigger by increasing its presence in the industry, and you're quite willing to challenge the market leadership head-on to do it. Perhaps your strategy includes an aggressive price-cutting campaign to gain as much market share as you can. Maybe you back up this campaign with a rapid expansion of distribution outlets and a forceful marketing effort. The strategy requires deep pockets, will, and the skill to force a market leader to blink, but in the end, it could make you the leader of the pack.

✔ **Turn a few heads.** In this situation, your company is certainly not one of the market leaders, but it's successful in its own market niche, and you want it to stay that way. So although you're careful not to challenge the market leadership directly, you're fierce about defending your turf. You have strengths and advantages in your own market segment because of the uniqueness of your product and customer loyalty. To maintain this position, you focus on customer benefits and the value that you bring to the market.

✔ **Just tag along.** It's easy to point out companies that have settled into complacency. Frankly, they're usually in rather boring industries in which not much ever happens. These companies are quite happy to remain toward the end of the pack, tagging along without a worry. Don't count on them to do anything new or different in the marketplace. (If you find yourself in a company like this, you may want to think about making a change while you're still awake.)

Remember the following when checking out strategic alternatives.

✔ A successful strategy must take into account what your competitors are up to.

✔ Vertically-integrated companies control many aspects of their business and can streamline their operations.

✔ Companies that concentrate on one or two activities are more flexible and can focus on what they do best.

✔ Market leaders set the agenda for the industry and shape the competitive landscape.

✔ Market followers aren't in the driver's seat, but they work hard, think big, and sometimes become leaders of the pack.

Coming Up with Your Own Strategy

If you feel a bit overwhelmed by all the possibilities for devising a strategy for your own company, stop and take a deep breath. Remember one important thing: Strategy isn't a test that you take once and have to get a perfect score on the first time. Instead, it's the way that you decide to do business over the long haul. Strategy is an ongoing process, so don't be alarmed if you can't see how all the pieces fit together all at once.

Coming up with the right strategy is something that you have the chance to work on over and over again – rethinking, revising, reformulating. If you approach strategy in the right way, you probably won't ever finish the task.

As you begin to shape your own strategy, the following pointers can guide you:

✔ Never develop a strategy without first doing your homework.

✔ Always have a clear set of goals and objectives in front of you.

✔ Remember what assumptions you make, and make sure that they hold up.

✔ Build in flexibility, and always have an alternative.

✔ Understand the needs, desires, and nature of your customers.

✔ Know your competitors, and don't underestimate them.

✔ Leverage your strengths and minimise your weaknesses.

✔ Emphasise core competence to sustain a competitive advantage.

✔ Make your strategy clear, concise, consistent, and attainable.

✔ Trumpet the strategy so that you don't leave the organisation guessing.

These guidelines are not only helpful for creating a strategy, but also useful for reviewing and revising one as well. Make sure that you return to them on a regular basis as part of your ongoing commitment to the strategy and planning process.

Companies that take strategy and business planning seriously know that to reach a target, it's 'ready, aim, fire' – not 'ready, fire, aim'. It's that simple. In other words, almost any strategy is better than no strategy at all. Companies that have clear strategies don't hit the bull's-eye every time; no strategy can promise that. But these companies succeed in the end because they subscribe to a strategic process that forces them to ask the right questions and come up with good answers – answers that are often better than their competitors' answers.

Chapter 14

Managing More Than One Product

. . . .

In This Chapter

▶ Working with the product life cycle

▶ Expanding your market

▶ Extending your product line

▶ Diversifying into new businesses

▶ Identifying strategic business units

▶ Managing your product portfolio

. . . .

*W*atching over a product or service as it makes its way through the cold, cruel marketplace is an awesome responsibility. It requires a major commitment of time and resources, as well as a great deal of careful planning. First, you have to understand what's required for the product to be successful. Which attributes and aspects should you stress? How do you make sure that people take notice (and like what they see)? What must you do to support and guide your product or service along the way, getting it into the right hands? You want to take advantage of opportunities as they appear. At the same time, you have to worry about the threats and competitive pressures that are lurking out there.

Does this sound a lot like rearing a child? Well, your product's your baby, and as any parent will tell you, there's going to be one blessed thing after another. Think how many times you've heard a parent say, 'You think they're difficult now? Just wait!'

Products and kids have a great deal in common; both of their worlds are continually changing, yet they eventually manage to grow up. For decades, the Dr Spocks of the business world have poked, probed, pinched, and studied products at all ages, and they've come up with a useful description of the common stages that almost all products go through. When you create a business plan, you have to plan for the changes in your own product's life cycle.

In this chapter, we explain the product life cycle and what it means for your company. We talk about ways to keep your company growing. We show you how to expand into new markets with existing products, as well as how to extend your product line to better serve current customers. We explore the opportunities and pitfalls of trying to diversify. We talk about strategic business units (SBUs) and introduce several portfolio tools to help you plan and manage a family of products.

Facing the Product Life Cycle

If you could use only one word to describe what it feels like to be in business and to compete in a marketplace, that word probably would be *change*. The forces of change are everywhere, ranging from major trends in your business environment to the shifting tastes and demands of your customers and the unpredictable behaviour of your competitors.

You may think that all these factors, stirred together, create a world filled with chaos and uncertainty. Not so. The experts have stumbled onto some basic patterns, and the cycles that they've created do a good job of describing what happens in the face of all the market turmoil and confusion.

One of these patterns – the *product life cycle* – illustrates what happens to a new kind of product or service after you launch it in the market. The product life cycle describes four major stages that your product is likely to go through:

- An introduction period
- A growth period
- Maturity
- A period of decline

Most product life cycles look something like Figure 14-1.

The curve traces your product sales volume over time. You can think about the sales volume in terms of the revenue that you take in or the number of units that you sell, and you may end up measuring the time scale in weeks, months, years, or even decades.

Every stage of your product's life cycle presents a unique set of market conditions and a series of planning challenges. The different stages require different management objectives, strategies, and skills. The following sections discuss what you should think about at each stage.

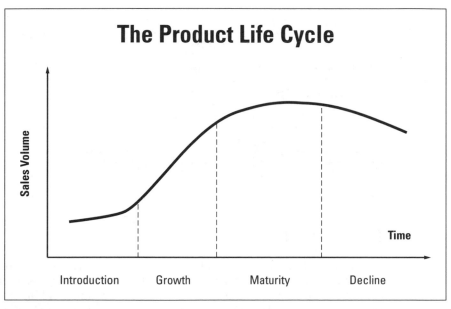

Starting out

You introduce a new kind of product or service in the market, and it begins to generate revenue. Because costs are relatively high at this stage, you usually don't find too many competitors around. Growth is limited instead by your company's ability to make the product, generate market awareness, and get customers to accept and adopt the new product.

At this stage in the product life cycle, efforts focus on getting your product out the door or on rolling out the new service and ensuring that everything works the way that it's supposed to. At the same time, you have to drum up lots of interest and struggle to create a brand-new market. Table 14-1 points out many characteristics of the introduction stage.

Table 14-1	Major Characteristics of the Introduction Stage
Component	*Characteristics*
Industry	One or two companies
Competition	Little or none
Key function	Research and development

(continued)

Table 14-1 *(continued)*

Component	Characteristics
Customers	Innovators and risk-takers
Finances	High prices and expenses
Profits	Non-existent to negative
Objectives	Product adoption
Strategy	Expanding the total market

Growing up

Your new product or service gains a reputation during the growth stage. Demand rises rapidly, and sales increase. Competition increases as well, as competing products jump into the fray to take advantage of an expanding market. Customers begin to develop brand loyalties, and companies tweak their product features to better serve customer needs – needs that are now easier to recognise.

As the growth stage kicks in, your priorities turn toward meeting growing product demand, improving your product or service, and targeting specific groups of customers. Along the way, you have to fend off a growing crop of competitors. Table 14-2 highlights characteristics of the growth stage.

Table 14-2	Major Characteristics of the Growth Stage
Component	**Characteristics**
Industry	Many companies
Competition	Growing strength and numbers
Key function	Marketing
Customers	Eager to try products
Finances	Variable prices and costs
Profits	Growing rapidly
Objectives	Sales growth and market share
Strategy	Establishing and defending position

Middle age

The growth of your product or service begins to slow in the maturity stage, as market demand levels off and new customers become harder to find. New competitors are also harder to find, and the competition stabilises. Profits keep on growing, however, as costs continue to fall. Changes in market share reflect changes in product value and often come at the expense of competing products.

As maturity sets in, your attention turns toward reducing costs and finally reaping the benefits of stable profits. Although it's easy to feel comfortable at this stage, you need to think about what's going to happen next. Table 14-3 identifies the characteristics of the maturity stage.

Table 14-3	Major Characteristics of the Maturity Stage
Component	*Characteristics*
Industry	Not as many companies
Competition	Stronger, but stable
Key function	Operations
Customers	The majority of buyers
Finances	Competitive prices and lower costs
Profits	At or near peak
Objectives	Cash flow and profit
Strategy	Maintaining competitive position

Senior stretch

At some point in your product's life cycle, sales start to fall off, and revenue begins to decline. Competitors drop out of the market as profits all but disappear. The decline stage may be triggered by large-scale changes in the economy or technology, or it may simply reflect changing customer needs and behaviour. Products still on the market in this stage are either redesigned, repositioned, or replaced.

As the decline stage looms, you have to get back into the business trenches. Your work shifts to redesigning your product or redefining its market, or maybe coming up with new uses or different kinds of customers. If all these attempts fail, you have to concentrate on ways to get out of the market and not lose too much money. Table 14-4 shows various characteristics of the decline stage.

Table 14-4	Major Characteristics of the Decline Stage
Component	*Characteristics*
Industry	Few companies
Competition	Declining in number
Key function	Finance and planning
Customers	Loyal, conservative buyers
Finances	Falling prices and low costs
Profits	Much reduced
Objectives	Residual profits
Strategy	Getting out alive

Where you are now

Take your own product or service and see whether you can come up with its estimated position on the product life cycle curve (refer to Figure 14-1 earlier in this chapter). If you're stumped, ask yourself the following kinds of questions:

- How long has the product been on the market?
- How rapidly is the market growing?
- Is the growth rate increasing, decreasing, or flat?
- Is the product profitable?
- Are profits heading up or down?
- How many competitors does the product have?
- How fast are product features changing?
- Are there more or fewer competing products than there were a year ago?

Perhaps you feel confident about where your product is in its life cycle. That's good. Just make sure, though, that you take the time to confirm your analysis. Chances are that you're going to get mixed signals from the market-place, and the clues may even contradict one another. No two products ever behave the same way when it comes to the product life cycle. Unfortunately, acting prematurely on the evidence at hand can lead to hasty planning and a self-fulfilling prophecy.

Suppose that the widget manager at Global Gizmos Company detects a slow-down in widget sales. As a faithful believer in the absolute law of the product life cycle, she comes to the obvious conclusion that the growth stage for wid-gets is finally coming to an end. What does she do? For one thing, she begins to think about ways to reduce costs. Maybe she cuts the advertising budget and begins to phase out incentives for the sales force. What happens? Sales of wid-gets decline even further, just as she predicted. So she pats herself on the back for being the first to recognise the early stages of a worldwide widget decline.

But what if the sales slump is actually reversible, simply caused by a bit of bad weather, some delivery problems, or any number of other reasons? By substituting blind faith in a business textbook for her own good judgement and careful analysis, the widget manager actually caused the outcome that she so confidently predicted in the first place.

What good is a business concept if you can't really count on it? Well, don't get us wrong here. The product life cycle is a powerful planning tool if you use it to support – not replace – your own solid skills. When it's deployed as an early warning system, the product life cycle alerts you to potential changes, allowing you time to plan for a different business environment and to respond quickly when your product finally enters a new stage in its life cycle.

- ✔ Your product or service goes through a life cycle that includes introduc-tion, growth, maturity, and (alas) decline.

- ✔ When you introduce a new kind of product, costs are high, but competi-tors are few.

- ✔ During your product's growth stage, demand increases fast, but so does competition.

- ✔ At maturity, competition stabilises, and as your costs continue to decline, profits grow.

- ✔ When decline sets in (as new technologies come along or customers' habits change), sales, revenue, and profits head south.

Finding Ways to Grow

Let's face it – your product simply isn't going to be the same tomorrow as it is today. You may not plan to do anything to it at all, but everything around your product is going to change. The world will take another step ahead. The economy, technology, your industry, and the competition will all change a bit. As a result, your customers will think about your company and your product a bit differently, even if you see yourself as being exactly the same.

The road not taken

If you had to name the single product that's had the greatest impact on the 20th century, it would have to be the car, hands down. But you wouldn't have guessed that in the early days. In the 1890s, bizarre four-wheel contraptions were lurching around everywhere, sputtering, sometimes careening forward, propelled by steam turbines, gasoline engines, electric motors, you name it – probably even by nuclear power, had it been around at the time. But the fledgling automotive industry faced a hurdle: getting people to try these strange horseless carriages in the first place.

By 1905, after a bit of coaxing, the idea of cars as serious transportation began to catch on. Henry Ford introduced his Model T in 1908 and sold 10,000 of them for a hefty $825 each. In five years, annual sales were up to a half million cars, and by the mid-1920s, 15 million Model Ts had rolled off Ford's factory floor. Ford Motor Company drove the Model T up the product life cycle growth curve and straight into its maturity. Ford was producing almost half the cars in the world. Although the price of a T had fallen to $260 by 1925, the assembly-line efficiency and sheer volume of cars sold allowed profit margins to remain high. Business was good.

Business was *too* good, as it turned out. Henry Ford was successful at introducing, growing, and maintaining his product for many years. But he was so intent on continuing to reduce costs and expand capacity that he failed to see the early signs of a decline setting in. He didn't see that his beloved Model T was going out of fashion.

Ideally, Ford would have looked ahead, adjusting his objectives and strategies for a new set of ground rules – rules governed by consumers who wanted more features and options. But he didn't. As a result, he was forced to shut down operations for almost a year as he retooled to compete against General Motors in a changed marketplace. During the course of that year, Ford lost $200 million and laid off at least 60,000 workers.

How does your company find ways to grow and prosper in the face of almost-certain product mortality? You probably have every intention of creating a new business plan (beyond turning off the lights and locking all the doors) as your product begins to age. But which way do you turn? Mark Twain had a bit of tongue-in-cheek advice for people who prefer to keep things just as they are:

Put all your eggs in one basket . . . and watch that basket!

Trouble is, the eggs are going to hatch, and the chicks will probably run away. So doing nothing except watching and waiting is not really an option. But what are your alternatives?

Fortunately, you don't have to invent the alternatives yourself; planning for long-term growth has been a philosophical favourite of management gurus for decades. One of the pioneers of business-growth techniques was a man named Igor Ansoff, who came up with a simple matrix to represent the possible directions of growth (see Figure 14-2).

Figure 14-2:
The Growth
Directions
Matrix
describes
different
ways in
which your
company
can grow,
based on a
combination
of products
and
markets.

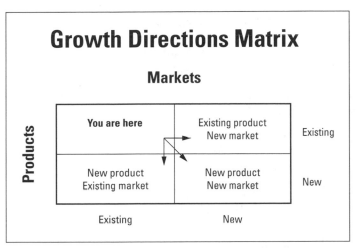

The Growth Directions Matrix really captures nothing more than basic common sense: it says that if you want to make your business grow, you have to start somewhere. The logical place to begin is to take advantage of where you are today and what you have to work with. How fast you grow in any of these directions has everything to do with your own capabilities and resources, as well as the rate of change in your industry. Consider the following ways in which you can move your company ahead:

- ✔ **You are here (existing product and market).** Continue to grow by doing what you're already doing, but do it a little bit better, so that customers use more of your product or service more often and in more ways than before. Encourage people to use more toothpaste, for example, by brushing their teeth (or even their dog's teeth) more often.

- ✔ **New market, existing product.** Grow in the near term by finding a fresh market for your existing product, either by expanding geographically or by reaching out to completely different kinds of customers. If you make baking soda, for example, get people to put baking soda in their refrigerators to keep them odour-free.

- ✔ **New product, existing market.** Grow by developing additional product features, options, or even a related product family with the intention of enticing your existing customers. Think of the array of apple drinks that are available these days – everything from Appletize to apple-flavoured water.

- ✔ **New market, new product.** Grow over the long term by going after new and unfamiliar markets with new and different products. Ford Motor Company, for example, used to make and sell prefabricated homes.

Without getting bogged down in a lot of details, try to come up with a dozen different ways to grow your company. Get yourself into the right frame of mind by first reviewing your company's mission and vision statements. (Don't have 'em? Flip to Chapters 2 and 3 for everything that you need to know.) Then complete the following steps:

1. **Identify three things that you can do right away to stimulate demand for your existing product in your current markets.**

   These things may include cutting costs, offering rebates, or maybe coming up with some new product uses.

2. **List three steps that you can take in the next six months to capture new markets for your existing product.**

   Some ideas include radio or television ads that target new customers, direct-mail campaigns, and stepped-up appearances at trade shows.

3. **Specify three development efforts that you can launch over the coming year to extend your current product line.**

   These efforts may include enhancing product features or adding options.

4. **Describe three directions that you can take over the next three to five years that will move you into new products and markets.**

More than one or two experts believe that any talk about brand-new products for completely new markets is really none of your business as a manager. These financial gurus think that managers are simply too biased to be objective when it comes to assessing totally new opportunities. They argue that you should return all your extra profits to investors and let them decide where to place their bets on the future. You probably don't agree with them; after all, investors have made monumental mistakes in the past. But they do have a good point. It's probably worth remembering that growth in new directions is a tricky business, no matter how it's done or who ends up doing it.

Same product, same market

Many successful big-name companies have become as big and successful as they are by relentlessly pursing a single business, a single market, or even an individual product decade after decade. When you hear the name BT, for example, you think of picking up a telephone. When you see a Coca-Cola sign, you imagine drinking a Coke. And when you pass a McDonald's, you probably picture a Big Mac. But these companies haven't turned into billion-pound corporations simply by launching their flagship products and letting the marketplace take care of the rest. Companies that largely depend on a single product spend enormous amounts of time and effort to continually rejuvenate and revitalise their core markets.

If you glance back at the Growth Directions Matrix shown in Figure 14-2 earlier in this chapter, you notice that these companies invest heavily in the top-left box. How do they manage to do that successfully? They use the four main strategies described in the following sections.

Encourage greater product use. A company increases demand by encouraging its customers to consume more of a product or service every time they use it. Maybe that means getting customers to feel good about buying more or giving them a better deal when they do. Customers may do the following things:

- Buy larger bottles of cola because they can save some money

- Apply for more insurance coverage because you carefully show them that it's the prudent thing to do

- Stay on the phone longer because the rates are lower

- Opt for a packaged computer or stereo system with all the components because it's simpler to assemble

Generate more-frequent product use. A company stimulates sales by getting customers to use its product or service more often. That may mean making the product more convenient, introducing it as part of customers' regular routine, or offering incentives to frequent customers. Customers may do the following things:

- Use toothpaste after every meal because they think it's hygienic

- Regularly drink wine at dinner because they think it's healthy

- Join a frequent-flyer programme and take an extra trip just to build more miles

Devise new uses. A company expands its market by coming up with new ways for customers to use its product or service. That may include getting customers to use the product at different times, in different places, on novel occasions, or in unconventional ways. All of a sudden, customers may do the following things:

- Snack on breakfast cereal during the day because it's handy and tastes good

- Put a radio in the shower and a TV in the car because they're convenient

- Make videos of every imaginable event from childbirth to pet funerals

Woo customers away from competitors. A company can also increase demand for its product or service the old-fashioned way: by taking customers away from the competition. Although the result is sometimes a fierce and unwanted response from competitors, companies can do the following things:

> ✔ Create incentives to switch from competing products and give rewards for staying put
>
> ✔ Concentrate on becoming a low-cost provider with the best prices around
>
> ✔ Package a product so that it's distinctive and stands out in the marketplace
>
> ✔ Focus on meeting or exceeding the needs of specific customer groups

Companies that manage to grow in the same old market with the same old product do so by continually generating new demand as well as maintaining or even increasing their market share. Often, these companies succeed in slowing the product life cycle, extending its maturity stage almost indefinitely. In some cases, they even manage to reset the life cycle, pulling the product back into the growth stage by inventing new and creative product uses. But steady and sustained market penetration based on a single product doesn't always work forever, and companies sometimes have to look in new directions for growth.

New market or new product

At some point in the life of your company, a single product or service may not be enough to sustain an attractive level of growth in your business. Where do you turn? The Growth Directions Matrix (refer to Figure 14-2, earlier in this chapter) suggests that the most reliable and productive paths point to market expansion in the near term, as well as to extending your product line. These two directions for growth have the distinct advantage of building on capabilities and resources that you already have. Market expansion leverages your current product expertise, and product extension builds on your experience and knowledge of current customers and the marketplace.

Successful big-name companies such as BT, Coca-Cola, and McDonald's usually are much bigger than just the flagship products that we associate with them, and if you look closely at the ways in which they grow, they almost always do so through a combination of expanding into new markets and extending their product lines. BT looks for new customers in both local and foreign markets, and it also offers a range of calling services (including direct-dial, collect, and third-party calling; messaging; paging; and now Internet access service). Coca-Cola enters new markets throughout the developing world by offering a family of cola beverages that includes Classic Coke, Diet Coke, and Caffeine-free Coke. And McDonald's is open for breakfast, lunch, and dinner with Egg McMuffins, Big Macs, and Chicken McNuggets, whilst at the same time making subtle variations to its products to fit in with local market needs: salads and wine in France, and even English language tuition for children in Japan, using the menu as the vocabulary.

How to make a bigger Mac

Mac and Dick McDonald were destined to change the way in which many of us eat. After struggling for years to make a go of their drive-in restaurant, they decided to throw in the towel. But instead of boarding everything up, they turned their drive-in into a self-service hamburger joint. The place: San Bernardino, California. The year: 1948. The result: a fast-food empire.

It turned out that fast food was in tune with the times. Americans were on the go – too much to do and never a free moment. What could be better than a hamburger, fries, and cola, wrapped up and ready to go in two minutes or less? Quick, efficient, and tasty to boot. Ray Kroc, for one, thought that the concept had real promise. So he bought exclusive franchising rights from the McDonald brothers in 1954 and opened his first McDonald's restaurant in Des Plaines, Illinois.

For the first two decades, McDonald's grew easily and quickly by expanding its market in all directions – first to the American suburbs; then to the cities; next to the rural towns; and finally to Europe, Asia, and the rest of the world. Hamburgers were the product, and McDonald's proudly displayed on its golden arches a running count of how many hamburgers it had sold. But geography has its limits, and McDonald's soon began to search for new kinds of customers and for new products that would extend the company's growth.

So along came Filet-O-Fish and McChicken sandwiches. The move into fish and poultry reduced the risk that McDonald's would be a one-product chain. The company also took advantage of market opportunities. McDonald's went on to leverage its resources– location, facilities, equipment, and loyal customers – to expand into the breakfast market, extending its product line to include Egg McMuffins, along with all the other early-morning fare. The company is now the world's leading food service retailer, with more than 30,000 restaurants in 118 countries serving 46 million customers each day.

McDonald's also owns Aroma Café (except in the UK, where they disposed of this business in 2003), Boston Market, Chipotle, and Donatos Pizza and they have a minority ownership in Pret A Manger.

That's not to say that going after new markets doesn't involve risk. New markets force you to conduct business on a larger scale. New markets mean wooing new customers and dealing with new competitors. When you enter a new market, you're the new kid on the block again, and you have to prove yourself at every step.

New market

Expanding into a new market is something that your company can do rather quickly, because it can take advantage of its current business model, copying many of the activities that it's already engaged in – producing, assembling, and distributing products, for example.

You can expand your market in two basic ways: move into new geographical areas or go after new market segments.

- **Geography.** The most obvious way to grow beyond your core product and market is to expand geographically, picking up new customers based solely on where they live and work. This kind of expansion has many advantages. You not only do business in the same way as before, but you also have a head start in understanding many of your new customers, even with their regional differences. Because geographic expansion may require you to do business in unfamiliar areas or even new countries, however, you have to pay special attention to how your company must change to accommodate the specific demands of your expanded market.

- **New market segments.** Sometimes you can expand the market for your product or service by finding new kinds of customers. If you're creative, maybe you can identify a group of customers that you've neglected in the past. Look carefully at your product's features and packaging, how it's priced and delivered, who's buying, and why they buy. Also, reassess the customer benefits that you provide. Then ask yourself how attractive a new market segment is in terms of its size and potential to grow. What strengths do you bring to the market? What competitors are already there? How do you plan to gain an advantage over the long haul?

New product

Extending the number of products or types of services that you offer is something that you should plan for well ahead of time. All too often, companies develop new product features, options, and major product enhancements without giving much thought to the implications for the company's future direction and growth. Instead, a customer asks for this or that special feature, or a distributor requests a particular option or accessory, and before you know it, you have additional products to support.

The good news, of course, is that you already have customers. But you also have to be sure that those customers represent a larger market that benefits from your product extension and that the additional products make sense in terms of your own business strategy and plan.

You can extend your product or service in two basic ways: offer new features and options or create related families of products.

- **New features and options.** The most common way to extend a product line involves adding bells and whistles to your product and giving customers the chance to choose which bells and whistles they want. The advantages are easy to tick off: You work from your existing strengths in product design and development, and you use real live customers to help you decide which incremental changes to make. It sounds like the perfect game plan.

The danger comes from losing track of the bigger picture – where you want your company to end up. Individual customers, no matter how good they are, don't always reflect the direction of larger markets. So avoid creating a bunch of marginal products that you can't really sell or support. Instead, plan to develop a smaller number of products with features and options that are designed to meet the needs of specific market segments.

✓ **Related product groups.** You may create a group of products based on a common element of some sort. You can develop a product family to use the same core technology, to meet a series of related customer needs, or to serve as accessories for your primary product.

You want the product group to look stronger in the market than the individual products do separately. That way, the risks inherent in product development are reduced, and the rewards are potentially greater. Take time to understand just how products in the group actually work together. Also, make sure that you address the separate challenges that each product poses in terms of customers, the competition, and your own company's assets and capabilities.

Before you put your plans for growth into action, make sure that they draw on your company's strengths, reflect the capabilities and resources that you have available, and help maintain your competitive advantage. Ask yourself the following questions:

✓ How well are you doing in the markets that you're already in?

✓ In what ways is the expanded market different from your current market?

✓ What parts of your business can you leverage in the expanded market?

✓ What functions and activities have to change to accommodate more products?

✓ How well will your extended product line meet specific customer needs?

✓ Is your extended product family stronger than each product by itself?

✓ How easy is it to scale up your business to meet the expected growth?

✓ How will your competitive environment change?

New product and new market

Has your company hit a midlife crisis? Do you find yourself searching for attractive new customers, sexy technologies, and aggressive competition? Well, it's not unusual for a company to think about rejuvenating itself from time to time. A plan to move in new directions often involves diversifying the company, moving down into the bottom-right corner of the Growth Directions Matrix (refer to Figure 14-2 earlier in this chapter). That corner, after all, is where the grass always looks much greener – and the profits look greener, too.

But you have to balance the potential rewards against the challenges and risks that go along with diversification. Too many companies end up looking foolish as they try to learn new tricks in unfamiliar businesses without much time to practise – and they often face the financial consequences.

To better your odds of success, start by doing your homework, which means researching all the new issues and new players. If this task sounds daunting, it's meant to. The stakes couldn't be much higher.

Your chances of success improve substantially when you identify the ways that a potential new business is related to what your company already does. But even without the benefit of any existing product or market expertise, you can often discover aspects of a new business opportunity that play right into your company's core competence (flip to Chapter 9 for more on that). Here's what to look for:

✔ **Name recognition.** If your company has worked hard to create a name for itself, you can sometimes make use of its brand identity in a new business situation. Name recognition is particularly powerful when the associations are positive, clearly defined, and can be carried over to the new product and market. Luxury-car companies such as BMW, for example, now give their names to expensive, upmarket lines of touring and mountain bikes.

✔ **Technical operations.** The resources and skills required to design, develop, or manufacture products in your own industry – or perhaps the technical services that you offer – may be extended to support additional product areas. Japanese electronics giants such as Sony and Mitsubishi, for example, are experts in miniaturisation, automation, and quality control. Given those skills, they can acquire original technology or experimental products and then go on to create product lines based on their expertise.

✔ **Marketing experience.** If your company has a great deal of marketing expertise available, you can often put that expertise to good use to expand the awareness and strengthen the positioning of a new product. Examples include the creative software products that small, independent developers produce and then sell to larger companies such as Symantec or Netscape – companies that have the marketing muscle to successfully advertise, promote, and distribute those products.

✔ **Capacity and scale.** Sometimes you can take the excess capacity that your company has in production, sales, or distribution and apply that capacity directly to a new business area. That way, you reap the benefits of a larger scale of operations and use your resources more efficiently. Many car dealerships around the UK, for example, reached out in the 1980s to show, sell, and service Toyotas and Hondas, permanently adding them to their British car lines. Now, of course, that's all that UK motor dealerships have to offer, so their new products eventually became their main and only products.

✔ **Financial considerations.** Persistent demands on your company's revenue, cash flow, or profits may inevitably point you in a new business direction. Although a financial opportunity by itself offers a fairly flimsy link to your existing products and markets, a new business may – just may – be justified on the basis of financial considerations alone. Large tobacco companies, for example, use their huge cash reserves to diversify into unrelated business areas that have brighter, smoke-free futures.

The temptation to set off in new directions and diversify into new businesses, creating brand-new products for brand-new markets, has bewitched and bothered business planners for decades. Unfortunately, the failure rate for new products can be as high as 75 per cent. And the most perplexing part of the puzzle is the fact that in the beginning, everything looks so good on paper. Here are some examples:

✔ Campbell Soup Company thought that it had a winner when it decided to launch a family of juice drinks for kids. But its Juice Works brand had trouble, in part because so many competitors had better brand-name recognition in the juice business.

✔ Federal Express set out to create the future of immediate document delivery by introducing a new computer network-based product. But customers turned to FedEx to send hard copy, not e-mail, and the company got zapped by its Zap Mail service.

✔ Laura Ashley, co-founder with her husband Bernard of the firm of the same name, never liked the concept of fashion, insisting instead that her clothes and furnishings were designed to endure. In the 1960s, the company's fresh cotton print dresses offered a clear alternative to the miniskirts of Mary Quant. In the late 1980s, following Laura Ashley's tragic death, the company made the mistake of trying too hard to get with it, downplaying its heritage, neglecting its long print tea-dresses and Viyella checks. The flirtation with fashion was a disaster, heralding a decade or so of revolving doors at management level, and strategic twists and turns that make fascinating, if depressing, case study material for MBA classes the world over.

A few companies, however, manage to succeed with new products and markets time and time again. Think Tesco, and you could be forgiven for thinking of value food in the UK. But the company has successfully introduced thousands of non-food products in the past decade – everything from fashion clothing, to microwaves: they even have a substantial personal finance business, and perhaps the world's only profitable Internet home delivery service. Tesco's stated goal is to bring value, choice and convenience to customers, notice that there is no mention of food here. It is a goal it pursues with vigour in Asia, Central and Eastern Europe, and the US.

✔ One way to grow is to encourage customers to use more of your existing product more often and in more ways.

✔ To grow in new directions, your company has to look to new products, new markets, or entirely new businesses.

✔ When you expand into a new market, you can take advantage of expertise in creating and delivering your existing product.

✔ When you extend your product line, you can take advantage of your knowledge of customers and the marketplace.

✔ When you go after a totally new business (new product, new market), the stakes are high, so do your homework.

Managing Your Product Portfolio

When you decide that it's time to branch out into new products and markets or to diversify into new businesses, you're going to have to learn how to juggle. You no longer have the luxury of doting on a single product or service; now you have more than one product and market to deal with. You have to figure out how to keep every one of your products in the air, providing each one with the special attention and resources that it needs, depending on which part of the product life cycle it's in.

Strategic business units

Juggling usually requires a bit of preparation, of course, and the first thing that you want to find out is how many oranges and clubs – or products and services, in this case – you have to keep in the air at one time. It's easy to count oranges, and counting clubs isn't tough, either. For products and services, though, the following questions tend to pop up. Often, these questions have no right answer, but just taking time to think through the issues helps you better understand what you offer.

✔ Just how many products or services does your company have?

✔ When you add another feature or an option to your product, does the addition essentially create a new product that requires a separate business plan?

✔ When you have two separate sets of customers using your service in different ways, do you really have two services, each with its own business plan?

✔ When you offer two different products to the same set of customers, each of which is manufactured, marketed, and distributed in much the same way, are you really dealing with one larger product area and a single business plan?

General Electric struggled with these questions in the late 1960s. The company had grown well beyond the original inventions of its founder, Thomas Edison; it wasn't just in the electric light bulb business any more. In fact, it was a diversified giant, with businesses ranging from appliances and aircraft engines to television sets and computers. The company had to decide the best way to divide itself up so that each piece was a manageable size and could be juggled with all the other pieces.

The managers at General Electric hit on the clever idea of organising the company around what they called strategic business units. A *strategic business unit* (SBU) is a piece of your company that's big enough to have its own well-defined markets, attract its own set of competitors, and demand tangible resources and capabilities from you. Yet a SBU is small enough that you can craft a strategy with goals and objectives designed to reflect its special business environment. By using the SBU concept, General Electric transformed nearly 200 separate, independent product departments into fewer than 50 strategic business units, each with its own well-defined strategy and business plan.

Consider ways to reorganise your own company around strategic business units. Each time you outline a separate business plan, you identify a potential SBU. How do you get started? Because strategic business units often refer to particular product and market areas taken together, begin with the following steps:

1. **Break your company into as many separate product and market combinations as you can think of.**

2. **Fit these building blocks back together in various ways, trying all sorts of creative associations of products and markets on different levels and scales.**

   Think about how each combination may work in terms of creating a viable business unit.

3. **Keep only those combinations of products and markets that make sense in terms of strategy, business planning, customers, the competition, and your company's structure.**

4. **Step back to determine how well these new SBUs mesh together and account for your overall business.**

   If you don't like what you see, try the process again. Don't make the changes for real until you're satisfied with your new organisation.

Aiming for the stars

Rather than juggle a set of who knows how many ill-defined products, practise your juggling technique on the strategic business units (SBUs) that you identify instead.

Start by dividing your SBUs into two basic groups, depending on the direction of their cash flow: put the ones that bring money into your company on one side and the ones that take money out on the other side. Maybe you're surprised that you have two sides here. Because every product goes through a life cycle that's likely to include an introduction stage, growth, maturity, and then decline, different SBUs naturally have different cash-flow requirements. You must invest in products during their introduction and growth phases, and your mature products end up paying all the bills. So as a successful juggler, you always need at least one mature SBU aloft to support the SBUs that are coming along behind.

Some of this juggling stuff may sound familiar if you've ever tried to manage your own personal savings or retirement accounts. Every financial adviser tells you the same thing: spread your investments out to create a more stable and predictable set of holdings. Ideally, financial advisers want to help you balance your portfolio based on how much money you need to earn right away and what sort of nest egg you expect to have in the future. Given your financial needs and goals, planners may suggest buying blue-chip stocks and bonds that generate dividends right away, and also investing in more speculative companies that pay off well down the road.

Your company's strategic business units have a great deal in common with a portfolio of stocks and bonds – so much, in fact, that the SBU juggling that we're talking about is called *portfolio management*. To manage your own SBU portfolio as professionally as financial experts track stocks and bonds, you need some guidance, which is where portfolio analysis comes in. *Portfolio analysis* helps you look at the roles of the SBUs in your company and determine how well the SBUs balance one another so that the company grows and remains profitable. In addition, portfolio analysis offers a new way to think about strategy and business planning when you have more than one strategic business unit to worry about.

You could make your first attempt at simple portfolio analysis with two SBU categories: those that make money and those that take money. Then all you have to do is make sure that the first category is always bigger than the second. But the two categories don't give you much help in figuring out what's going to happen next. Fortunately, the people at the Boston Consulting Group came up with an easy-to-use portfolio-analysis tool that provides some useful planning direction.

The Boston Consulting Group's Growth-Share Grid (see Figure 14-3) directs you to divide your SBUs into four groups.

You base your portfolio analysis on two major factors: market growth and market share.

✔ **Market growth.** Is the SBU part of a rapidly expanding market, or does it fall somewhere in a slow- or no-growth area? You use market growth to define your portfolio because it forces you to think about just how attractive the SBU may be over the long haul. The exact point that separates high-growth and low-growth markets is rather arbitrary; start by using a 10 per cent annual growth rate as the midpoint.

✔ **Relative market share.** Does your SBU command a market-share advantage over its nearest competitors, or does its market share place it down the list relative to the competition? You use relative market share as a major characteristic to define your SBU portfolio because all sorts of evidence suggests that a strong market-share position is closely tied to the profitability of the SBU. Separate your SBUs into those where you have the highest market share and those where you don't.

Here's a review of the types of SBUs:

Problem children. *Problem children* are SBUs that have relatively low market share in high-growth markets. Problem children often represent newer businesses and are sometimes referred to as *question marks*, because you aren't quite sure which path these SBUs may take. Because problem children are in expanding markets, these SBUs require lots of cash just to tread water, maintaining what market share they already have, but their relatively low sales tend to generate little or no revenue in return. If you can substantially increase their market share over time – and that means shelling out even more cash – problem children can blossom into stars. If not, you may have to give them up.

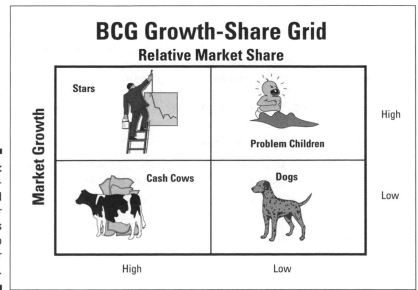

Figure 14-3:
The Growth-Share Grid divides your company's SBUs into four major groups.

Stars. *Stars* are SBUs that have a dominant market-share position in high-growth markets. Every SBU wants to be a star. Stars usually have an expensive appetite for the cash to fund continual expansion and to fend off competitors that are eager to get a piece of the turf. But their market-share advantage gives these SBUs an edge in generating revenue, high margins, and profits. On balance, stars usually support themselves, both producing and consuming large amounts of money. You shouldn't hesitate to step in and support a star SBU, however, if additional resources are required to maintain its market-share lead.

Cash cows. The name *cash cows* says it all – these SBUs have a major market-share position in low-growth markets. Because of their market-share advantage, these SBUs generate a great deal of cash, and the best part is the fact that they don't require much in return. Their low-growth markets usually are mature, and the products are already well-established. The bottom line: You can milk cash cows to produce a cash surplus and then redirect that cash to fund promising SBUs in other quadrants.

Dogs. *Dogs* are SBUs that deliver low market share in low-growth markets – and little else. Although many of us are dog lovers, it's hard to love this particular breed. Revenue and profits usually are small or non-existent, and the SBUs are often net users of cash. Although they require periodic investments, these marginal businesses usually never amount to much, so it may be best to turn your attention to more-promising SBU candidates.

It's time to put all the pieces together so that you can construct a Growth-Share Grid to represent your own portfolio of strategic business units. Ideally, of course, you see mostly stars and cash cows, with enough problem children (the question marks) to ensure your company's future. Ideally, you have few dogs to contend with.

But the world isn't always ideal. Fortunately, you can also use the Growth-Share Grid as a tablet to sketch out what you plan to do with your SBUs to balance them in the future. Here's what you do:

1. **Sort through your company's SBUs, and get ready to put them in a blank Growth-Share Grid.**

   To see the grid format, refer to Figure 14-3 earlier in this chapter.

2. **Place each SBU in its proper quadrant, given what you know about market growth and the SBUs relative market share.**

3. **Draw a circle around each SBU to represent how big it is in relation to your other SBUs.**

   Base the size of your SBUs on revenue, profits, sales, or whatever measure is most convenient.

4. **For each SBU in the grid, forecast its movement in terms of overall market growth and market-share position.**

   Use a time frame that's appropriate for your industry and its rate of change.

5. **To capture this forecast, draw arrows indicating the direction of movement and where you plan to have each SBU end up in the future.**

   Arrows that point outside the grid indicate that you plan to get rid of the SBUs in question.

The BCG Growth-Share Grid, with its quirky cast of characters and its black-and-white view of the world, is hard to resist, because it makes the complex, difficult job of juggling several businesses seem to be almost effortless. After it first caught on nearly 30 years ago, however, the model became so widely overused and misapplied that the entire business of understanding business portfolios went out of fashion. Today, of course, we understand that portfolio-analysis tools have their place, but they have to be used sensibly. As the saying goes, if something looks too easy to be true, it probably is.

Before you start moving your SBUs around the Growth-Share Grid like pieces on a chessboard, remind yourself that the following strings are attached:

- ✔ Market growth is singled out as the only way to measure how attractive a market is and to determine whether or not you'd like to be in business there. But growth isn't the only interesting variable. Markets may turn out to be attractive because of advances in technology, changes in regulation, profits – you name it.

- ✔ Relative market share alone is used to describe how competitive you are and how profitable your company is likely to be. But market share is really relevant only when you're competing on the basis of size and sales volume. There are other ways to compete, including making your product unique in some way, focusing on a particular group of customers, or concentrating on service.

- ✔ The SBUs in the Growth-Share Grid are linked only by the flow of cash in and out of the different businesses. But there are many other ways to think about how strategic business units may relate to one another and function together, including views that stress the competition or focus on market risk factors.

- ✔ The differences between a star and a cash cow (or a problem child and a dog) are arbitrary and subject to all sorts of definition and measurement problems, so without careful analysis and a dose of good judgement, it's easy to cast your SBUs in the wrong roles. You may end up abandoning a problem child too soon, for example, because you think that the SBU is a dog, or you may neglect and hurt a star SBU by assuming that it's a cash cow that you can milk for money.

Looking strong and attractive

If you feel that the Growth-Share Grid doesn't represent your own business situation (if you'd like something in Technicolor, maybe with a few more bells and whistles), dozens of other models, methods, and tools are available, all of which promise to guide you to the right answers with little fuss. Many of the other models claim to work particularly well for certain industries or in specific business conditions, and one of them may be just right for your company. But before you turn to the pros for guidance, however, you may want to take one more step in analysing your SBU portfolio on your own.

During the 1960s, General Electric (with the help of the consulting gurus at McKinsey and Company) came up with a portfolio-analysis framework that's a little more complicated than the Growth-Share Grid. But the GE Framework is richer and can be applied successfully in a wider range of business situations.

To make use of the GE Framework, start by examining the complicated-looking box shown in Figure 14-4.

Don't worry; we'll help. The GE Framework creates two primary categories that shape your SBU portfolio analysis: industry attractiveness and your business strengths. Unlike the Growth-Share Grid, the GE Framework requires you to go on and define exactly what you mean by *industry attractiveness* and *business strengths*.

Figure 14-4:
The GE framework arranges your company's SBUs into three bands and nine boxes, based on the strength of each SBU and its industry's attractiveness.

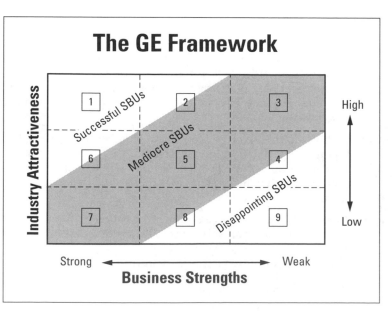

Coming up with what's attractive and what's a strength can be more ambiguous and less obvious than dealing with market-growth figures and relative market-share numbers. These definitions should help you get started:

Industry attractiveness. This category may include any number of components, depending on your industry. In most situations, however, you want to emphasise the factors that are likely to lead to fatter returns on your own SBU investments. Some of the things that you should look at (in addition to the overall market growth rate) are:

- ✔ Industry size
- ✔ Industry ups and downs
- ✔ Intensity of competition
- ✔ Customer and supplier relationships
- ✔ Average revenue and profits
- ✔ Rate of innovation
- ✔ Entry and exit barriers (see Chapter 7 for more details)
- ✔ Government regulations

Business strengths. This category should be based on your specific business situation relative to your industry. Instead of relying on relative market share as the only indication of your company's capability to compete, you should include other factors that reflect your company's particular strengths and advantages, such as the following:

- ✔ Product uniqueness
- ✔ Service quality
- ✔ Customer loyalty
- ✔ Brand recognition
- ✔ Costs and profitability
- ✔ Manufacturing capacity
- ✔ Research and development
- ✔ Patents
- ✔ Organisational skills

Rearrange your SBU portfolio so that every strategic business unit falls somewhere in one of the nine newly-minted boxes (flip back to Figure 14-4 for your template). Depending on the location of each box, the GE Framework presents a set of planning guidelines. Here are the options that the numbered boxes suggest:

1. **Protect position.** Concentrate your resources and efforts on maintaining your strengths. Invest to grow at a fast but manageable pace.

2. **Try harder.** Challenge the market leaders. Build up the aspects of your company that are strong and reinforce areas in which the company is vulnerable.

3. **Be choosy.** Seek ways to overcome your business weaknesses. Keep an eye open for new opportunities if the risks are low.

4. **Harvest.** Limit your investments, and try to reduce costs to maximise your profits. Back away if you begin to lose ground.

5. **Manage carefully.** Maintain your existing programmes. Concentrate any new investments in promising areas in which the risks are manageable.

6. **Grow wisely.** Build on your competitive position. Invest in attractive areas in which you can gain or need to maintain an advantage.

7. **Regroup.** Try to preserve your current cash flow. Defend your strengths, and focus on areas that remain attractive.

8. **Coast along.** Keep any further investment to the bare minimum. Protect the position that you have, and try to sustain revenue.

9. **Get out.** Cut your costs to the bare bones, and avoid making any new investments. Bide your time until you can sell to the highest bidder.

✔ If you offer more than one product or service, manage your offerings like a portfolio, with an eye toward how the components work together.

✔ A strategic business unit (SBU) is a particular product/market combination that typically requires its own business plan.

✔ You can divide SBUs into stars, problem children, cash cows, and dogs, depending on market growth and market share.

✔ Place your bets on SBUs in attractive industries that take advantage of your company's strengths.

Part V
A Planner's Toolkit

In this part . . .

Whatever the task you're involved in, no matter how big or small, there comes a time when you have to roll up your sleeves and get down to the real business at hand. Once you know where you're headed and what you're going to do, you must go out and do the task itself. The best plans in the world aren't worth anything if you can't carry them out.

In this part, we help you put your business plan to work. First, we look at ways to organise your company, and develop the procedures and systems that allow you to carry out your plan as efficiently and effectively as possible. Second, we talk about ways to encourage leadership, develop business skills, and create a company culture so that you can achieve your plan. Finally, we show you an entire sample business plan, so that you have a better idea of exactly what lies ahead for your company.

Chapter 15

Making Your Business Plan Work

Congratulations – you're close to completing your business plan! As much as we'd like to help you finish, we're not going to stand over your shoulder right now. Just remember that you've already done the really hard parts; at this point, it's up to you to bring them together. If you need a little nudge to get under way, flip to Chapter 1 for a sketch of what your written plan should look like, or check out Chapter 16 for a good example of someone else's business plan.

Unfortunately, you don't have much time to celebrate a job well done. Did you ever hear the story about the man who fell off a 20-storey building? As he passed the fifth floor, he shouted, 'So far, so good!'

Clearly, that man wasn't thinking his situation all the way through. Too many companies are guilty of the same optimism when it comes to business plans; they fail to see how critical (and sometimes difficult) it is to actually carry out a completed plan. More than a few of these companies ultimately self-destruct – not because they don't have a business plan, but because they assume that when the plan is finished, everything else will simply take care of itself. Preparing for what comes next, after your own plan is on paper, is important. It's not enough just to make your business plan; you also have to make it work.

In this chapter, we help you understand what you need to do to carry out your business plan. We show you ways to shape your company and prepare your people, using your business plan as your primary guide. We explore how you can create an effective organisation and then come up with business procedures that promote the goals and objectives in your plan. Finally, we talk about how you can encourage the people around you to take on leadership roles, develop the skills that they need, and create a strong company culture to make your business plan a reality.

Shaping Your Company

When your business plan is ready, it's time to take the next step, which means carefully arranging all your company's resources to put the plan into action. If you were designing a chair, a desk, or a sofa, rather than your company, you'd probably be reminded of the adage

> *Form follows function.*

It's really why chairs look the way they do – and look different from sofas. The function of your company is set out in your business plan, and it's up to you to design a form for your company to support that function.

For decades, business consultants have made their names and fortunes by coming up with different ways to design companies and organisations. What a surprise! We're quite sure that any number of these consultants would be happy to tailor a design just for you. But before you call one of them (and sign a big fat cheque), you may want to see what you can put together on your own. Then, if you decide that you really do need professional help, you'll know the right questions to ask.

As you come up with ways to design your company, you need to consider the six major areas shown in Figure 15-1. Three of these areas shape your company; the other three prepare the people around you.

Living the plan

When you have your business plan down on paper, take the time to read it – and we mean *really* read it. Don't just check for typos and bad grammar; remind yourself of what it actually says. An amazing number of companies have business plans that nobody reads. At least, nobody in those companies seems to know much about what the plans say (other than the all-important numbers in the budget, of course).

Perhaps you feel that there's nothing you don't already know about your own business plan. Because you're so close to all parts of it, however, you can sometimes forget the big picture. So step back and pay special attention to the broad sweep, below:

✔ Read your company's mission and vision statements as though you were seeing them for the first time.

✔ Consider the goals and objectives that you set for your company, and ponder what they really mean.

✔ Review the strengths and weaknesses that you identify, and consider what they say about your company's capability to make the plan work.

✔ Think about the different ways in which your company provides value to its customers and how these ways add up to your long-term advantage.

If you expect everyone who's involved in your company to take the business plan seriously, you need to start with yourself. As you put your business plan into practice, stop and take a step back on a regular basis. Ask yourself these sorts of questions:

✔ Do the procedures that you come up with make sense in terms of the kind of organisation that you're creating?

✔ Does your leadership promote the sort of company culture that you'd like to see?

✔ Does the shape of your organisation encourage the skills that you need your employees to have?

✔ Do the procedures that you put in place make your company culture stronger and more focused?

✔ Do the skills that you emphasise add to the leadership qualities that you want to develop?

✔ Does every last thing that you do support the business plan that you're working toward?

Making Your Business Plan Work

The Company You Are

Plans

Organization   Procedures

Leadership   Culture

Skills

The Company You Keep

Figure 15-1: The six major areas of your business that make a business plan work can be divided into two groups.

Growing fast is hard to do

GEC was a red hot company in the 1970s. The company was build up by a series of acquisitions by the legendary Arnold (Lord) Weinstock.

Weinstock ran a very tight ship, some say too tight. After a couple of decades of buying up most of the UK's electronics industry he sat tight, running the empire using a grid of handful of accounting ratios. A summary of these ratios for every business was in his office each month, and any executive not up to the mark followed close behind.

When he retired, his successor George Simpson (Lord Simpson of Dunfeld), a man of undoubted energy and passion, changed strategic direction overnight, going hell for leather for growth. Seduced by the Internet bubble he sold off GEC's famous defence business and other segments of the old conglomerate, and bought heavily into telecoms companies around the world just as the sector was going into massive overcapacity. Simpson delighted in his selling and spending spree, declaring that he intended to reduce Weinstocks carefully stewarded assets "as fast as I can". To be absolutely fair he was, in part, reacting to the decades of critism Lord Weinstock had had to suffer for sitting on his cash and buying nothing. As 2001 began, the newly renamed Marconi had 11 new companies in its stable, and an untried Oracle e-business system, to replace Weinstocks handful of hand produced key ratios, to manage all the financial details together.

The system failed to work as expected, and the board lost track of the dismal performance of the new businesses. From a peak of £12, the shares fell to less than 4p. Simpson and John Mayo, Marconi's finance director, walked the plank, and under new management the group secured a debt-for-equity swap that shifted control to creditors, leaving shareholders with just 0.5 per cent of the business.

In barely nine months from the end of 2000, the once powerful Marconi, formerly GEC, lost 95 per cent of its market value. From a £4bn cash mountain built up by Lord Weinstock, it had heaped up the same amount of debt.

Looking back it is easy to see what went wrong:

- The company's management didn't really understand the new business sectors they were going into.

- Their business systems were not up to running the newly acquired companies.

- They got their timing spectacularly wrong entering sectors in their death throws.

Now, under Mike Parton, the business is slowly recovering, but it is still a shadow of the empire it was endowed with.

Putting together an organisation

If everybody in your company can fit comfortably into a Honda hatchback, you're going to have a fairly easy time coming up with an organisational structure; you can arrange two or three people in only so many ways. But the mere fact that a structure is straightforward doesn't mean that it's not important. Whether you have two or 2,000 employees, the way that you design your organisation plays a major part in your success in making your business plan work. No matter how big or small your company gets, everybody in it still needs to know what his or her job is. All employees have to understand the special roles that they play in carrying out the business plan and in achieving company goals and objectives.

Where do you start? You can put together an organisation in several ways. The following sections discuss several of the most common structures.

Basic design

The simplest way to organise your company is to put somebody at the top – an owner or senior manager – and let everybody else do all the jobs that have to be done. Describing how everyone fits in is easy, because everybody's equal to everybody else.

- **Advantages.** You can usually find someone who's willing to do a job whenever it needs to be done. Because you're not devoting many extra resources to managing the organisation itself, the basic design is cost-effective, too.

- **Disadvantages.** The basic design really works only if your company has fewer than about 20 people. If the company is any larger, the person at the top can't keep track of everybody. So if your company is growing, at some point you're bound to outgrow your organisation. The basic design isn't always efficient, either. People end up doing jobs that they've never done before, and experience often gets lost in the shuffle.

Functional model

If you organise your company around business functions, you divide people into groups, depending on what they do. You take all the engineers and put them together in one area, and lump the marketing types together in another area. You put the operations people together in one area and all the financial folks in another. You need to make sure that some sort of general manager coordinates the various activities of the functional groups, of course.

- **Advantages.** A functional organisation works well if your business involves only one type of product or service. The organisation is efficient, because people get really good at their particular tasks and each function performed is done only in one place. Also, everybody knows exactly what he or she is responsible for. The jobs in your company are well defined, and you have a clear-cut way to measure how everyone's doing.

- **Disadvantages.** Unfortunately, a functional organiation can too easily turn into a bunch of separate boxes stacked on top of one another. Each box houses a different functional area; the boxes aren't connected well, and without good communication, the functions begin to have separate goals. Operations, for example, wants to make the same product over and over, whereas Marketing wants to sell different products to different customers. Each function might be efficient by itself, but both functions taken together aren't terribly flexible or effective in carrying out a larger business plan.

Divisional form

If your company is big enough to be in more than one business, the best approach may be to organise by divisions. Each of your company's divisions may be responsible for a particular product, a market, or a geographic area. If your company is even bigger, your divisions may cover strategic business units, or *SBUs,* which are specific product-market combinations. (Refer to Chapter 14 for additional information on SBUs.) The major divisions in your company usually are divided up further, often into separate business functions within each area.

✔ **Advantages.** An organisation made up of divisions that are based on products, markets, or SBUs encourages your company to focus all its energy and resources on the real businesses that you're in. Senior managers can tend to the larger issues of how the divisions work together. Managers inside the divisions can concentrate on their own sets of customers, competitors, and company issues.

✔ **Disadvantages.** Because the separate divisions within your company often represent entire businesses, they sometimes compete with one another, perhaps going so far as to fight over the same customers. Also, separate divisions usually mean additional overhead costs, because each division invariably has its own set of management layers and business functions (research, operations, marketing, service, sales, and finance) that are bound to overlap. As a result, your company ultimately is less efficient and less capable of taking advantage of any economies that result from combining tasks.

Matrix format

The matrix format organises people along two dimensions, rather than just one. In a matrix organisation, everybody has two bosses and wears two hats. One hat might be functional; a person might be in the programming or auditing group, for example. The other hat might relate to special projects, such as one that needs a programmer and an auditor for six months. In this case, the programmer and the auditor report to both a functional manager and a project manager.

✔ **Advantages.** The matrix format allows you to share talent, expertise, and experience among different parts of your company to see that these resources are applied when and where they're needed. A matrix organisation can be quite flexible in responding to business needs. At the same time, you maintain some of the efficiencies that you gain from arranging people by functions.

✔ **Disadvantages.** A matrix organisation can be tricky to manage – and sometimes even disastrous. The format violates an important management rule: Don't give people two bosses at one time. Tension is bound to occur between the project manager and the functional manager, for example, and your people will be caught in the middle. If you're not careful, the matrix format can lead to opposing priorities, clashing goals, and diverging ideas about how your company's business plan should be carried out.

Your own way

After you decide *how* to organise your company, you have to decide *how much* you want to divide it up. Ask yourself a simple question: If the guy who mails letters has a suggestion to make, how many people do you want the suggestion to go through before it gets to the top of the organisation? In other words, how many management levels do you want to have?

The number of tiers in your management cake depends a great deal on how big your company is and how it's organised. Managers can manage only so many people directly if they want to do a good job, and certain organisational structures simply require more managers than others do. Always keep in mind one general rule. The more management levels you have in place:

- ✔ The more control is concentrated at the top of your company
- ✔ The less flexible your organisation is in the face of change
- ✔ The more costly your organisation is to maintain

How do you know what kind of organisation – and how much of it – is right for you? Unfortunately, the answer isn't always obvious. Depending on your company's size, how fast the company is changing, and the nature of your competition, certain ways of organising seem to have an edge over others. The ones that work best in practice seem to be the ones that combine aspects of several of the common options described in the preceding sections.

Some companies try to stay efficient, flexible, and on target by keeping their organisations as simple as possible, using informal project teams when necessary and reorganising whenever changes in their industries and markets require it. A simple organisational structure tends to keep costs under control. Informal, temporary project teams create much of the flexibility of the matrix format without all the management confusion. Willingness to reorganise when things change can be a real strength, if you reorganise in the right way and for the right reasons.

Why do small companies stumble so often? A major stumbling block turns out to be an unwillingness on the part of people at the top to change the organisation as a small company grows bigger. Small companies tend to organise around a basic design, in which the owners or senior managers have their fingers in everything that the company does. Bigger companies just won't work that way for long, and if the owners can't let go when it's time to reorganise, the situation usually spells failure for an otherwise healthy enterprise.

Be sure to explore all your options as you go about creating or recreating your organisation. Try to come up with a structure for your company that makes sense to you. Only then can you put together an organisation that allows your company to work better and makes it easier for the company to fulfil its business plan.

Developing procedures

After you spend the time and effort to put together a business plan, it's natural to assume that running your business will automatically be easier. If your company's small, you may not have given any serious thought to what comes next. Now that you know what you have to do, you just go out and do it, right? Whether it's making a sale, negotiating with a supplier, or keeping track of expenses, you just get the job done, even if you have to change the procedure (or make up a new one).

Informal procedures such as these (especially the ones that always change) don't work for long, however, even if your company's just you. Your customers want to know what to expect when they deal with you, no matter how big or small your company is, and so do your suppliers. (So do the tax people, for that matter.) Nobody likes to deal with lots of rules and regulations, unless they're in the army. But all companies eventually have to come to terms with the set of guidelines that they're going to use to remind everybody how they are supposed to operate.

When you start thinking about the procedures that you use to get things done in your company, you'll keep discovering new ones. To start, ask yourself how your company does the following things:

- Keeps track of customer sales orders
- Manages credit control
- Manages its cash flow and bank accounts
- Invoices and credits customers
- Handles customer complaints
- Recruits and trains new employees
- Determines wages, salaries, and benefits
- Reimburses employee expenses
- Develops capital and operating budgets
- Manages product inventory
- Creates new products and services
- Monitors the industry and the competition

And don't forget business-planning procedures. For years, managers and management gurus alike pretty much ignored the systems and procedures that made companies run. Let's face it – systems and procedures are b-o-r-i-n-g. As a result, many of the standard operating procedures across industries were thought up decades ago, at a time when business meant manufacturing, distributing, and selling products. Full stop. But the times have changed – and companies have changed with them.

During the late 1980s, businesses began to wake up to the fact that some of these boring old systems were holding them back. Enter *re-engineering* – the smart idea that you should take a close look at all of your company's procedures to see whether they really make sense, given what your company actually does. When companies jumped on the re-engineering bandwagon, they discovered that they were doing all sorts of things just because they'd always been done that way. Today, doing things the same old way is simply not good enough, especially when your competitors are breathing down your neck.

Try to take the basic idea of re-engineering to heart when you develop your own business procedures. Do things in your company because they make sense, not because that's just the way things are or the way they were in your last company. It's worth taking a moment to think about a few of the essential systems that you're most likely to need as you go forward.

Accounting system. The right accounting methods, principles, and even software can mean the difference between really knowing what you have and losing track of where your money is coming from and where it's going. Profit & Loss Accounts, cash-flow statements, and balance sheets are indispensable to your business. (Turn to Chapter 10 for all the financial information that you'll ever want.) You have to have a reliable accounting system in place if you want to be able to put your financial records together in a way that you can trust.

Budgeting system. You need to develop procedures that allow you to create a complete financial picture today, as well as project your future needs (refer to Chapter 11 for more on financial planning and budgeting). You should make sure that your budgeting process covers your short-term needs, but it's just as important to make sure that the budgeting system encourages long-term investments.

Human Resources system. People are a big part of your company, even if you're the only employee right now. No matter how many people you count in your company, you should have a system in place that rewards employees for their hard work and also encourages them to think about their continued contributions over the long haul.

Information systems. There's no quick-and-dirty way to keep up with what's going on in your industry and markets; you need to have a process to capture information when and where it's available. You also need an information system to make sense out of the information that you capture. Consider your customers. You should keep track of everything that you know about what customers want, what you've done for them in the past, and what they expect from you in the future. While you're at it, set up a similar system to keep track of your competitors.

Planning system. We spent this entire book talking about business plans. But all the great planning ideas that you come up with may as well remain in your head if you don't set up a system to develop them inside your own company. Once you have a business plan, you also have to put a planning process in place to keep the plan alive.

- ✔ As you put your plan into practice, make sure that your organisation, procedures, and people all work together toward the same goals.

- ✔ How you organise – by function, product, market, or division, for example – plays a big role in making your plan work.

- ✔ With more management levels in place, you gain control but lose flexibility as a company.

- ✔ Be ready to change the way that your company is organised as the company grows or business circumstances change.

- ✔ Don't say, 'That's just the way things are done.' Make sure that every procedure that you adopt makes good business sense.

Preparing Your People

What makes up your company, anyway? Maybe you think of your company mainly in terms of the products that you offer or the services that you provide. Maybe the image that first comes to mind is of a building or a warehouse with your name and logo on top. Perhaps you think of the organisation, your way of doing business, and the reputation that you've tried to cultivate.

Your business really is all these things put together, and more. Ultimately, your company is defined by the people around you – who they are, how they act, and what they are capable of doing. If you want your company to be successful, you have to figure out how to encourage leadership roles at the top. You have to make sure that the people around you develop all the skills that they need to do their jobs better. Finally, you must create a company culture that promotes your business plan and ensures that it gets accomplished.

Encouraging leadership

If you want the people around you to follow you into the future that you lay out in your business plan, you have to lead them there. But what does it really mean to be a leader, and how can you encourage others to take on leading roles?

We should be clear about one thing right from the start: Leadership abilities and management skills are two very different things. Leadership certainly is part of what it takes to be an exceptional manager. But leadership also describes a more general capacity to influence others and persuade them to behave in certain ways. The world has seen its share of political leaders and spiritual leaders, as well as business leaders.

Effective leaders lead in different ways, depending on the circumstances at hand. As you find yourself in different business situations, you have to be prepared to alter the way that you lead as well. Consider the following leadership styles.

The boss. In certain situations, you have to tell people what to do, either because they simply don't know how to proceed or because you have definite ideas about what has to happen next. Even while you're being the boss, however, remember that you're going to get the most out of people by giving them good reasons why they're being asked to do something.

The adviser. If you want people around you to take on responsibility over time, you have to be prepared to let them go off and try to accomplish the tasks that you give them on their own. In your advisory role, timing is everything, because you need to develop a sixth sense for stepping in with support and giving just the right amount of advice. You should also develop procedures so that your people know how to ask for help when they know that they need it. Sometimes you lead best when you allow people to make mistakes, realising that they'll learn and grow from the experience.

The colleague. As you bring people into your company and develop strong working relationships over time, your leadership may become almost invisible. On the surface, you behave more like a colleague – one among equals. In this case, you lead in subtle ways and often by example. If you demand the best of yourself, others excel, too. If you meet deadlines, others meet them, too. This brand of leadership is based on mutual respect, and it can turn into one of the most powerful forces and potent assets that you have in making your company work.

As you reflect on your own leadership talents and those of the people in your company who are closest to you, you may wonder whether leaders are born or whether they can be made. It's hard to say which statement is true, of course. Some people are natural leaders. It's certainly easier to think about how you teach someone basic management skills, for example, than how you go about instilling leadership abilities in them.

The Army claims that it can create leaders out of raw recruits. Although we might argue about its success rate, the Army has come up with leadership techniques, procedures, and programmes, as well as with one simple piece of wisdom.

Don't ask those you lead to do anything you wouldn't be willing to do yourself.

Come to think of it, that's pretty good advice for aspiring leaders in any situation and in every walk of life.

Developing skills

At some point, you have to turn your attention to your employees, who are the ones who will turn your business plan into reality. Employees can't be just any bunch of random people who are willing and able to work (not if you want your plan to work, that is). The people you bring on board must have the right skills to do the kinds of jobs that you ask them to do.

The right skills today are different than they were just ten or 15 years ago. Oh, your people should still be top in their own areas, whether their areas are engineering or operations, marketing or sales. But they also need to have more general abilities that allow them to succeed in the company that you're putting together for the future. In many industries, the people around you must also excel in the following activities.

Managing information. Employees should be able to deal with an avalanche of information on almost every imaginable aspect of your company. You need people who can not only organise the bits and pieces of data, but also make sense out of them and then go on to make business decisions that take advantage of the information.

Thinking independently. Employees should be able to tackle and resolve business issues as they crop up. You can't afford to have people around you who do only what they are told to do. If you want to get the most out of your company, your people have to take initiative, think on their own, and come up with answers to the business problems that they face every day.

Working in teams. Employees should be able to get things done as part of a group. The need for speed in a complex business world makes it hard to get anything big accomplished without pooling resources, talent, and expertise in a team. Whether you need to solve a technical problem, assemble a product, or deal with a strategic issue, you count on a team of your people to get the job done.

Dealing with change. Employees should be able to do things in different ways, take on new responsibilities, and adapt to unfamiliar situations. Industries don't stand still anymore, and if your company is going to keep up, you need people around you who feel comfortable in a world in which the only constant is change.

Acquiring new skills. Employees should be able to keep on learning. If you want your company to move forward, those around you have to be willing to move ahead as well. Your people have to take the time and make the effort to master new skills.

A leader on leadership

Jack Welch was the CEO of General Electric, one of the largest corporations in the world, with 1996 revenue of almost $80 billion and a work force that's 240,000 strong. Welch is a leader who understands the value of surrounding himself with other leaders. What does it take to be an effective leader at General Electric? According to Welch, leaders at GE have the following qualities:

✔ A passion for excellence

✔ Hate bureaucracy

✔ Are open to new ideas

✔ Self-confidence

✔ Involve everyone around them

✔ Enormous energy

✔ Energise other people

✔ Set aggressive goals

✔ Reward progress

✔ Understand commitment

✔ See change as being opportunity

✔ Know how to build diverse and global teams

As your company grows and changes, you have to decide how your employees can acquire these skills. Do you invest in training to develop all the business skills that you need from inside your company, or do you go out and buy the necessary expertise, bringing in new people who already have the backgrounds that you're looking for? Going outside is certainly faster, but developing and promoting people from within your company can create a more dedicated work force and a much stronger organisation in the long run.

Creating a culture

Creating a culture in your company doesn't mean forcing everybody to go to the opera and symphony on a regular basis. Your *company culture* comes from the common attitudes, beliefs, and behaviour of the people who are involved in your organisation. In that sense, company culture is a great deal like a nation's culture. But people aren't born working for your company, and they don't grow up in it either. When you attempt to create a company culture, you bring together people who have different backgrounds and try to give them a common outlook.

Your own company culture might focus on one or more of the following points of view:

✔ To offer the best technology around

✔ To deliver the finest-quality products available

✔ To provide the highest level of customer service

✔ To be the most innovative company in the business

✔ To have the lowest costs in the trade

✔ To be the fastest-growing company in the industry

You want these attitudes to translate into the way in which your employees act. If employees' behaviour is based on a set of shared beliefs, you can always count on the people around you to do the right thing in any business situation. Company rules and regulations look good on paper, but a company culture provides a sturdier set of guidelines for encouraging employees to behave the way that you think they should.

Unfortunately, you can't order people to have a particular point of view, so you have to take advantage of less direct methods to change people's attitudes and influence their behaviour. Leadership has a powerful role to play in this task. The strongest company cultures often occur in companies that also have effective leaders – Virgin and Richard Branson, for example.

Here are some ways that you can use your own leadership skills to create a strong company culture.

Mission, values, and vision. Use your position in the company to talk about your company's mission, the values that you think are important, and the vision that you have for the business. Reinforce the things that really matter. Make sure that everybody is always aware of why you think each person is a part of your company and what each person is ultimately supposed to accomplish.

Actions and activities. Set an example for everyone around you to follow when it comes to the attitudes that you'd like to see and the behaviour that you'd like to promote. If you want your company culture to value customers, for example, go out and visit customers. If you want people to focus on profits, ask questions about profitability every chance you get. If innovation is critical to your company's success, search out the innovators, acknowledge them, and reward them.

Rituals and rewards. Set up rewards inside your organisation to support the company culture and the behaviour that you want to promote; then endorse and identify yourself with that behaviour. Offer customer-satisfaction awards, for example, and attend the ceremonies. Set profit targets, and hand out bonuses when they're met. Make a big deal out of innovations that work, and see to it that nothing bad happens when something new doesn't work out.

Your company culture can be one of the keys to making your business plan work. If you're not careful, however, it can also turn into a stumbling block. You can't change your company culture overnight, so you have to pay close attention to the attitudes and outlook of the people around you. You have to put in the time and effort that's required to encourage the shared behaviour that you expect to see across the company.

- Leadership is the capacity to influence other people and persuade them to behave in certain ways.

- Different business situations demand different leadership styles.

- Choose people who can manage information, think independently, work in teams, deal with change, and acquire new skills.

- Develop and promote people from within the company to foster dedication and a strong organisation.

- With a company culture that reflects your vision and values, you can always count on your people to do the right thing.

Chapter 16

Learning from Others: A Sample Business Plan

· ·

In This Chapter

▶ Viewing a sample business plan

▶ Following a business-plan template

▶ Learning about the tourism industry

· ·

Sometimes, you have to see something up close and personal before you really understand what it's all about. Viewing a real live business plan should get you much closer to putting your own plan down on paper.

Your written business plan says something about all the important parts of your company. After all, you want to convince people – and yourself – that your company knows what it's doing. If you want to persuade people of anything, however, they have to actually sit down and read what's in front of them. So you want to be clear, concise, and to the point, and it doesn't hurt to spend some time with your prose, either.

In this chapter, we show you a sample business plan. (We changed the names and some of the numbers to protect the innocent.) By reviewing the plan in some detail, you can learn a bit about how to construct a business plan of your own, and as a bonus, you'll pick up some tips on the tourism industry. But please don't rely on any of the data; it is provided simply to illustrate the business plan and not to help you kick start your way into the tourism business.

Safari Europe: Business Plan

~ *Executive Summary* ~

For the past five years Karen Kehoe has been a founder director of a very successful outdoor clothing shop in Bristol: Adventure Works. Last year that business made £120,000 profit on sales of £850,000 and employed seven people.

Adventure Works recently took on an agency from European Adventure Holidays, one of the largest and most respected tour operators in the market. With virtually no marketing effort some 200 adventure holidays have been sold by Karen in the past six months, netting £40,000 in commissions. Sales of insurance policies and other services have added to this total, and could potentially add much more. From desk and field market research carried out on 300 clients, Karen is certain that there is considerable potential in the adventure travel business. In particular one important segment of that market, the professional 25- to 35-year-olds who want to adventure travel in Europe, is not having their needs properly met.

Karen Kehoe plans to sell her shares in the clothing shop and invest the proceeds in a new business, Safari Europe. The business will operate from a self-contained facility within the existing shop, with its own entrance and shop window onto the main street.

The company believes that by concentrating on one market segment, the 25- to 35-year-old professionals, and one geographic destination, Europe, it will be able to deliver a significantly superior service to anything currently on the market.

Published research shows that tourism is a fast-growing business sector and Europe is the favoured location for most travellers. Adventure holidays, though a relatively new and small market, looks set for explosive growth.

Karen has selected a small team, some of whom have worked with her in the clothing shop for several years. She has worked as the manager of a branch of a high street travel agent and other members of the staff have extensive travel, selling, and computer skills, all of which will be invaluable to the new venture.

Safari Europe expects that by concentrating full time on selling adventure holidays, clients will increase from the present level of 200 in six months, achieved with only a part time effort, to at least 660 in the first year, 1,400 in the second, and 2,100 in the third. To help achieve this growth Karen has identified three other tour operators she wishes to represent and has begun negotiations with them. Selling between two and three holidays a day will allow the business to reach cash-flow break even in year one, while making a modest profit. This compares with the 1.3 holidays currently being sold each day.

By year 2 post-tax profits should be £180,000, and in year 3 nearly £300,000.

To achieve these results the company needs to invest in Web site and database software and systems, and in refurbishing the shop premises. Our market research demonstrates that sales of travel services via the Internet accounts for approaching £3 billion a year's worth of business. It is the fastest growing business to consumer activity on the Internet.

In all, about £75,000 will be needed to fund the business during its formative months. A further £10,000 needs to be available to deal with unforeseen events, although a sensitivity analysis has been carried out which shows this is unlikely to be required.

Karen will be investing £25,000 of her own money in the business, and seeking £60,000 from outside. The purpose of this business plan is to attract other shareholders to invest in a highly profitable venture. Return on shareholders' capital by year 3 will be close to 100 per cent. This opportunity may appeal to Karen's partners in the clothes shop or to a business angel.

Alternatively, we are considering loan finance made up of a £25,000 short-term loan and an overdraft facility of £35,000.

~ The Business and Its Management ~

Increasingly, shop customers have asked for advice on adventurous places to go on holiday. Last year Adventure Works took on an agency from European Adventure Holidays, one of the largest and most respected tour operators in this market, and began to promote and sell their products. In the six months that we have been selling travel agency products, some 200 holidays, at an average cost of £2,000, have been sold. Adventure Works' commission on the sales has been £40,000 (10 per cent commission). In addition, 35 insurance policies have been sold at an average price of £100, yielding £1,050 (30 per cent commission).

▶ *Mission*

To be the leading provider of hassle-free European adventure holidays to the 25- to 35-year-old young professionals market. The business will initially operate within a 25-mile catchment area, but quickly start to sell its services worldwide, via the Internet. Sales of travel services is the fastest growing category of business to consumer activity on the Internet. In 2000 the value of this market will be an estimated £2.7 billion.

The emphasis will be on providing a complete specialist service based on having a detailed knowledge of the holiday destination and adventure activities being offered. Our market research shows that the major criticism our type of client has of existing travel agencies, is that they "know nothing about their products, they just open the catalogue and read", to quote one of the many disappointed adventure holidaymakers.

Also, by using our experience in the Adventure Works clothing shop, we will be able to both advise and direct our clients to sources of the type of travel equipment they will need to get the very best out of their holiday experience.

▶ *Objectives*

Our financial objectives are to be operating at, or close to, cash flow break even by the end of the first year. We aim to be profitable from year 1 onwards, then we will aim to earn at least £180,000 post-tax profit in the second year, and nearly £300,000 in the third. Our profit margin on sales by year 3 will be a respectable 7 per cent.

We also intend that the business should be fun. The present staff are passionate about adventure holidays, and we intend to maintain their enthusiasm by constant product and skill training. We will only recruit new people who share our vision.

▶ *Legal Structure*

The business will be set up as a limited company in the next few weeks. This structure will clearly separate the travel business from the shop and make it possible to attract the risk capital that will be required when the business starts to grow. For example, an Air Travel Operators License (ATOL) will eventually be required, which in turn calls for a business to have a minimum paid-up share capital of £25,000.

At a later stage the business may wish to sell and issue airline tickets and to create its own charter holidays. This will require membership of the International Air Traffic Association (IATA) and an Association of British Travel Agents (ABTA) bonding. However, in the period covered by this business plan we intend to operate only as the appointed agents for a number of tour operators. As such, we can shelter under their licenses and bonds.

~ *Products and Services* ~

▶ *Tour Agency Products*

We currently are appointed agents for European Adventure Holidays (EAH), a leading supplier in the market. Currently EAH offer some 40 different adventure holiday packages throughout Europe, covering such areas as: horse trekking in Iceland; above-the-clouds trekking on islands and remote mountain regions in such areas as Corsica and Norway; van-supported inn-to-inn bicycling; mountain biking and hiking adventure tours throughout France, Germany, Italy, and Austria; ballooning across the Alps.

We intend to seek to be appointed agents by three other major adventure holiday tour firms, with whom we are currently in negotiation.

▶ *Services*

We will offer a comprehensive range of complementary services to support the adventurous holidaymaker that will ensure they have a safe, enjoyable, and memorable experience. These services will include: insurance, both personal and effects; pre- and post-holiday briefing packs; a directory of advice and information services covering each country and adventure activity.

▶ *Proprietary Position*

Whilst at present we are offering only other company's adventure holidays we have protected our position in a number of ways.

Firstly, we have a two-year agency agreement with European Adventure Holidays which gives us access to all their holiday products, both existing and new. This contract is dependent on our achieving sales of at least 250 holiday packages a year. We intend to negotiate similar agreements with future suppliers, although sales targets with them will be lower to reflect their relative market position.

Secondly, we intend to maintain a high service element to our business, extending our range of value added services. In this way we will seek to build up a high level of repeat business. Customer loyalty is vital to our profitable growth.

▶ *Guarantees and Customer Protection*

Our clients will be protected financially against either our or our tour operators' failure, by virtue of the ABTA bonding held by our principals. We will only use holiday providers who can provide 24-hour emergency support services for clients whilst on holiday.

~ *Markets and Competitors* ~

▶ *Markets, Projections, and Market Segments*

The world travel market is forecast to expand at a 4.1 per cent average annual growth rate until 2010. This is faster than economic growth generally, which is expected to be around 2.4 per cent per annum.

The European market, whilst not the fastest growing, will be the most important destination, accounting for over 50 per cent of all international arrivals. France, Italy, and Spain are the most important destinations within Europe. This is why we have selected as our initial partners, tour operators with appropriate products in these countries.

Figures for the size and projected growth of adventure holidays are sketchy, but one recent study (World Adventure Travel Data Corp.) gave these figures.

Adventure Travel Holidays — World Forecast (Million Arrivals) : 1990 – 2010

Destination	1990	1997	2003	2010
Europe	0.25	0.60	1.60	2.35
N. America	0.45	0.60	1.40	2.20
Rest of World	0.10	0.25	0.95	1.10
Total	**0.85**	**1.45**	**3.95**	**5.65**

Age	1990 %	2010 %
16-24	61	38
25-35	20	31
36-45	15	25
46+	4	6
	100	**100**

Our own market study confirms that Europe is likely to be the largest destination market for adventure holidays. Our study shows only 30 per cent of adventure travellers to be under 24, whilst the World Adventure Travel Data study claims 61 per cent. We feel the difference is caused by our survey sample being confined to relatively affluent people who had spent at least £200 in adventure clothing.

One further emerging market-segment for adventure holidays is corporate clients. Our market research suggests that up to 20 per cent of adventure holidays are sold at this top-price end of the market.

▶ *Competition and Competitive Advantage*

There are no adventure holiday specialist travel agents in the Bristol area. However, there are many in capital and secondary cities such as London, Paris, Lyon, Madrid, Barcelona, and Frankfurt. There are also a number of direct marketing and Internet providers. These are the types of competitors we expect to face:

General travel agents, who have added adventure holidays to their range. These agents often have little or no knowledge of adventure destinations or activities. They sell literally from the page, offering limited advice, information, and support. According to our market study 40 per cent of adventure holidays are booked through these general travel agents, but only 33 per cent of clients would use them again.

Adventure tour operators advertise their holidays in the press, attracting about 25 per cent of all adventure holiday clients. However, clients have to shop around several tour operators to find what they want, and they cannot get unbiased advice, or much help with information. Only 45 per cent would go back to a tour operator for their next holiday.

Independent travellers make up 15 per cent of those going on adventure holidays, and 65 per cent of those would travel that way again. We need to persuade this group that our superior product-knowledge and service is worth their consideration.

Internet providers sell only 5 per cent of adventure travel holidays. However, 70 per cent would buy their next holiday via the Internet. There is plenty of scope to offer a superior Web site. We believe that by having daily face-to-face contact with clients we will be better able to manage a fresh, vital, and relevant Web site aimed at the specific needs of our market segment.

Specialist adventure travel agencies only sell about 15 per cent of holidays at present, but we feel that this is due partly to lack of client awareness and partly to the comparative rarity of such outlets.

Some 65 per cent of those using specialist adventure holiday travel agents would use them again, which is many more than would use either a tour operator direct or a general travel agent.

However, these agents were criticized for having such a wide range of activities and destinations, that their sales agents knew little about them. Our research shows that whilst 41 per cent of clients take adventure holidays in Europe only 23 per cent of the 5,000 adventure tours on offer are for European destinations.

We feel that by concentrating on European destinations, which is the largest market for both holidays in general and adventure holidays in particular, we will be able to have superior product knowledge. We will only need to know perhaps 100 destinations and activities well, rather than have only a passing knowledge of the 5,000 adventure holidays on offer.

Our market research has also shown that many adventure travel agents are catering for the backpacker market, consisting mostly of very cost-conscious under 24-year-olds. This can lead to very different types of clients ending up at the same destination, with some consequent dissatisfaction. It is also evident that the backpacker market requires a much lower level of service and information, than do the more affluent professional 25- to 35-year-olds.

▶ *Customer Needs and Benefits*

We believe that by concentrating on the European market, offering a limited but extensive range of types of holiday, and aiming our service specifically at affluent professionals, we can meet the needs of our clients in a way not being achieved by any of our competitors.

Our market study has shown that this group has specific needs that are not currently being met, as 65 per cent of those taking adventure holidays would not buy from the same source again. In particular they want their travel agent to have comprehensive knowledge of the destination (87 per cent); to have an efficient administration system in which they can have confidence (84 per cent); to go on holiday with similar professional people (81 per cent); and to be offered useful advice and ancillary services such as insurance (79 per cent).

~ Competitive Business Strategy ~

▶ *Pricing Policy*

The normal commission paid to travel agents for this type of holiday is in the 10 to 15 per cent range. Whilst European Adventure Holidays, the first agency we have been appointed to, pay us at the lower end of the scale, they are a prestigious firm to represent. Having them in our portfolio will enable us to negotiate much higher commissions from our new principals. Accordingly we are planning on an average travel agency commission of 11 per cent rising to 13 per cent by the end of year 3. Commission on insurance and other services will be 30 per cent, throughout.

▶ *Promotional Plans*

Our market research shows that editorial has the greatest impact on people's choice of an adventure holiday, closely followed by having the right 'shop window', and having a recommendation from a friend, relation, or colleague. General press advertising seems to be fairly ineffective in this sector, and even specialist press advertising only draws in 14 per cent of clients.

Accordingly, our promotional plan is as follows:

Public Relations (PR). We will put considerable effort into preparing and disseminating a regular flow of press releases. These will be based on stories about our destinations, activities, corporate clients, and our staff. We will use a freelance PR adviser to help us write copy and target editors.

Shop Front. We plan to have an exciting, informative, and actively managed display window. There will be a video display showing holidays in progress. Different destinations can be selected from outside the window via a control panel, otherwise the scenes will rotate on a random basis.

Web Site. We will have a well-managed Web site. This is fast becoming a major promotional channel and we believe it will increase in importance over time. Also it is the easiest way for us to have a global presence at the outset.

Advertising. We will undertake a small amount of specialist-press advertising in order to enhance our PR activity. There is considerable research to support the argument that the more often a potential client hears about you, the more likely they are to approach you when they have a need for your type of service.

Database. Our database will retain full details of all our clients, the holidays they have taken, and their post-holiday appraisal data. We will use this data to provide incentives to our delighted clients prompting them to recommend our services to friends, relatives, colleagues, and employers.

Direct Mail. We will write to all past shop clients announcing the establishment of the travel business, and offering them a special introductory adventure holiday package.

▶ *Wider Factors Affecting Strategy*

The general economic climate in this city is good. A large influx of new businesses relocating from London and its surrounds, has added to the area's prosperity. There is now a large and growing young-professional population.

Tourism in general looks set to grow, Europe looks like continuing to be the major destination, and the Internet will be an important channel into this market.

Tourism is becoming a heavily regulated business sector. Whilst we have avoided most of the regulatory problems by becoming an appointed agent for a large established tour operator, in the future we will need our own ABTA bonding and ATOL registration.

~ *Operations* ~

▶ *Sales*

Excellent selling skills are vital in our type of business, so everyone will be fully trained in selling. Every month we will audit each other by observing half a day's selling activity and giving feedback on strengths and weaknesses in skills.

▶ *Record Keeping*

We will keep records of every sales contact. Data such as source of enquiry; client's needs; previous holidays; and job, income, and status, will be recorded. By having superior information on clients and prospects we intend to offer a truly personal service.

▶ *Premises*

It is vital that the travel business has both a shop front facing onto the main street, and a visible separate entrance. It is intended that clothing-shop clients will be able to move between the premises without going outside. We will be renting 70 sq m (750 sq ft) of space at a cost of £18,000 per annum, fully serviced. In addition, we will need to spend £15,000 on internal refurbishments. We plan to do some of this work ourselves. Also a further £2,500 will be needed for office equipment such as desks and chairs.

▶ *Capacity*

Our offices can accommodate five sales desks. Each sales desk has a capacity to handle 4 clients per hour, which means over the year we could handle up to 40,000 enquiries. With our average conversion rate of 1 in 5 we could service 9,600 clients from our present facilities. This is well above the numbers we are anticipating in the business plan.

▶ *Equipment*

We will be renting an integrated telephone and database system from the outset. This will allow any of up to 10 sales staff to answer calls and have full on-screen data on clients and products. As service is one of our key differentiators, it is essential that all of us have full access to all relevant data speedily and efficiently.

▶ *Staffing*

From the outset, all staff will have job descriptions, a career and training history file, and a record of appraisals. New staff will take the travel agency psychometric aptitude test, and then spend time with each member of the Adventure Works Travel team.

All staff will undergo full product training, and will spend at least four weeks a year on site at key travel destinations. We plan to start with three full-time staff, including the founder, and one part timer. We plan to be operating with six staff during the third year of trading.

▶ *Quality Control*

We will be developing outline scripts to help sales staff manage enquiries. This will ensure that all incoming phone calls are dealt with in the same way and to a similar high standard.

We will encourage people enquiring about holidays to give us feedback on:

Our ability to handle their enquiry.

The way we manage between booking the holiday and taking the holiday.

The client's reactions to the holiday, in terms of whether it meets their expectations.

~ *Forecasts and Financial Data* ~

▶ *Sales Forecast*

Our enquiry to sales conversion rate on the adventure travel holidays sold to date, whilst operating within the outdoor clothing shop, has been 33 per cent. For the purposes of our sales forecast, we are assuming that only 20 per cent of enquiries will actually result in an adventure holiday being booked. This is a very conservative estimate.

We expect there to be a steady build up of clients coming from the clothing shop to talk to us about holidays. However, the number of new enquiries generated by our promotional activity will also build up during the year, gradually overtaking enquiries from the clothes shop. This is a trend we expect to continue.

Based on the projection below, we are forecasting to sell 660 adventure travel holidays next year at an average price of £2,125.

Once insurance and other service sales are added in we expect to generate an income of £160,948 over the 12 months.

Sales Forecast Projection

	Q1	Q2	Q3	Q4	Year Total
Enquiries Generated Through Promotion	200	425	425	750	1,800
Adventure Shop Enquiries	300	300	450	450	1,500
Total Enquiries	**500**	**725**	**875**	**1,200**	**3,300**
Holidays Sold	100	145	175	240	660
Average Holiday's Cost	2,000	2,000	2,250	2,250	2,125
Commission Received	20,000	29,000	43,312	59,136	151,448
Commission on Insurance & Other Services Received	1,000	2,000	3,000	3,500	9,500
Total Commission & Fees Earned	**21,000**	**31,000**	**43,312**	**62,636**	**160,948**

In year 2 we are forecasting commission of £373,843, and in year 3 we plan to reach £590,926.

▶ *Cash Flow Projections and Sensitivity Analysis*

The cash flow projections for year 1 show that after the owner has put in £25,000 the business will need additional short-term financing of about £50,000. For the last two months of the year we are forecasting a positive cumulative cash flow, and a year-end cash surplus of £11,937.

We have also done a sensitivity analysis to assess the impact on cash flow, if our sales of holidays were 10 per cent less than projected. We do not believe this to be a likely event. But even if it were to occur, our short-term financing needs would still not exceed £50,000 in any month. However, this scenario would leave the company with a small (£1,450) negative cash position at the year end.

In our cash flow projection we have assumed the whole £50,000 additional financing has come from a bank loan. We have allowed for interest on the full amount for the whole period. In practice, we would hope to finance part of this at least by an overdraft amount equal to the money actually required. In this way we believe we have made a prudent, conservative provision.

▶ *Profit and Loss Account*

We expect to make a small after-tax profit in the first year of £21,898. This is before the owner's drawings. Any owner's drawings will be contingent on performance being better than that expected in the plan.

Projected Profits in Years 1 to 3

	Year 1	Year 2	Year 3
Turnover	1,416,071	3,115,356	4,545,588
Less Cost of Sales	1,255,123	2,741,513	3,954,662
Gross Profit	**160,948**	**373,843**	**590,926**
Less Expenses	133,575	145,750	207,000
Profit Before Tax	**27,373**	**228,093**	**383,926**
Provision for Tax	5,474	45,619	87,276
Proft After Tax	**21,898**	**182,474**	**296,650**

▶ *Balance Sheet*

The balance sheet at the end of year 1 shows a healthy surplus of current assets over current liabilities. We have shown a conservative funding position, which does not include any of the additional capital that we hope to secure.

▶ *Performance Ratios*

We plan to move our gross profit up from 11 per cent in year 1, to 13 per cent in year 3. These figures look quite low, but it should be remembered that our income is really the sales commission we earn, not the full price of an adventure holiday.

Our profit before tax is a more accurate measure of performance. This we expect to move from 2 per cent at the outset, up to 8 per cent by year 3.

Commission generated and profit per employee will be amongst the highest in the industry. At Brooker's Travel, for example, profit per employee never exceeded £19,500.

	Year 1	Year 2	Year 3
Gross Profit (%)	11	12	13
Profit Before Tax %	2	7	8
Commission Generated per Employee	£45,985	£83,076	£98,487
Profit per employee	£7,535	£41,471	£63,987

▶ *Break Even*

To break even we will need to sell between 2 and 3 holidays a day. This compares with our present sales of 1.3 holidays a day, based on our part-time effort out of the clothing shop. So we feel confident that break even can be attained within a reasonable period.

~ Financing Requirements ~

▶ *Funds Required and Timing*

The two major investments we plan to make are:

Web Site and Database Development (this will cost us £25,000). The database system is one of our key differentiators. It will allow us to offer superior service and ensure a high level of repeat business and referrals.

The Web site is vital if we are to reach this wide and disparate global market. The group of potential clients we have chosen as our target market (affluent, professional 25- to 35-year-olds) are prime users of the Internet. Even those people in our locality will expect to be able to research our offers on the Internet before coming to the shop.

Shop Premises Development (this will cost us £17,500). We have to look professional and to have an efficient work environment. If our staff do not have the right tools we can hardly expect them to deliver superior performance. If clients see an amateur premises, they will not be inspired to spend thousands of pounds and entrust their adventure holiday plans to us.

Both these investments need to be made at the outset to ensure the business creates the right impression from the start. We only get one chance to make a first impression.

We have decided to lease our telephone and computer systems as this is a rapidly changing area and we need to have access to the very latest technology. Financing packages from equipment suppliers are currently very attractive.

▶ *Funding Options*

The owner plans to invest £25,000 of her own money (the proceeds of the sale of her share of the clothing shop business). The cash flow projections show that the business will require a further £50,000 of working capital during the early months of the first year's trading. We think we should provide for £60,000 to allow for unforeseen eventualities. We are considering two options for raising this.

Option 1: The sale of equity, perhaps to the original shop partners, of between £25,000 and £100,000. This would provide some capital to allow for growth. Any shortfall could be funded by overdraft or a bank loan.

Option 2: Approach our bank with a view to raising a medium-term loan of £25,000 and an overdraft facility of £35,000. Karen Kehoe could, with family help, provide any lender with security for part, if not all, of this facility.

~ *Business Controls* ~

▶ *Financial*

We will be using a computer-based financial management system. This will allow us to analyse the profitability of sales of different holidays through each tour operator. In this way we can review our sales and marketing activities on a regular basis. It will also allow us to reward staff on the basis of profit achieved rather than just on sales.

▶ *Sales and Marketing*

We will also be using a contact-management system that will allow us to monitor the effectiveness of different promotional strategies and of different marketing messages. The cornerstone of our strategic advantage lies in having superior data on prospects and clients.

▶ *Appendix: Market Research*

International Arrivals by World Region

Indicators of Tourism Demand

Summary of Findings From our Market Research

Adventure Works Travel Market Research Questionnaire

International Arrivals by World Regions: Updated Forecast for the Year 2010 (Millions)

	1975	1995	1996	2000	2010	Average annual growth rate 1990 - 2010
Europe	153.8	338.2	347.4	397	525	3.1
East Asia/Pacific	8.7	84.5	90.1	122	229	7.6
Americas	50.0	110.1	115.5	138	195	3.7
Africa	4.7	18.7	19.4	25	37	4.6
Middle East	3.6	11.3	15.1	14	21	4.9
South Asia	1.6	4.5	4.5	6	11	6.7
World Total	**222.3**	**567.4**	**592.1**	**702**	**1,018**	**4.1**

Indicators of Tourism Demand in 2004

	International tourist arrivals (x 1,000)	Nights spent by foreign tourists (Mill)	International tourism receipts (Mill, ECU)
Austria	17,173	63.8	11,168
Belgium	5,560	12.8	4,776
Denmark	1,614	10.8	2,814
Finland	835	3.3	1,320
France	60,110	54.3	20,993
Germany	14,847	35.5	12,408
Greece	10,130	39.6	3,138
Ireland	4,231	14.0	2,059
Italy	31,052	113.0	20,993
Luxembourg	767	2.3	4,776
Netherlands	6,574	19.7	4,946
Portugal	9,706	22.2	3,330
Spain	44,886	107.8	19,431
Sweden	683	7.9	2,652
United Kingdom	22,700	164.9	14,366
EU	230,868	672.0	124,143
Iceland	190	0.8	127
Liechtenstein	59	0.1	n.a.
Norway	2,880	7.1	1,826
EEA	233,997	680.0	126,096
Switzerland	11,500	34.0	7,236

~ *Summary of Findings from Our Market Research Survey* ~

▶ *Part 1*

Summary of Findings From Market Research Sample of 300

300 clients of Adventure Works were surveyed, who had made purchases in excess of £200 in the past six months.

The key responses were as follows:

Percentage of Sample Taking and Not Taking Adventure Holidays

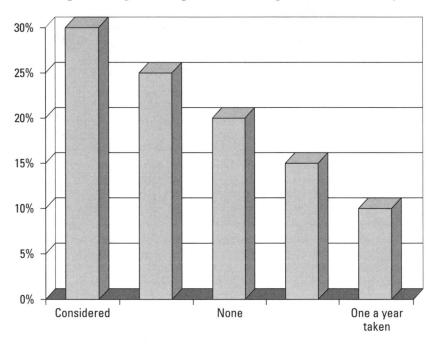

From this we can see that only 20 per cent of our sample had never taken or considered taking an adventure holiday. 30 per cent, whilst they had not yet taken such a holiday, had at least actively considered doing so. 10 per cent are regular users, taking at least one adventure holiday each year.

▶ *Part 2*

A Summary of Findings About Those 186 Respondents Who Have Taken at Least One Adventure Travel Holiday

Gender:	Male 65%	Female 35%
Status:	Married 21%	Single 79%

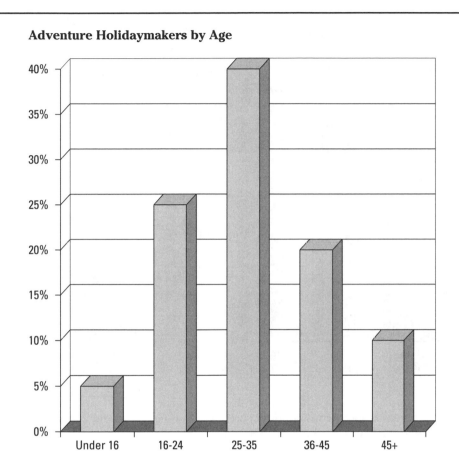

Adventure Holidaymakers by Age

The 25- to 35-year-olds appear to be the largest group, accounting for 40 per cent of adventure holidaymakers.

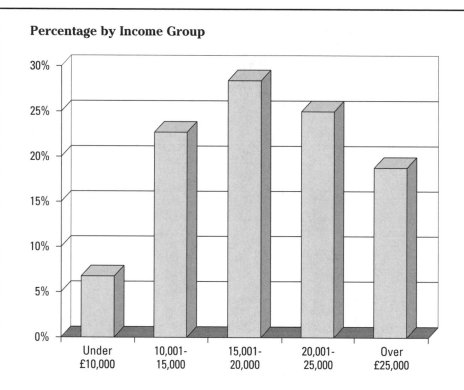

Percentage by Income Group

Over 40 per cent of adventure holidaymakers are in the £20,000 plus, income bracket. Nearly 20 per cent earn in excess of £25,000.

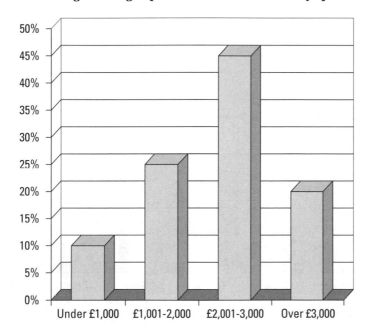

Percentage Average Spent on Adventure Holidays per Head per Holiday

Most of those taking adventure holidays spend in excess of £2,000 per head per holiday. Those spending over £3,000 per head tend to be 25- to 35-year-old professionals. Those spending under £2,000 are in the lower income and lower age groups.

Percentage by Destination

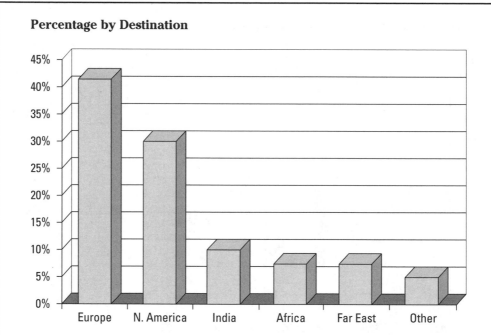

Europe	1,200
North America	1,000
India	600
Africa	810
Far East	675
Other	715

The 5,000 Major Tours Offered by Region. Adventure Research, May 2004.

Our research shows that Europe is the most popular destination for adventure holidaymakers. However, only 1,200 of the 5,000 adventure tours on the market are for European destinations. Africa, which only attracts 7 per cent of the market, has 16 per cent of the tours aimed at it.

It follows that the European market has scope for expansion, and that if we concentrate on that market we only have to have detailed knowledge of upmarket European tours, rather than all 5,000. In that way we can have the advantage of superior knowledge in our chosen market.

Percentage by Source of Purchase of Last Adventure Holiday and Whether They Would Use Again

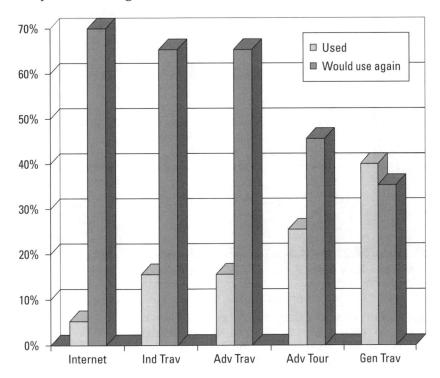

This finding is one of the most powerful results of our research. Whilst general travel agents may be the most likely to be used by those taking an adventure holiday, they are the least likely place for those clients to return to.

Whilst specialist adventure travel agents, such as the business we are setting up, only account for 15 per cent of the market, 65 per cent of clients would use them again. We aim by superior service to better this ratio.

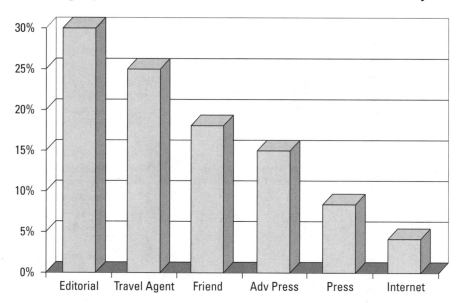

Percentage by Where You Heard About Your Last Adventure Holiday

These findings demonstrate the power of editorial comment. The next most effective way to reach potential clients is via the travel agent's shop window. Both the general press and the adventure-travel press do not appear to have much effect on buyers in this market.

Part VI
The Part of Tens

In this part . . .

In The Part of Tens, we list the ten most important questions to ask yourself about your business plan while you're working on it. We also point out the ten things you never ever want to be caught doing (while you're business planning, of course). Then we take a look at ten (or so) of the best-planned organisations around, pointing out why we think they're so good at what they do.

Chapter 17

Ten Questions to Ask About Your Plan

In This Chapter
▶ Looking over what you've done
▶ Making the necessary changes

*I*t never hurts to step back every once in a while and take stock of where you stand. With that in mind, we've filled this chapter with all sorts of questions to mull over before you show your business plan to the world.

Are Your Goals Tied to Your Mission?

Look at the goals that you set for your company. These goals are the results that you absolutely, positively intend to achieve, and to a large extent, these goals determine how you set priorities and how you run your company. Your goals have to be consistent with one another so that you're not running in different directions at the same time. In addition, you have to tie your goals to your company's mission so that you're heading in the direction in which you really want to go.

Can You Point to Major Opportunities?

If you want your company to grow and prosper in the long haul, you have to take advantage of business opportunities as they come along. Your business plan should point out the major opportunities that you see heading your way (in technology, markets, and distribution, for example) and outline the actions that your company intends to take now so as to be in a position to take advantage of those opportunities down the road.

Have You Prepared for Threats?

It's easy to paint a rosy picture of what the future holds for your company, but having a rosy picture doesn't necessarily mean that it's going to come true. Your company is in much better shape if you paint an objective picture – including the bad news along with the good. That way, you're prepared for the dangers that are bound to be there.

Your business plan should point out the biggest threats that loom on the horizon (a market slowdown, new regulations, or increasing competition, for example) and offer ways to prepare for them. If you recognise threats before anybody else does, you can often turn a threat into a real business opportunity.

Have You Defined Your Customers?

The more you know about your customers – who they are, how they act, what they want – the more you know about your company. Customers tell you how to succeed in the marketplace.

Describing your customers is much easier if you think about dividing them into separate groups. Each group, or market segment, has its own unique profile and places its own set of demands on your company.

Your customers are so important to your company that you can't afford to leave them out of your business plan. You should answer three questions:

- Who is buying?
- What do they buy?
- Why do they buy?

Your plan should explain how your company intends to serve those customers better than anyone else out there.

Can You Track Your Competitors?

Your competitors are around to make life interesting. They're the companies that always try to woo your customers away, promising products or services that have better value (more benefits, lower prices), and you can't ignore them. You have to be able to identify who your competitors are, what they're doing, and where they plan to go in the future.

Competition represents a big piece of your business environment. Your business plan should cover what you know about your competitors and – more important – how you intend to keep track of them on an ongoing basis. Your plan should also address how you intend to use what you learn to choose competitive battles that you can win.

Do You Know Your Strengths and Weaknesses?

It's hard to be objective in making an honest assessment of what your company does well and what it could do better. But your company's strengths and weaknesses determine its odds of success as you look ahead. Strengths and weaknesses refer to your company's capabilities and resources and how well they match up with the capabilities and resources that your company really needs to have in place to be successful.

Your business plan should list your company's capabilities and resources – from management skills or research expertise to operations and distribution strength or loyal customers. But the plan must go on to describe how each of these capabilities or resources is either a strength or a potential weakness, given your business situation and the industry in which you compete.

Does Your Strategy Make Sense?

Strategy has to do with how you intend to make your business plan happen. For starters, you have to pull together your company's strengths and weaknesses, the opportunities and threats that your company faces, and the business goals that you set. Then, given all these pieces of the puzzle, you have to figure out a way to get where you want to be, in spite of all the things that stand in your way.

It should be clear, from beginning to end, that your business plan is based on an overall strategy that makes sense. Your company should have a strategy that's grounded in reality and that makes reasonable assumptions about what's happening and what's about to happen – a strategy that's logical and rational about what can be accomplished and how long it's going to take.

Can You Stand Behind the Numbers?

Think about all your financial statements as your company's report card – one that answers some big questions. Do your customers love you? Are your competitors afraid of you? Are you making the right business choices? A profit and loss account presents the bottom line, the balance sheet shows what your company is worth, and the cash-flow statement keeps track of the money.

Your current financial statements tell everybody how well you're doing. But many people are more interested in your financial forecasts, which say what you expect to happen in the future. Just because these forecasts include official-looking numbers, however, doesn't mean that the predictions will necessarily come true. If you want to paint an honest picture of your company, your business plan should include a realistic financial portrait, based on assumptions that you believe in and numbers that you trust.

Are You Really Ready for Change?

If one thing remains constant in the business world, it's change. Although some industries change faster than others, everything around you – from technology to competition to your market – is going to be a little different tomorrow than it is today, no matter what business you're in. If you want to keep up, you have to think two or three steps ahead. You must look carefully and continually at what may happen in the world and how it may affect your company.

Although your business plan paints an honest picture of how you see your company and what you see happening down the road, the plan should also acknowledge the fact that you don't have a crystal ball. So present some options. Include one or two alternative business scenarios, asking – and answering – the question 'What if. . . ?'

Is Your Plan Clear, Concise, and Up to Date?

Your plan should certainly capture all the things that you think are essential to know about your company and its situation – everything important that you learn in the process of planning your company. But none of the information that you present is going to be of any use to anyone else if your business plan is too long, impossible to read, or out of date.

Read over your own plan. Is it easy to understand? Is it easy to navigate? How long did it take you to read? Did you know where to find all the details? Did the details get in the way?

Your plan is a living document, so make sure that it's in a form that's easy to change when you need to make changes. If you have to start from scratch each time, your plan is destined to be old news.

Chapter 18

Top Ten Business-Planning Never-Evers

. . . .

In This Chapter
▶ Reviewing what to watch out for
▶ Fixing things that are broken

. . . .

*T*his chapter lists a few of those 'I can't believe I did that' planning miscues that are all too easy to make. We list the top ten here so that you have a better chance of not making these mistakes yourself. But if you happen to make them anyway, at least you'll know that you're not alone.

Failing to Plan in the First Place

We're probably preaching to the converted here, because you're already reading this book. But neglecting to plan is a business sin so grave that it's always worth a short sermon. Planning isn't easy. After all, there are no right or wrong answers, and nothing's guaranteed. But the planning process is bound to leave your company better prepared to face an uncertain future.

Although a business plan may not solve all your problems, it can help. Planning makes you a better manager and makes your company, no matter how large or small it is, more competitive and more likely to succeed in the long haul.

Shrugging Off Values and Vision

There's nothing more invigorating than jumping right into the thick of things. You're itching to line up your products and services, seize the opportunities that are right in front of you, and face down your competitors one by one. This situation is the business version of a roller-coaster ride, and we won't deny that it's exciting: ups, downs, hairpin corners. But roller coasters end up right back where they start – and so will your company, if you don't stand back and spend some time on the values and vision that set you off in the right direction.

Your company's values and vision statements are there to remind you where you want to go and what you want to become. Together, these statements are your business compass, so you don't want to start your journey without them.

Second-Guessing the Customer

Everybody knows the cliché, 'The customer is always right.' Well, it's not a cliché for nothing. Whether you're trying to satisfy an individual customer face-to-face or attempting to figure out what an entire segment of the market needs and wants, you ignore what customers tell you at your own peril.

This idea seems so obvious that it's hardly worth repeating. But you may be surprised how many companies approach the marketplace with a 'We know just what you're looking for' attitude. Just remember that if you're not listening to your customers, one of your competitors is.

Underestimating Your Competition

Sometimes you can get so involved in working on your own product or service that you forget the other smart people out there who are trying to develop and market the same product or service. The more competitive your industry is, the smarter the competitors are and the more of them there seem to be.

Watching your competitors is just as important as listening to your customers. After all, if you want to stay ahead of the pack, you have to know what the rest of the pack is up to. The more you know about your competitors, the more you can use what you know to beat them at their own game.

Ignoring Your Own Strengths

Why does the grass always seem a little bit greener in the other company's garden? It usually isn't all that green when you get up close and look carefully, of course. But there's a real temptation in business to think that other companies have all the right answers, the better way of doing things, the correct approach.

Oh, you can always learn things from your competition – no doubt about it. But what's right for one competitor isn't necessarily going to be the best way for you to do things. So don't forget to catalogue your company's own unique strengths and use them to your own advantage in the marketplace.

Mistaking a Budget for a Plan

Putting together your company's budget is one of the most critical steps in the business-planning process. A budget, after all, is where you make all the really big decisions about how much money to spend and where to spend it. Your budget plays a large role in determining what your company will do in the months and years ahead.

But don't ever mistake this budget for your business plan. The bulk of your plan is all the work that you do up front, before you begin to put your budget together in the first place. All that analysis of your industry, customers, competitors, and yourself makes your financial decisions the right ones – the ones that move your company closer to your larger business goals.

Shying Away from Reasonable Risk

Some people jump out of planes; others won't ride a big wheel. Some of us are willing to bet the house; others have trouble buying a lottery ticket. But no matter how you feel about risk, nothing's risk-free, especially in today's competitive markets.

Doing business means taking risks, and creating a business plan is one good way to manage those risks. Don't shy away from making a bold business move – after you've done your homework, assessed the risk, and know that it's a reasonable step to take.

Allowing One Person to Dominate the Plan

Nobody has all the right answers (at least, no one we've met personally). So no matter how big or small your company is, don't create a business plan all by yourself. Even if you're the only one running the show, get other people you trust involved in your planning process – at the very least, to review what you've done and provide an outside perspective. If your company's bigger, involve as many people with different points of view as you can in your planning process. The more viewpoints you get, the stronger the business plan will be.

Being Afraid to Change

We all end up making changes in our lives. Sometimes we're not given much choice in the matter, and most of us would prefer to go on doing the same things that we've always done, especially if we're really good at them. Companies aren't much different. It's not easy to change the way that you do business or the kind of business that you do, and change is particularly hard if you're really successful. But a good business plan alerts you to changes that your company should make before you're forced to make them – changes that allow you to be more responsive to customers, more competitive, more efficient, and more successful.

Forgetting to Motivate and Reward

A business plan isn't useful if it never gets out of your head or off the page. Your business blueprint has to be translated into the efforts and activities of all the people in your company – and it has to make sense to every one of them.

You have to link your strategy to your vision; link your vision to the company mission; link your mission to the goals and objectives that you set. Then you have to link all these pieces of the plan to the way in which you motivate and reward the people around you.

Chapter 19

Ten of the Best-Planned Organisations Around

- -

In This Chapter

▶ Checking out a few of the best organisations

▶ Making a choice of your own

- -

Here are lots of organisations out there – millions, really – so we can't claim to have looked at every one of them in the search for our own Top Ten. But we think that the following companies, countries, teams, and personalities stand out for their unique approaches to planning. We can all learn something from each of them.

Amazon

Jeff Bezos, Amazon.com's founder, came up with the idea for selling books online while he was working as a senior vice president of D.E. Shaw, a New York-based investment management firm. Bezos was assigned to come up with profitable ideas for selling over the Internet. Bezos concluded that online book selling would be a good business because two of the largest book distributors in the United States already had electronic lists.

Bezos' firm was not willing to invest in the idea, so he started it himself. He and his wife then drove across country to Seattle to start the company. Bezos typed the business plan on his computer while his wife drove. Bezos recruited one of the programmers he had met through his investigations for D.E. Shaw, Shel Kaphan, to become his first employee.

Kaphan and a contractor named Paul Barton-Davis built a prototype of the Amazon.com Web site in a converted garage of a rented home in Bellevue, Washington. Bezos raised the first $1 million of seed capital from fifteen wealthy individual investors.

The naming of Amazon.com was based on the importance of its relative size. Bezos reasoned that the Amazon River was ten times as large as the next largest river, which was the Mississippi, in terms of volume of water and Amazon.com had six times as many titles as the world's largest physical bookstore.

Bezos focused on ways to enhance Amazon.com customers' experiences. He planned the Web site to make people to feel as though they are visiting a place rather than a software application.

Bezos spends hours thinking about the future, to make sure he keeps his business proposition fresh and competitive. He is always on the look out for new ideas, which he garners by talking to employees, researching competitors and surfing the Internet.

To put Amazon's winning ways to work, read the following:

- ✔ Preparing for opportunities and threats (Chapter 4)
- ✔ Applying a strategy that offers something unique (Chapter 13)
- ✔ Working with the product life cycle (Chapter 14)

Harvard University

Founded way back in 1636, Harvard University is on everybody's shortlist of the best universities in the world. The university has educated six US presidents, and its faculty members have included 33 Nobel laureates. With more than 250,000 living alumni in every country on the planet, a faculty of 2,000 professors, an endowment of $6.2 billion, and an annual operating budget of roughly $1.3 billion, Harvard is definitely at the top end of the education business.

Harvard's enduring success is due in part to a clear mission and vision of its own role as a leader in higher education and to the image that it has developed around that vision. Graduating from Harvard is viewed as being a special accomplishment. The university creates an atmosphere of academic excellence by combining a 360-year tradition with a world-class faculty (no, we're not among them) and top-notch students. The traditions are carefully maintained, the faculty members are well rewarded, and the students are selected from among the best and the brightest.

This sort of thing doesn't come cheap, of course, but the university remains a financial powerhouse, largely because of an industrial-strength fundraising organisation. Harvard works hard at keeping track of and supporting its extensive network of alumni and friends, and the school rakes in enormous amounts of cash from them.

Harvard's long-lasting capabilities and resources should allow it to continue planning for the next 400 years.

To put Harvard's winning ways to work, cruise to the following:

✔ Creating a mission and vision for the future (Chapter 2)

✔ Focusing on your core competence (Chapter 9)

✔ Keeping track of finances (Chapter 10)

The LEGO Group

Who would have guessed that an entire corporate empire could be built on a foundation of brightly coloured plastic bricks? The LEGO Group is one of the ten largest toy manufacturers in the world, employing almost 10,000 people in 30 countries. LEGO toys, of course, are those plastic building sets that kids go wild over – 515 different sets, to be exact. The sets are sold in more than 60,000 retail outlets around the globe.

Why is LEGO so popular with the younger crowd? In Danish, *LEGO* combines words that mean to 'play well'. Since 1934, the company has focused its energies on figuring out new ways to help kids play better by using their own creativity and the skills required to build things. And build things they do. LEGO bricks are small technological marvels in themselves, with a patented design dating back to 1958. Kids use them to build everything, including LEGO towers – the current world record stands at just over 76 feet! The company is also constructing entire LEGO theme parks out of the plastic bricks.

A big part of The LEGO Group's success stems from its capability to stay focused on a specific group of customers who have very particular needs. The company is devoted not only to children's toys, but also to children themselves. The LEGO Group spends time and money on understanding how kids play, how they learn, and how they grow.

The company's basic respect for children extends to broader issues around the world. The LEGO Group funds the LEGO Prize, an international award given each year to an organisation that has made special efforts to improve the conditions under which children live.

To put The LEGO Group's winning ways to work, check out the following:

✔ Identifying market segments you can serve (Chapter 6)

✔ Focusing on a specific group of customers (Chapter 13)

✔ Extending your product line (Chapter 14)

Republic of San Marino

The Republic of San Marino traces its origins to the waning years of the Roman Empire, making it the oldest country in Europe and certainly the longest-running republic in the world. It also happens to be the smallest independent nation on the planet, with a population of fewer than 25,000 people living in an area of about 60 square kilometres.

Legend has it that the country was founded by a stonecutter named Marinus (later, Saint Marino), who fled to Mount Titano in 301 AD to escape persecution from Rome. The small city-state of San Marino based its earliest form of self-rule on the principles of democracy, and the workings of its government have stayed pretty much the same ever since. The country's steadfast belief in individual freedom so moved Abraham Lincoln that he wrote to the captains regent (the head of state and chief executive) in 1861, saying, 'Although your dominion is small, nevertheless your state is one of the most honored throughout history.'

What accounts for the Republic of San Marino's longevity? Location, location, location, for one thing. The tiny country is rugged, mountainous, and relatively easy to defend. But just as important are the ideals and values embraced by the people and reflected in the way that the government is organised and has functioned for more than a millennium.

To put San Marino's winning ways to work, jump over to the following:

- ✔ Learning why values are so important (Chapter 3)
- ✔ Recognising critical success factors (Chapter 4)
- ✔ Putting together an organisation that works (Chapter 15)

General Electric Corporation

'What's the Dow doing?' This question is asked every day in hundreds of languages. The Dow Jones Industrial Average, which combines the stock price of 30 major US corporations, is watched around the globe. The oldest company on that list – and the only Dow stock remaining from the original 'dirty dozen' back in 1900 – is General Electric Corporation. Today, the company has revenues of $80 billion, a workforce of 240,000 employees, and operations in more than 100 countries.

Over the past century, General Electric has come up with many of the bright ideas that have become a standard part of modern business planning. The company invented new ways to scan the business environment, divide an organisation into strategic business units, and manage product portfolios.

Along the way, General Electric also created a strong and dynamic company, with visionary leadership at the top and with a commitment to develop and promote people up through its ranks. The company's training programmes are the envy of many business schools, and when their then CEO Jack Welch speaks, the corporate world listens. Today, GE is a management and organisation role model that big companies worldwide imitate. To put GE's winning ways to work, see the following:

✔ Identifying strategic business units (Chapter 14)

✔ Managing a product portfolio (Chapter 14)

✔ Encouraging leadership roles (Chapter 15)

Manchester United

Manchester United Football Club is one of 20 teams in the top English football competition, the Premier League. The football club was established in 1878, under the name of Newton Heath LYR Football Club, and joined the First Division of the Football League in 1892. In 1902 the name of Manchester United was adopted and in 1910 the football club relocated to Old Trafford, where it has played its home matches ever since. The club has won more than 25 major league trophies, including more than a score of Premier League or its equivalents, since 1908. Manchester United's shares were listed on the London Stock Exchange in 1991 with an initial market capitalisation of £47 million. By the beginning of this millennium the company was worth £623 million and was ranked 210th by market capitalisation in the FTSE Top 500. According to accounting firm Deloitte and Touche (Deloitte), Manchester United is the largest football club in the world.

To be successful at football, you have to combine teamwork, team players, and team management – perhaps more than in any other sport. For a team to win game after game, the players must have a consistent strategy, chemistry, and an organisation that's flawless. And the team must understand exactly who they're up against every single time they face a competitor. But to be on top for 90 years calls for strategic management of the highest order, an achievement unequalled by many businesses.

From player selection to preseason preparation, from drills and practice to the games themselves, the Manchester squad is a disciplined football-playing machine with well-defined goals in front and clear objectives to back them up. Individual players who were talented to begin with are moulded into a nearly unbeatable team. From the beginning Manchester United developed an organisational culture in which winning was simply expected. In the process, they redefined the meaning of victory in sports and created a model for how sports dynasties are made.

To put Manchester United's winning ways to work, look at the following:

- ✔ Setting your own goals and objectives (Chapter 2)
- ✔ Knowing who the competitors are and what they can do (Chapter 7)
- ✔ Creating an organisational culture to support your goals (Chapter 15)

Your Local McDonald's Restaurant

Absolutely nothing is left to chance at this global fast-food franchise. The McDonald's in your town is one of more than 25,000 restaurants worldwide, each of which is run with the precision of a Swiss watch. Go to a Golden Arches on your high street or to one halfway around the globe, and – for good or bad – you won't be able to tell the difference in what you're eating. Is this consistency simply a coincidence? No way.

This company understands the supreme value its customers place on knowing exactly what they're going to get at a McDonald's, anywhere in the world. And to ensure there are no surprises, McDonald's demands uniform quality standards. These standards are maintained through strict procedures and systems that leave absolutely nothing to chance. Everything that McDonald's does reflects the significance that the company places on careful planning.

McDonald's store managers are initiated into the art of assembly-line food-making at Hamburger University, the company's in-house training facility. New recruits are shown how to do things right the first time and every time. They learn that French fries must be cut and cooked just right and that the pickle, mustard, and ketchup have to be placed just so. They also learn that the precise amount of this or that spells the difference between a Big Mac and a pretender.

Even the location of a McDonald's restaurant is the result of a textbook-like lesson on where to put a retail outlet. Food suppliers are selected only after the most rigorous testing and retesting to ensure guaranteed consistency and quality. Staff training is clearly a science. The company has shown its competition the importance of planning in a tough business environment. McDonald's is the model to emulate when it comes to making a go of it in the food-on-the-go industry.

To put the winning ways of McDonald's to work, check out the following:

- ✔ Constructing a value chain to gain an advantage (Chapter 9)
- ✔ Creating effective procedures and systems (Chapter 15)
- ✔ Developing the necessary business skills (Chapter 15)

Madonna Louise Ciccone

Don't laugh – Madonna is an organisation unto herself. Born in Michigan in 1958, one of eight children, this ambitious and complex entertainer has so completely mastered the world of show business that she has been called 'America's smartest businesswoman'. Using what can fairly be described as mediocre talent and competent performance skills, she has managed to move to the top of her industry – and stay there – by continually reinventing herself. She has transformed herself from dancer to pop singer, video performer to author, actress to global superstar. Through it all, Madonna has demonstrated that the careful planning and management of an image can be just as powerful as raw talent in the media business. It's hard to argue with success. After all, the earnings of Madonna, Inc. now top a quarter of a billion dollars.

How has she accomplished all this at such a young age? Planning, personal discipline, and constant attention to detail are among her wide array of talents. She manages her own career, chairs her own group of companies, and charts her own path, based on an uncanny instinct for knowing what the public wants and what it will tolerate. She always goes to the edge, but she never falls over. A leading Hollywood mogul noted, 'I would take her street-smart business sense over someone with a Harvard MBA any day.'

To put Madonna's winning ways to work, see the following:

✔ Understanding customer perceptions (Chapter 5)

✔ Identifying your own strengths and weaknesses (Chapter 8)

✔ Anticipating change and assessing risks (Chapter 12)

easyJet

You have to be a bit crazy to think seriously about competing in the airline industry today, because the dice are loaded against airlines as money-making propositions. The fixed costs of doing business are extremely high, so nearly everything that an airline does has to be paid for in advance, before a single passenger plonks down money and boards a plane. In addition, there's hardly any brand loyalty in airline travel. Throw in the fickleness of the weather, and what you have is a recipe for disaster rather than profits.

None of these problems fazed Stelios Haji-Ioannou, who founded easyJet in 1995. The inaugural flights from London, Luton to Edinburgh and Glasgow was supported by the advertising campaign 'Making flying as affordable as a pair of jeans – £29 one way.' At this time, the airline had two leased Boeing 737-200 aircraft and essentially acted as a 'virtual airline' which contracted in everything from pilots to check-in staff. Early on, Stelios Haji-Ioannou came to the conclusion that many passengers just want to get from point A to point B at the lowest possible price, so he started an airline without frills. easyJet offers no commissions to travel agents and has even eliminated meals during flights. The company was quick to take advantage of Internet reservations and ticketless travel to reduce costs even further.

But the real savings at easyJet are in turnaround time. Stelios Haji-Ioannou realised early on that the key to profits is keeping planes in the air, so he came up with a new way to operate. easyJet flies only short-haul routes and the company uses only one type of aircraft to minimise parts stock, training, and maintenance costs – and to reduce downtime. easyJet has been selected as a Business Superbrand by the Superbrand Council which recognises companies with an outstanding brand name. Other Superbrand companies include such globally-recognised names as Virgin, Coca-Cola and Manchester United and *Marketing* magazine described the launch of easyJet as 'one of the 100 great marketing moments of the 20th century'.

To put easyJet's winning ways to work, read the following:

- ✔ Determining customer needs and motives (Chapter 5)
- ✔ Constructing financial forecasts and budgets (Chapter 11)
- ✔ Applying a low-cost leadership strategy (Chapter 13)

(Insert Your Own Nominee Here!)

That's right – it's your turn. See whether you can come up with a good candidate for one of the best-planned organisations around. We've given you nine to think about; now it's time for you to add the tenth.

How should you begin? Start by rereading Chapters 1–18. (Just kidding.) Actually, you can start by thinking of an organisation that you really admire. Then ask the same sorts of questions that we've raised all through the book. In particular, consider these questions:

- ✔ What are the company's mission and vision?
- ✔ How does it satisfy its customers' needs?
- ✔ Who are its competitors?
- ✔ What are the company's critical success factors?
- ✔ Where is the company's competitive advantage?
- ✔ What is the company's strategy for success?

Glossary of Business and Accounting Terms

- -

Account(s): Usually annual financial records of a business.

Accrual: A system of accounting in which revenues and expenses are recorded as they are earned and incurred, not necessarily when cash is received or paid.

Added value: The difference between sales revenue and material costs. See also *value added*.

Adoption curve: A graphic representation of the classification of users or buyers of an innovation according to the time of adoption. These categories are as follows: innovators, first 2.5 per cent; early adopters, next 13.5 per cent; early majority, next 34 per cent; late majority, next 34 per cent; laggards, last 16 per cent. Research has shown that these adopter groups have different characteristics, for example social class, age, education, and attitudes. Those launching new products or businesses have to pay particular attention to the characteristics and behaviour of the innovator group in order to identify the most likely early customers, and so focus initial marketing on them.

Ad valorem: Literally means 'according to value'. Any charge that is applied as a percentage of value.

Advertising: The central purpose of all advertising activity is to secure as many favourable buying decisions as possible. As a concept, advertising has been around too long for its origins to be precisely traced. As an institutionalised business it has existed in the UK since the 1700s, when newspapers began to feature advertisements. The UK's oldest advertising agency, Charles Baker, was founded in 1812. The most surprising fact about advertising is not how much money is spent on doing it (although that is quite surprising) but how much money is misspent. Lord Leverhulme is reputed to have said, 'Half the money I spend on advertising is wasted, but I can't find anyone to tell me which half!' For the smaller firm, leaflets and brochures consume the greater proportion of advertising expenditure. Answering the following five questions before committing to any expenditure can usually ensure that this intangible activity has some concrete results:

- ✔ What do you want to happen? (for example, X people to buy Y quantity of produce Z)
- ✔ How much is that worth?
- ✔ What message will make it happen?
- ✔ What media should be used?
- ✔ How will the results be checked?

Advisory, Conciliation and Arbitration Service (ACAS): ACAS is mainly concerned with preventing disputes before they can get to the public eye. They also offer advice on recruitment and selection, payment systems and incentive schemes, and manpower planning. It is in these areas that they can prove particularly helpful to new firms, and over a quarter of their 12,500+ advisory visits each year are to companies with fewer than 50 employees. ACAS has an extremely useful website www.acas.org.uk.

AIM: Alternative Investment Market. Market for small and new businesses to raise equity capital (see also *initial public offering*).

Angel: Someone who puts up risk capital for a theatrical performance, show, or film. A West End musical, for example, costs upwards of £500,000. *Starlight Express* cost over £2.2 million, so external funding is essential. These 'angels' must be prepared to lose their money and many do. The rewards, however, can be spectacular. Investors who bought into *Evita* have recouped their cash six and a half times. Those who put up money for the smash hit musical *Me and My Girl* recouped their money and received their first profit within ten months. The term has now been taken over by the venture capital industry to mean any private investor.

Animal spirits: A term coined by J. Maynard Keynes to describe the effects of entrepreneurial zeal on the healthiness or otherwise of an economy. Surveys such as those conducted by the Confederation of British Industry and the Small Business Research Trust regularly attempt to monitor some aspects of these animal spirits.

Annual report: see *audit*.

Arbitrage: Profiting from differences in the price of something that is traded on more than one market.

Asset: Something owned by the business that has a measurable cost.

Asset finance: Releasing cash into a business by selling fixed assets and leasing them back.

Audit: A process carried out by an accountant (auditor) on larger companies each year, to check the accuracy of financial records. The auditor cannot be the company's own accountant. The result is the annual report. Currently, UK companies may be audit-exempt if they qualify as small, have a turnover of not more than £5.6 million and have a balance sheet total of not more than £2.8 million.

Authorised capital: The share capital of a company authorised by law. It does not have to be taken up. For example, a £1,000 company need only 'issue' two £1 shares. It can issue a further 998 £1 shares without recourse to law. After that sum it has to ask the permission of its shareholders.

Back-up: Copies made of data and programmes to be available in the event of originals being corrupted, damaged, or lost.

Bad debts: The amounts of money due in from customers that either have become or are expected to become uncollectable. The accounting principle of conservation requires that all reasonably likely losses be anticipated. So debts that are almost certainly uncollectable are deducted from the total; debts that are reasonably likely to be uncollectable have a specific provision made against them; and in addition a general provision can be made against the rest of the debts, based on past experience.

Balance sheet: A statement of assets and liabilities of a business. This report does not indicate the market value of the business.

Bankruptcy: Imposed by a court when someone cannot meet his or her bills. The bankrupt's property is managed by a court-appointed trustee, who must use it to pay off the creditors as fairly as possible.

Barriers to entry: The way in which big businesses appear to pull up the drawbridge after them. The greater the barriers to entry, the fewer the opportunities for new firms to enter a market. Such barriers include economies of scale, access to distribution channels, high capital requirements, high spending on research and development, short product life cycles, break-even pricing, high advertising expenditure and government policy.

Benchmark: The performance of a business against some standard or standards that other comparable businesses have achieved. Usually ranked in such a way that a firm can see if it is in the top, middle, or bottom position.

Black economy: Usually refers to businesses run by the self-employed who illegally avoid tax and National Insurance. There is therefore no official record, and they are collectively referred to as the black economy.

Blue chip: In gambling, the high chips are usually blue. In business, this refers to high-status companies and their shares. They are usually large companies with a long successful trading history.

Bookkeeping: The recording of all business transactions in 'journals' in order to provide data for accounting reports.

Book value: Usually the figure at which an asset appears in the accounts. This is not necessarily the market value.

Bootstrapping: Getting a business underway with the minimum of finance. Literally pulling the business through by sheer effort. Improbable, but it can be done.

Break-even point: The volume of production at which revenues exactly match costs. After this point profit is made.

Browser: A World Wide Web client. An information retrieval tool.

Business Link: Business support, advice and information service managed by the DTI. A local presence across England, managed by business people for business people, means Business Link is able to identify business support services from across the government, voluntary and private sectors. Similar institutions exist in Scotland, Wales and Northern Ireland.

Business transfer agents: Analogous to estate agents, they help bring buyers and sellers of small and usually retail businesses together.

Cadillac syndrome: This occurs when entrepreneurs brush aside the vital price-volume issue and its relationship to the *break-even point*, with the explanation, 'We are the Cadillac of the field.' This leads to the setting of such an unreasonably high price that a market so small as to sink the business is brought about. Although the theoretical profit margin on each unit sold is high in percentage terms, the volume sold is too low to even recover the investment. For many inventors, financial failure is often of secondary importance to their 'artistic' success (unless it is their money at stake). The fact that their product is on the market is, in itself, sufficient success.

Capital: It has several meanings, but unprefixed it usually means all the assets of the business.

Cash: The 'money' assets of a business, which include both cash in hand and cash at the bank.

Cash flow: The difference between total cash coming in and going out of a business over a period of time.

Cash-flow break-even point: The point below which the firm will need either to obtain additional financing or to liquidate some of its assets to meet its fixed costs.

Caveat emptor: Buyer beware. The buyer must inspect and satisfy him or herself it is adequate for his or her needs. The seller is under no obligation to disclose defects but may not actively conceal a known defect or lie if asked.

Chairman / Chairperson (of the Board): The senior director of a company. In a small business this role is often combined with that of *managing director*. He or she is responsible for presenting the *annual report* to the shareholders, along with his or her own comments on how the business is performing in the light of world affairs.

Common shares: Securities that represent equity ownership in a company. Common shares let an investor vote on such matters as the election of directors. They also give the holder a share in a company's profits via dividend payments or the capital appreciation of the security.

Company director: A person elected by the shareholders of a limited company to control for them the day-to-day management of the business, and to decide on policy. The Companies Act sets out directors' duties and responsibilities. In most companies, one-third of the directors are required to retire from office each year. The directors who retire in any one year are those who have been longest in office since their last election. A retiring director can stand for re-election.

Company doctor: Someone brought in to turn around an ailing venture. The term can also apply to someone who makes a habit of buying up loss-making ventures and returning them to profitability. Usually the measures taken by a company doctor in restoring a business to health include large-scale redundancies, closing down loss-making units, and the sale of any parts of the venture peripheral to its main trade. This may account for why such people are reticent to assume the title, but they are well known on the acquisition/merger circuit.

Company secretary: Every limited company in the UK must have a company secretary. In public companies they must be professionally qualified and in a private company they must be 'suitable' but need not have professional qualifications. They are appointed by the board of directors to carry out the legal duties of the company such as keeping certain records, sending information to the Registrar of Companies, and generally to manage the administration of the company.

Computer-aided design (CAD): Software to produce two- and three-dimensional drawings on the screen and as hard copy.

Corruption: A distortion or elimination of data from the memory or disk, usually caused by electromagnetic impulses – such as when a disk is left near another electronic or magnetic device such as a loudspeaker.

Cost of goods sold: The costs of goods actually sold in any period. It excludes the cost of the goods left unsold, and all overheads except manufacturing.

Crash: What happens when a program refuses to continue. Usually the program has to be reloaded, with the loss of all work in progress – unless you have kept a *back-up*.

Creative accounting: The term used to describe the rather elastic treatment of accounting rules and concepts, usually in an effort to create a picture that is favourable to the entrepreneur. In its more extreme forms it becomes fraud.

Credit scoring: A statistical technique where several financial characteristics are combined to form a single score to represent a customer's creditworthiness.

Current assets: Assets normally realised in cash or used up in operations during the year. It includes such items as debtors and stock.

Current liability: A liability due for payment in one trading period, usually a year.

Debenture: Long-term loan with specific terms of interest, capital repayment, and security.

Debug: Computerese for 'troubleshoot'.

Demand, law of: An economic theory that suggests that, all things being equal, the lower the price, the greater the demand. The concept is much misunderstood by new entrepreneurs who believe the only thing that has to be done to beat a competitor is to have a lower price. The theory was put to good effect by the late Sir Jack Cohen of Tesco in his philosophy of 'stack it high and sell it cheap'. He understood the need for good promotion, a good range and mix of products, and above all good location for his stores, as well as having competitive prices. Unfortunately (or perhaps not!), the demand for all products or services is not uniformly elastic, that is, the rate of change of price and demand are not interlinked. Some products are not that price sensitive. For example, Jaguar and Rolls-Royce would be unlikely to sell any more cars if they knocked 5 per cent off the price – indeed, by losing snob value they may sell less. So if they dropped their price they would simply lower profits. However, people would quite happily cross town to save 5p in the £1 on fresh vegetables and meat. This concept is closely allied to working out the *break-even point*.

Depreciation: A way of measuring the cost of using a fixed asset. A set portion of the asset's cost is treated as an expense for each period of its working life.

Direct costs: Expenses, such as labour and materials, which vary 'directly' according to the number if items manufactured. Also called *variable costs.*

Downside risk: Everyone who goes into a business venture does so with the expectation of making a profit. After the excitement of calculating the size of the prospective fortune to be made, the prudent entrepreneur also takes stock of the likely maximum to be lost if it all goes wrong. This is called the downside risk. The Midland Bank's association with Crocker in the USA shows that more than just your original stake can be at risk. Crocker's loans were in the main secured against farm land values, which was fine while prices were rising, but became a catastrophe when they started to fall as they did shortly after the Midland (now HSBC) acquisition. Crocker's *bad debt* provision had to be topped up with extra money from the UK parent.

Earnings before interest and taxes (EBIT): A financial measure defined as revenues less cost of goods sold and selling, general, and administrative expenses. In other words, operating and non-operating profit before the deduction of interest and income taxes.

Earnings per share (EPS): A company's profit divided by its number of outstanding shares. If a company earned £1 million in one year and had 1 million shares of stock outstanding, its EPS would be £1 per share.

E-business: Any activity on the Internet that transforms business relationships or fundamentally changes the way in which business is done. It is not simply about selling things you already make or have, but a new way to drive efficiencies, speed up transactions, innovate new products and services, and create more value for your business and for your customers. In this respect the Internet should be seen as an 'enabling technology', such as the telephone or electricity, which themselves both improved a whole variety of processes and allowed whole new industries to become established. Unlike *e-commerce*, which usually only involves relationships between suppliers and customers, e-business involves a more complex series of relationships, both inside a business, for example to change the way work is done, and outside, to improve relationships along the whole value chain that links a business and its suppliers to the market.

E-commerce: One element of *e-business* that describes the trading relationship between companies and individuals exchanging goods and services using the Internet.

Economies of scale: The gain experienced by firms that can spread their costs over a large volume of output. Other advantages, such as more efficient buying, can accrue to big producers. It is one of the *barriers to entry*, inhibiting new firms from entering certain markets successfully. However, achieving economies of scale carries some penalties. For example, it makes such businesses relatively inflexible and less responsive to change than their smaller cousins.

E-economy: Also referred to as the 'Digital Economy' or 'Cyberspace', this is the whole virtual environment in which electronic business is conducted. It is here that goods and services are exchanged, relationships initiated and established, and money changes hands. Activities in the e-economy can mirror similar activities taking place in the conventional marketplace. So, for example, a major food retailer may have alongside its 'bricks' activities, as its physical trading has become known, an Internet or 'clicks' business. In measuring the e-economy, only the 'clicks' portion of business would be counted.

Electronic Fund Transfer Systems (EFTS): A variety of systems and technologies for transferring funds (money) electronically rather than by cheque. Includes BACS (Banks Automated Clearing System).

Enterprise Agency: Independent, but not for profit, Local Enterprise Agencies are committed to responding to the needs of small and growing businesses by providing an appropriate range of quality services, particular, but not exclusively, targeting pre-start, start-up and micro businesses and assisting in building their ability to survive, to sustain themselves and to grow.

Enterprise Investment Scheme: The scheme provides income tax relief for new equity investment by external investors and business *angels* in qualifying unquoted companies, and capital gains tax exemption on disposal of shares.

Entrepreneur: An entrepreneur is someone who recognises an opportunity, raising the money and other resources needed to exploit that opportunity, and bears some or all of the risk associated with executing the ensuing plans. Entrepreneurship can be more correctly viewed as a behaviour characteristic than a personality trait, which explains why the 'typical' entrepreneur is difficult to describe – or to detect in advance using questionnaires.

Equity: The owner's claims against the business, sometimes called the shareholders' funds. This appears as a liability because it belongs to the shareholders and not to the business itself. It is represented by the share capital plus the cumulative retained profits over the business's life. The reward for equity investment is usually a dividend paid on profits made.

Escrow account: An escrow account is a special bank account into which earnings from sales (such as convertible currency proceeds from exports) are accumulated. These revenues are set aside for subsequent acquisition of goods and services from a foreign supplier. The escrowed money, usually interest-bearing, is disbursed by the bank to the foreign supplier under payment terms and against documents specified in the supplier's sale contract.

Experience curve: A graphical description of what happens to costs as a business acquires history of experience of producing a product. Typically, for each doubling of experience, as represented by the absolute volume of output, unit costs can be expected to fall by 20–30 per cent. This axiom poses at least one threat and one opportunity for entrepreneurs.

Extraordinary general meeting (EGM): Meeting held within the rules laid down by company law and the company's own rules to deal with unusual events, such as responding to a takeover bid and changing the capital structure of a business.

Factoring: A range of products where finance is provided against the security of trade debts. Normally as an invoice is raised a copy will be sent to a factor who will then fund up to 85 per cent against the invoice in advance of the customer paying. The remainder will become payable either on a maturity date or when the customer pays. As the invoice is assigned to the factor, payment by the customer will be direct to the factor. Compare *Invoice discounting*.

Financial ratio: The relationship between two money quantities, used to analyse business results.

Financial year: A year's trading between dates agreed with the Inland Revenue. Not necessarily the fiscal year, which starts on 5 April.

Firmware: Computer instruction stored in read-only memory (ROM).

Fixed assets: Assets such as land, building, equipment, and cars, acquired for long-term use in the business and not for stock in trade. Initially recorded in the balance sheet at cost.

Fixed cost: Expenses that do not vary directly with the number of items produced. For example, a car has certain fixed costs, such as tax and insurance, whether it is driven or not.

Floating charge: The security given by a borrower to a lender that floats over all assets. So if the borrower fails to repay the loan, the lender can lay claim to any and all assets up until the time the full sum due has been recovered. This contrasts with a fixed charge.

Force majeure: The title of a standard clause in a contract exempting the parties for non-fulfilment of their obligations as a result of conditions beyond their control, such as earthquakes, floods, or war.

Forfaiting: Forfaiting is a form of supplier credit in which an exporter surrenders possession of export receivables, which are usually guaranteed by a bank in the importer's country, by selling them at a discount to a 'forfaiter' in exchange for cash. Forfaiters usually work with bills of exchange or promissory notes, which are unconditional and easily transferable debt instruments that can be sold on the secondary market. Differences between export factoring and forfaiting are:

- Factors usually want access to a large percentage of an exporter's business, while most forfaiters will work on a one-shot basis

- Forfaiters generally work with medium- and long-term receivables (180 days to seven years), while factors work with short-term receivables (up to 180 days).

See also *factoring*.

Free cash flows: Cash not required for operations or for reinvestment. Often defined as earnings before interest (often obtained from the operating income line on the income statement), less capital expenditures, less the change in working capital.

Funds: Financial resources, not necessarily cash.

Gearing: The ratio of a business's borrowings to its equity. For example, a 1:1 ratio would exist where a bank offered to match your investment pound for pound.

Going concern: Simply an accounting concept, it assumes in all financial reports that the business will continue to trade indefinitely into the future unless there is specific evidence to the contrary – meaning it has declared an intention to liquidate. It is not an indication of the current state of health of the business.

Goodwill: Value of the name, reputation, or intangible assets of a business. It is recorded in the accounts only when it is purchased.

Gross: Total before deductions. For example, gross profit is the difference between sales income and costs of goods sold. The selling and administrative expenses have yet to be deducted. Then it becomes the net profit.

Growth Directions Matrix: When planning for growth, entrepreneurs tend to be led by opportunity, which more often than not leads them to select diversification strategies at the outset. By their nature, diversification strategies are the most risky as they build neither on the company's proven product nor on market skills – they simply use surplus cash or borrowings to back a hunch. Successful diversification calls for strong management skills, a commodity in short supply in most small firms. The Growth Directions Matrix was developed in 1965 by Igor Ansoff to help companies cluster and analyse their strategies for growth and to assess their relative risk. The dimensions of the matrix are defined as product and market, each of which is defined in terms of the present position and the new position, resulting in four basic growth strategies: market penetration, market development, product development, and diversification.

HTTP: HyperText Transfer Protocol, the protocol used by Web servers.

Hyperlink: A link in a given document to information within another document. These links are usually represented by highlighted words or images.

HyperText Markup Language (HTML): The rules that govern the way documents are created so that they can be read by a *browser*. These documents are characterised by the .html or .htm file extension.

Income statement: See *profit and loss account*.

Initial public offering (IPO): A company's first sale of stock to the public. Securities offered in an IPO are often, but not always, those of young, small companies seeking outside equity capital and a public market for their stock. Investors purchasing stock in IPOs must generally be prepared to accept very large risks for the possibility of large gains. IPOs by investment companies (closed-end funds) usually contain underwriting fees that represent a load to buyers (see also *AIM*).

Insiders: These are directors and senior officers of a corporation – in effect, those who have access to inside information about a company. An insider is also someone who owns more than 10 per cent of the voting shares of a company.

Insolvency: A situation in which a person or business cannot meet the bills. Differs from *bankruptcy*, as the body involved may have assets that can be realised to meet those bills.

Invention promoter: A business offering support to inventors in exploiting their intellectual property. Not all provide value for money, and the Patent Office (www.patent.gov.uk) provides useful advice in this area.

Invisible hand: The cornerstone of the theory of economist Adam Smith (1723–90) on the way the capitalist system works, as expounded in his book, *The Wealth of Nations* (1776). The book lends credibility to entrepreneurial activity by proposing that if all individuals act from self-interest, spurred on by the profit motive, then society as a whole prospers, with no apparent regulator at work. It is, wrote Smith, as if an 'invisible hand' guided the actions of individuals to combine for the common wealth. Governments are 'selective' in the ways in which they demonstrate their belief in this theory and their all too visible hand is seen in the creation of more and more *red tape* that often seems only to inhibit enterprise.

Invoice discounting: Similar to *factoring* in that the invoice discounter makes up to 85 per cent of invoice value available immediately to the seller, the balance being paid when the buyer finally pays the invoice. However, with confidential invoice discounting, the seller retains control of its debtors.

Irrevocable: This is the most common instrument of credit in international trade, and carries an irrevocable obligation of the issuing bank to pay the beneficiary when drafts and documents are presented in accordance with the terms of the letter of credit. An irrevocable letter of credit, once issued, cannot be amended or cancelled without the agreement of all named parties. As such, it must have a fixed expiration date.

Junk bond: A bond with a speculative credit rating of BB or lower is a junk bond. Such bonds offer investors higher yields than bonds of financially sound companies. Two agencies, Standard & Poor's and Moody's Investor Services, provide the rating systems for companies' credit.

Just-in-time inventory systems: Systems that schedule materials/inventory to arrive exactly as they are needed in the production process.

Know-how agreement: This is a promise to disclose information to a third party. If the disclosure is made for them to evaluate the usefulness of the know-how, the agreement is called a secrecy agreement. If the disclosure is made to allow commercial production, it is called a know-how licence.

Letter of credit: A financial document issued by a bank at the request of the consignee guaranteeing payment to the shipper for cargo if certain terms and conditions are fulfilled. Three types of letter of credit exist:

- ✔ A Revocable Letter of Credit is subject to possible recall or amendment at the option of the applicant, without the approval of the beneficiary.

- ✔ A Confirmed Letter of Credit is issued by a foreign bank with its validity confirmed by a domestic bank. An exporter who requires a confirmed letter of credit from the buyer is assured payment from the domestic bank in case the foreign buyer or bank defaults.

- ✔ A Documentary Letter of Credit is one for which the issuing bank stipulates that certain documents must accompany a draft. The documents assure the applicant (importer) that the merchandise has been shipped and that title to the goods has been transferred to the importer.

Leveraged buy-out (LBO): A transaction used for making a public corporation private, financed through the use of debt funds: bank loans and bonds. Because of the large amount of debt relative to equity in the new corporation, the bonds are typically rated below investment grade, properly referred to as high-yield bonds or junk bonds.

Liabilities: The claims against a business, such as creditors, loans and equity.

LIFO (Last-in-first-out): The last-in-first-out inventory valuation methodology. A method of valuing inventory that uses the cost of the most recent item in inventory first.

Liquidation: The legal process of closing down a business and selling off its assets to meet outstanding debts.

Loan capital: Finance lent to a business for a specific period of time at either a fixed or varied rate of interest. This interest must be paid irrespective of the performance of the business.

Love money: Money put into a business by family, friends, or successful business neighbours. It is a US term that has less to do with love than it has to do with tax. In the US, anyone investing in a new enterprise can do so out of pre-tax income and so have that investment effectively subsidised by the marginal tax rate. See *Enterprise Investment Scheme*.

Management buy-out (MBO): A growing phenomenon whereby the managers of a company become its owners. They do this by setting up a new company that buys either all or, more usually, a part of their old company. The money to do so is raised from banks, venture capital funds, and from the managers themselves. The reason for the buy-out often stems from the desire of the parent company to pull out of a certain activity, or to demerge from a previous amalgamation.

Management consultant: 'Someone who borrows your watch to tell you the time – then charges you for the privilege.' A rather disparaging description, but one that is instantly recognisable by anyone that has used a consulting firm. Management consultants sell professional advice on most aspects of business, including financial management, marketing, market research, strategy formulation, and manpower planning. The have come into their own in the information technology area and in all aspects of managing change in organisations. Management consultants are much in evidence after takeovers where they are used to help the victor make sure of the spoils. In the UK there are about 5,000 management consultants, with 2,800 belonging to the Institute of Management Consultants, their professional body.

Managing director: A company director holding special powers to manage the day-to-day affairs of a company. The managing director is second in importance only to the chairman.

Marginal cost: The extra cost incurred in making one more unit of production.

Marketing mix: The combination of methods used by a business to market its product. For example, it can vary its price or the type and quantity of advertising; the distribution channels can be altered; finally, the product itself can either be enhanced or reduced in quality.

Marketing strategy: Philip Kotler, the US marketing theorist, identified four basic competitive marketing strategies. While strategy is classically a big business concept, there is no reason why those running small businesses should not profit by using the same principles. Indeed, there is much evidence to suggest they are more likely to succeed if they do.

Market segment: A group of buyers who can be identified as being especially interested in a particular variant of the product. For example, a cheap day return ticket for a train is a variant of a rail fare, especially attractive to people who do not have to get to their destination early in the day.

Market share: The ratio of a firm's sales of a product in a specific market during a particular period to the total sales of that product in the same period in the same market.

Memorandum of Association: A legal document drawn up as a part of the registration of a company in the UK. The memorandum must state the company's name, its registered office, its purposes, and its authorised share capital. The purpose of the business, as set out in the memorandum, is very broad, deliberately so, in order not to preclude any type of trade the company may choose to embark on in the future. The memorandum is sent to the Registrar of Companies, who must also be informed of any changes.

Multi-tasking: The capability for more than one program (in the case of a network, possibly used by more than one user) to run at the same time.

National Insurance: A state insurance scheme in the UK administered by the Department of Health and Social Security, by which every employer, employee, and self-employed person makes weekly payments to provide insurance against accidents, sickness and unemployment, and towards a pension and other benefits.

Non-disclosure agreement: An agreement that allows you to reveal secret commercial information – for example, about an invention – to a third party, and which prevents them from making use of that information without your agreement.

Non-executive director: A generally part-time director, who helps to plan and decide the policy of a company but who has no responsibility for carrying out such policies. Normally, companies raising capital through merchant banks and other financial institutions will be 'encouraged' to have a nominee of theirs as a non-executive director.

'Off the shelf' company: A company without a trading history that has been formed and held specifically for resale at a later date. Agencies keep a large stock of such companies in numerous categories of business. They cost around £130 each, and can be up and running in a day or so. An 'off the shelf' company may have an unsuitable name, but that can be changed later for a modest fee. A tailor-made company will cost more than an 'off the shelf' company, and it takes four to five weeks to set up. So if speed is of the essence, the 'off the shelf' is the first choice.

One per cent syndrome: Also known as the market research cop-out clause. This describes the situation in which a prospective business owner starts a venture on the premise that 'If we only sell 1 per cent of the potential market, we'll be a great success.' This argument is then advanced so that no time is wasted in doing basic market research – after all, the business only has to sell to this tiny percentage of possible buyers! In fact, this type of thinking leads to more business failures than any other single factor. If the market is so huge as to make 1 per cent of it very profitable, then inevitably there are large and established competitors. For a small firm to try to compete head-on in this situation is little short of suicidal. It can be done, but only if sound research has clearly identified a market niche, or if there is a particular industry 'lag' that would allow a new business to obtain a special place. However, more usually the idea itself is badly thought through – as are all ideas that do not take the customers' viewpoint – and this causes the business to fail to gain even the magical 1 per cent.

Opportunity cost: The value of a course of action open to you but not taken. For example, keeping cash in an ordinary share account at a building society will attract about 2 per cent less interest than a five-year term at the same society. So the opportunity cost of choosing not to tie up your money is 2 per cent.

Overheads: This is an expense that cannot be conveniently associated with a unit of production. Administration or selling expenses are usually overheads.

Overtrading: Expanding sales and production without enough financial resources – in particular, working capital. The first signs are usually cash flow problems.

Pareto principle: The rule which states that 80 per cent of effort goes into producing 20 per cent of the results. For a new business, this rule is usually observed first when it is seen that 20 per cent of their customers produced 80 per cent of sales by value. As this rule is almost impossible to change, it is only by widening the customer base and lowering the dependence on a few important customers that a new firm can hope to survive.

Piggybacking: Usually associated with firms that market other firms' products as well as their own, but the term can be used to describe any 'free riding' activity.

Poison pill: Anti-takeover device that gives a prospective acquiree's shareholders the right to buy shares of the firm or shares of anyone who acquires the firm at a deep discount to their fair market value. Named after the cyanide pill that secret agents are instructed to swallow if capture is imminent.

Preference shares: These usually give their holders the right to a fixed dividend and priority over ordinary shareholders in liquidation, and confer voting power only in matters concerning the varying of the shareholders' rights or in cases when dividends have not been paid. There are four types of preference share in the entrepreneur's 'capital' armoury:

- Cumulative preference shares, which give the right to payment of any past dividends not paid
- Redeemable preference shares, which are those that the company has agreed to repay on a specified date, often at a premium over issuing price

- ✔ Participatory preference shares, which, in addition to the right to a fixed dividend, allow further profit participation in good times
- ✔ Convertible preference shares, which have the right to be changed for ordinary shares at specified dates and prices

Product life cycle: A concept that states that every product (or service) passes through certain identifiable stages in its life. Understanding the implications of each of these stages for the company's *cash flow*, *profit*, and *marketing strategy* is an important element in successfully launching a new venture. The five stages are:

1. **Pre-launch:** All the work done to bring the product or service to market. This includes product development and market research.

2. **Introduction:** Usually featured by low sales and no profits. Innovators (see *adoption curve*) are the main customers.

3. **Growth:** If all goes well, and the product is accepted by the innovative customers, sales begin to grow, sharply at first.

4. **Maturity:** Sales growth stops, new competitors have probably arrived, and the original product is beginning to look a bit stale.

5. **Decline:** Unless the product is relaunched, by changing various elements in the *marketing mix*, sales will decline.

Profit: The excess of sales revenue over sales cost and expenses during an accounting period. It does not necessarily mean an increase in cash.

Profit and loss account: A statement of sales, costs, expenses, and profit (or loss) over an accounting period – monthly, quarterly, or annually. Also known as the *income statement*.

Pyramid selling: A form of multi-level distributorship which typically involved the manufacture or sale by a company, under its own trade name, of a line of products through 'franchises' which appear to be regular franchise distributorships. The pyramid may include three to five levels of non-exclusive distributorships, and individuals may become 'franchisees' at any level by paying the company a fee, and agreeing to buy stock, based on the level of entry. Once in, the individual earns a commission by selling the company's products, but at higher levels in the pyramid it is made more attractive to introduce new members. This product is sold down the chain at progressively higher prices, until the final person has to sell to the public. Since most people make a profit by merely being a link in the chain, the emphasis is placed on recruiting more investors-distributors, rather than on selling to end customers. The schemes, like chain letters, are lucrative for those at the top of the pyramid.

But inevitably, the market becomes saturated, no further participants can be recruited, and the system then collapses. Trading schemes become illegitimate and illegal if, while purporting to offer business opportunities, the sole purpose of the scheme is to make money by recruiting other participants, rather than trading in goods or services.

Receiver: Someone called in by a troubled company's creditors to try to sort out the company's financial problems. The receiver's aim is to get the company back on the straight and narrow without it going into liquidation.

Red tape: The excessive use of or adherence to formalities. Despite protestations to the contrary, it would appear to describe accurately the relationship between the government and an enterprise. Research by the Forum of Private Business has shown that an entrepreneur wishing to set up a limited company as an electrician needed to make 18 telephone calls, travel 127 miles to collect papers, and spend 24 hours reading 269,200 words to understand government regulations.

With the seemingly endless encroachment of legislation, it seems unlikely that government-inspired deregulation measures will be effective in the short run. The only hope in the foreseeable future is a computer with the appropriate software – alas, as yet unwritten.

Registered office: This need not necessarily be the same address as the business is conducted from. Quite frequently the address used for the registered office is that of the firm's solicitor or accountant. This is, however, the address where all official correspondence will go. EC regulations now require the name of the company to be prominently displayed at the registered office address.

Reserves: The name given to the accumulated and undistributed profits of the business. They belong to the ordinary shareholders. They are not necessarily available in cash, but are usually tied up in other business assets.

Revenue: Usually from sales. Revenue is recognised in accounting terms when goods have been despatched (or services rendered) and the invoice sent. This means that revenue pounds are not necessarily cash pounds. A source of much confusion and frequent cash flow problems.

Royalty: The money paid to the owner of something valuable for the right to make use of it for a specified purpose. Examples include payment made to the owners of a copyright for permission to publish, or the owner of a patent for permission to use a patented design.

Schedule E: Tax allowances for employed people.

Seasonality: A regular event, usually one that causes sales to increase or decrease in an annual cycle. For example, the weather caused by the seasons or events associated with the seasons, such as Christmas, spring sales, and summer holidays.

Secured creditor: Someone lending money to a business whose debt is secured by linking a default in its repayment to a fixed asset, such as a freehold building.

Share capital: The capital of the business subscribed for by the owners or shareholders.

Share option: A facility that allows top managers and employees to have shares in the companies for which they work, on special terms. The most effective way to improve employees' attitudes, productivity, and understanding of the company's position is by instituting a share option scheme. In this way they can participate in success (and failure), too. Half of all leading UK companies operate such schemes. Indeed, various Finance Acts from 1972 have relaxed the tax position in this area.

Six badges of trade: The list drawn up by the Royal Commission on the Taxation of Profits and Income, 1955 to distinguish whether an activity constitutes trading (and is therefore taxable), or is simply a hobby (and is not). These are:

- ✔ the frequency of the activity
- ✔ the value added, or amount of work done
- ✔ the motive
- ✔ the nature of the transaction
- ✔ the circumstances
- ✔ the methodology

Sleeping partner: Someone who has put up capital but does not intend to take an active part in running the business. They can protect themselves against the risk of unlimited liability by having the partnership registered as a limited partnership. The Limited Partnership Act of 1908 sets out the arrangements and relationships that apply in the absence of any formal agreement being reached by the various partners. In a company the 'sleeping partner' would normally be a shareholder and thus limit financial exposure in that way.

SME: Small- or Medium-sized Enterprise: Defined by EU regulations as independent businesses having fewer than 250 employees, and having either an annual turnover not exceeding ECU 40 million, or an annual balance-sheet total not exceeding ECU 27 million Such businesses may benefit from state aid in certain circumstances.

Spreadsheet: Computer document format designed to help financial planning. Spreadsheet software can be used to perform repetitive numerical calculations and a spreadsheet is sometimes referred to as a modelling tool. It comprises rows and columns into which numbers, formulae, and text can be entered.

Strategy: A general method of policy for achieving specific objectives. It describes the essential resources, and their amounts, which are to be committed to achieving those objects (see *tactics*).

Sweat equity: The value that accrues to a business by virtue of the time, energy, and intellectual effort required to get to the immediate pre-launch phase. It is a notional concept applied by venture capitalists to assess the commitment the entrepreneur has to his business idea; it is a substitute for the commitment that hard cash would demonstrate in the event that a proprietor has no money to put up.

SWOT analysis: SWOT is an acronym for Strengths, Weaknesses, Opportunities, and Threats, the four factors that have to be considered when developing a successful business *strategy*.

Synergy: A cooperative or combined activity that is more effective or valuable than the sum of its independent activities.

Tactics: The method by which resources allocated to a strategic objective are used.

Tax avoidance: Action taken to avoid having to pay tax unnecessarily, using legal means.

Tax evasion: Using illegal means of avoiding payment of tax and making a false tax declaration. About 70,000 small businesses are investigated by the UK Inland Revenue each year for irregularities in their tax affairs. Just short of £400 million in extra tax is recovered from these firms. Most proprietors who have gone through the experience of a tax investigation would be reluctant to do anything that might incur a repeat of the experience.

Tax loss: A loss that has been manufactured specifically to reduce or eliminate taxable profits. Such action usually consists of bringing forward expenditure. That unfortunately has the usual effect of increasing profits in the next year. However, for sole traders it can be attractive to have a loss in their first trading period as this forms the reference base for future tax.

Trade cycle: At times, the economy appears to behave like a rollercoaster, encouraging new ventures and expansion plans on the upswing, only to dash them on the rocks a short time later when the downturn comes. This effect is known as the trade cycle. No one is quite sure why there is this regularity – or rather, everyone is sure but for different reasons.

True and fair: Accounting terminology that indicates that the business financial reports have been prepared using generally accepted accounting principles.

Turnkey: Usually refers to a client-commissioned system, accepted only when you can 'turn a key' and are satisfied with the results, or output.

Unique selling proposition: Coined in 1940 by Rosser Reeves, advertising copywriter of the leading advertising agency, Ted Bates. His thesis was that from the launch of a product or service onwards you should always seek to identify and promote a unique selling proposition. This can be done by asking two questions: What is different about me, the seller, and what is different about our product or service? If nothing is different, why on earth should anyone want to buy from you? This is a particularly powerful concept at the outset of a new venture when a firm is short on market credibility.

URL: Uniform Resource Locator, the address to a source of information. The URL contains four distinct parts, the protocol type, the machine name, the directory path, and the file name. For example: `www.bbsrc.ac.uk/business/ skills/plan/Welcome.html`

User group: Organisation set up by computer users who have a common interest. This common interest may be a particular computer, a piece of software, or an activity. Usually there is a free exchange of ideas, programs, and tips, and quite frequently a magazine is produced and circulated to members.

Value: In accounting it has several meanings. For example, the 'value' of a fixed asset is its costs less its cumulative depreciation. A current asset, such as stock, is usually valued at cost or market value, whichever is the lower.

Value added: The difference between sales revenue that a firm gets from selling its products (or services), and the cost to it of the materials used in making those products.

Vapourware: A term, slightly derogatory in nature, used to describe wishful thinking in describing a business's advantages or strategies.

Variable costs: See *direct costs*.

Variance: The difference between actual performance and the forecast (or budget or standard).

Working capital: Current assets less current liabilities, which represents the capital used in the day-to-day running of the business.

Working life: The economically useful life of a fixed asset. Not necessarily its whole life. For example, technological development may render it obsolete very quickly.

Work in progress: Goods in the process of being produced, which are valued at the lower end of manufacturing costs or market value.

Index

• C •

• *F* •

• S •

FOR
DUMMIES®

The easy way to get more done and have more fun

UK EDITIONS

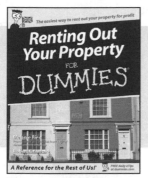

0-7645-7016-1

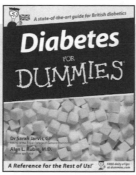

0-7645-7019-6

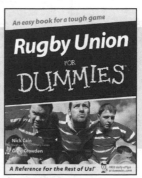

0-7645-7020-X

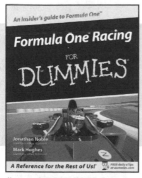

*   0-7645-7015-3

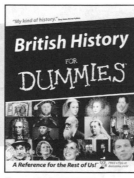

*   0-7645-7021-8

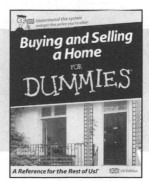

0-7645-7027-7
Due August 2004

0-7645-7023-4

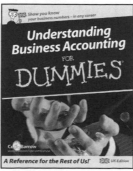

0-7645-7025-0

0-7645-7018-8

**Available in the UK at bookstores nationwide and online at
www.wileyeurope.com or call 0800 243407 to order direct**

* Also available in the United States at www.dummies.com

WILEY

6020

FOR DUMMIES®

The easy way to get more done and have more fun

GENERAL INTEREST & HOBBIES

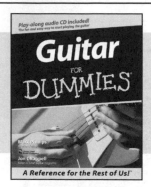

0-7645-5106-X

0-7645-5194-9

0-7645-5193-0

0-7645-5196-5

0-7645-5434-4

0-7645-1771-6

Also available:

Japanese For Dummies®
0-7645-5429-8

Architecture For Dummies®
0-7645-5396-8

Rock Guitar For Dummies®
0-7645-5356-9

Anatomy and Physiology For
Dummies®
0-7645-5422-0

German For Dummies®
0-7645-5195-7

Weight Training For
Dummies®, 2nd Edition
0-7645-5168-X

Project Management For
Dummies®
0-7645-5283-X

Piano For Dummies®
0-7645-5105-1

Latin For Dummies®
0-7645-5431-X

Songwriting For Dummies®
0-7645-5404-2

Marketing For Dummies®
2nd Edition
0-7645-5600-2

Parenting For Dummies®
2nd Edition
0-7645-5418-2

Fitness For Dummies®
2nd Edition
0-7645-5167-1

Religion For Dummies®
0-7645-5264-3

Selling For Dummies®
2nd Edition
0-7645-5363-1

Improving Your Memory For
Dummies®
0-7645-5435-2

Islam For Dummies®
0-7645-5503-0

Golf For Dummies®
2nd Edition
0-7645-5146-9

The Complete MBA For
Dummies®
0-7645-5204-X

Astronomy For Dummies®
0-7645-5155-8

Customer Service For
Dummies®, 2nd Edition
0-7645-5209-0

Mythology For Dummies®
0-7645-5432-8

Pilates For Dummies®
0-7645-5397-6

Managing Teams For
Dummies®
0-7645-5408-5

Screenwriting For Dummies®
0-7645-5486-7

Drawing For Dummies®
0-7645-5476-X

Controlling Cholesterol For
Dummies®
0-7645-5440-9

Martial Arts For Dummies®
0-7645-5358-5

Meditation For Dummies®
0-7645-5166-7

Wine For Dummies®
2nd Edition
0-7645-5114-0

Yoga For Dummies®
0-7645-5117-5

Drums For Dummies®
0-7645-5357-7

**Available in the UK at bookstores nationwide and online at
www.wileyeurope.com or call 0800 243407 to order direct**

Also available in the United States at www.dummies.com

WILE

FOR DUMMIES®

The easy way to get more done and have more fun

FOR DUMMIES®

The easy way to get more done and have more fun

TRAVEL

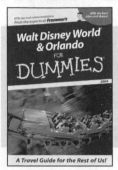

Walt Disney World & Orlando
A Travel Guide for the Rest of Us!
0-7645-3875-6

Germany
A Travel Guide for the Rest of Us!
0-7645-5478-6

Ireland
A Travel Guide for the Rest of Us!
0-7645-5455-7

Spain
A Travel Guide for the Rest of Us!
0-7645-5495-6

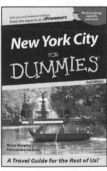

New York City
A Travel Guide for the Rest of Us!
0-7645-5451-4

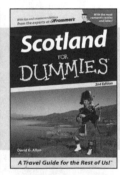

Scotland
A Travel Guide for the Rest of Us!
0-7645-5477-8

Paris
A Travel Guide for the Rest of Us!
0-7645-5494-8

Italy
A Travel Guide for the Rest of Us!
0-7645-5453-0

Florida
A Travel Guide for the Rest of Us!
0-7645-1979-4

Also available:

Alaska For Dummies®
1st Edition
0-7645-1761-9

Hawaii For Dummies®
2nd Edition
0-7645-5438-7

Arizona For Dummies®
2nd Edition
0-7645-5484-0

California For Dummies®
2nd Edition
0-7645-5449-2

Boston For Dummies®
2nd Edition
0-7645-5491-3

New Orleans For Dummies®
2nd Edition
0-7645-5454-9

Las Vegas For Dummies®
2nd Edition
0-7645-5448-4

Los Angeles and Disneyland
For Dummies® 1st Edition
0-7645-6611-3

America's National Parks For
Dummies® 2nd Edition
0-7645-5493-X

San Francisco For Dummies®
2nd Edition
0-7645-5450-6

Europe For Dummies®
2nd Edition
0-7645-5456-5

Mexico's Beach Resorts For
Dummies® 2nd Edition
0-7645-5781-5

Honeymoon Vacations For
Dummies® 1st Edition
0-7645-6313-0

Bahamas For Dummies®
2nd Edition
0-7645-5442-5

Caribbean For Dummies®
2nd Edition
0-7645-5445-X

France For Dummies®
2nd Edition
0-7645-2542-5

Chicago For Dummies®
2nd Edition
0-7645-2541-7

Vancouver & Victoria For
Dummies® 2nd Edition
0-7645-3874-8

**Available in the UK at bookstores nationwide and online at
www.wileyeurope.com or call 0800 243407 to order direct**

Also available in the United States at www.dummies.com